Why Hackers Win

Why Hackers Win

Power and Disruption in the Network Society

Patrick Burkart and Tom McCourt

UNIVERSITY OF CALIFORNIA PRESS

University of California Press
Oakland, California

Cataloging-in-Publication Data is on file with the Library of Congress.
Library of Congress Control Number: 2019950171

ISBN 978-0-520-30012-5 (cloth)
ISBN 978-0-520-30013-2 (paperback)
ISBN 978-0-520-97165-3 (e-edition)

Manufactured in the United States of America

28 27 26 25 24 23 22 21 20 19
10 9 8 7 6 5 4 3 2 1

For David and Jane

CONTENTS

ILLUSTRATIONS

TABLES

FIGURES

PREFACE

Contemporary geopolitics are in flux as their norms shift and institutions realign. Information increasingly is employed as both hard and soft power in struggles that cross the social and technical boundaries of long-standing networks. These struggles are central to what we term the "Network Society."[1] *Why Hackers Win: Power and Disruption in the Network Society* examines the pressures that have driven global law and policy into ambiguous territory. While many popular and scholarly accounts posit hacking as a means to wobble the trajectory of late capitalism, we argue the inverse is true. Hacking (offensively through exploits and defensively through cybersecurity) extends and deepens state and corporate proclivities to control social realities. We define "hacking" as unauthorized trespass, breach, or bypass of "trusted systems" for purposes of surveillance and potential theft, manipulation, or destruction of information.[2] These systems are based on communication networks in which service providers and users must be authenticated to access goods and services. Therefore, user trust in their security and reliability is essential.[3] We focus on the hacking of trusted systems—and not other kinds of readily accessible systems—because the template for their protection has been refined in key areas of law, technology, and society.

We posit hacking as a generalized symbolic medium, like power and money, which can be collected and mobilized to influence communication systems. In the process hacking affords opportunities to bypass existing law and policy through force. Our purpose in *Why Hackers Win* is to examine hacking as a corporate and state strategy for managing risk. Ulrich Beck claims that "being at risk is the way of being and ruling in the world of modernity; being at global risk is the human condition at the beginning of the twenty-first century" (2006, 330). Given the immense complexity of the Network Society, state and corporate actors seek greater self-awareness and certainty. Hacking enables these actors to seek out their blind spots in online boundaries and activities. This knowledge is valuable for maintaining systems and exposing risks. Hacking (offensively through exploits or defensively through cybersecurity) reflects common social impulses to survey, to measure, to model, and to predict. While hacking often is viewed as essentially disruptive to social structures, we argue the inverse is true. States and corporations seek to maintain their standing and seek competitive advantage through hacking campaigns. The creation of markets for exploits and cybersecurity also affords new opportunities to develop and exchange commodities. Consequently, to preserve national-security prerogatives and develop global markets for hacking technologies, states have resisted legal regimes to contain hacking by institutions—even as they have enacted draconian laws against hacking by individuals.

We find that hacking and cybersecurity reinforce and accelerate each other in trusted systems. While ostensibly antagonistic, both increasingly share a common grounding in intellectual property. For hackers the value of hacking victims, or "data subjects," is not so much in their personally identifiable information, which is gathered and commodified by trusted systems. Instead, hackers exploit the "intellectual property" that gathers and commodifies this information within these systems to squeeze revenues through phishing and fraud. A secondary value is that hacking provides data for valuing insurance products and refining cybersecurity products already in use. In turn, cybersecurity offers possibilities for developing intellectual property in the military and civilian sectors, particularly in software and services. Both private security firms and state military and police forces claim to have evolved cybersecurity and cyber warfare into a "science," in which knowledge and expertise are increasingly institutionalized in higher education and corporate management. Both markets and militaries view offensive hacking techniques (intrusion software like malware and botnets) and defensive countermeasures as new opportunities to generate power and money and manage risk.

Much like the "dual-use" nature of exploits themselves and consistent with other domains in the Network Society, the boundaries between private and public are blurred and indeterminate. In the neoliberal era the economic system has assumed more and more responsibility for allocating risk through the market function of pricing, and the state has turned more areas of social welfare over to markets in an elaborated process of risk management and deregulation.[4] Similarly, states increasingly outsource both hacking and cybersecurity as a means of managing risk. Internet service providers perform state surveillance by proxy, and states (including the United States) frequently employ independent spyware and hacking firms to supplement their operations. Innovations such as insurance against corporate hacking and identity theft also reflect the commodification of hacking risks. When these responsibilities are outsourced to the market, risks are distributed in patterns that can reinforce social inequalities. The economy provides markets for risk management, but "with the economic exploitation of the risks it sets free, industrial society produces the hazards and the political potential of the risk society" (Beck 1992b, 23).

Through all these means hacking represents an interface between technical code (the structure of trusted systems), legal code (the laws that govern their access and use), and social code (their impact on society, particularly in terms of privacy and sanctioned activity). As a growing portion of the global economy is based in digital trusted systems, we find a proportional growth in the vulnerabilities inherent to these systems: the buggy software, the unprotected account access, and the availability of personally identifying information to others on the internet. Although hacking ostensibly undermines their own security, corporations and states paradoxically use hacking for gain. Hacking can suit a broad spectrum of purposes, including gathering intelligence, managing crises, and accumulating competitive advantages over rivals. Some "exfiltration" hacks have successfully stolen data such as business plans, while some failed episodes have landed spies in jail (Landau 2013). The "hack-back," an attempt by victims of cyberattacks to get into the hacker's computer, can try to ascertain the fallout from the initial breach, as well as knowledge about any new schemes and risks of future breaches. While examining abuses of power through computer vulnerabilities and exploits, we have not found "master conspiracies" of surveillance and espionage, or even a systematic imposition of will, in coordinated hacking campaigns. Instead, we see a proliferation of agents contributing to offenses and defenses played in long games and embedded in global networks. In our view hacking has become a mundane, "business as usual" application of force for many enterprises.

The development of hacking and cybersecurity together also foregrounds paradoxes for social systems. Hacking is now integrated into state and corporate activities, especially where business or security interests are invested in maintaining trusted systems. Organizations may hack for advantages over rivals by exploiting vulnerabilities in trusted systems. At the same time organizations may hack their own trusted systems or invite others to hack them (sometimes called penetration testing or "pen testing") for purposes of cybersecurity. "Red Team v. Blue Team" exercises take pen testing to active warfare levels—one team trying to break in while the other defends. (In cybersecurity gospel "Red team ALWAYS wins eventually. Blue just holds on as long as they can.") "Red teaming" is embraced and institutionalized by the U.S. Department of Defense, where "in the cyber world, offense and defense stemmed from the same tools and techniques" (Kaplan 2016, 260). In all these scenarios hacking activity provides recursive knowledge about trusted systems and the communication systems in which they are embedded. In turn, these reflexive processes can exercise coercive force in these systems. Whether or not they encounter defenses, an exploit delivered through the right attack vector can contribute to cybernetic feedback loops within systems. These loops appear to be generated with increasing frequency, as hacking campaigns (or cyberattacks) proliferate together with mass data breaches.

Our approach to technology foregrounds the role of human agents and institutions in communication. We argue that technologies are socially constructed rather than deterministic and autonomous. Notwithstanding the impact of technological change on the economy and society, even our most powerful technologies do not operate independently of human controls such as market exchange, law, policy, and cultural norms. *Why Hackers Win* takes a sociological perspective on hacking, viewing it as one of many activities that constitute communication in social systems. If we view the cybernetic arena as a social system, hacking serves to differentiate the components of this system, which then adapts accordingly. The system as a whole is reconfigured, with consequences for political, economic, and legal systems, among others. Hacking and its codependent, cybersecurity, therefore contribute to encoding communication in social systems rather than undermining them. This idea is informed by Jürgen Habermas's (1984, 1987) theory of communicative action and his dualistic "system and lifeworld" analysis of modern societies. Accordingly, hacking is related to digital piracy as a means of cultural reproduction (Burkart 2011, 2014). In the absence of a tightly regulated market for cybersecurity and component exploits, hacking has greater freedom to "steer" interactions between states, markets, and laws. If the legal system were to suppress the proliferation of commercial hacking tools and spyware, the risks perpetuated by cyber insecurity might improve. But the legal system is not designed to do this; in fact, it contributes to systemic risk by enabling legal or gray markets for vulnerabilities. We argue that the conjoining of intellectual property and cyber defense in copyright law and policy adds additional levels of risk for society as a whole. This is in part because hacking and data breaches are not just episodic bugs; rather, they are routine and institutionalized features of the system. The growth of cybersecurity software and related industries also impact these institutions and routines, contributing social effects in the process.

Although social-technical systems for media, business and finance, and defense are increasingly globalized, the nation-state still provides the basis for law and policy governing hacking. But the coherence and continuity of law and policy within nation-states can fall on a continuum from anarchic to totalitarian. Hacking therefore illustrates "governance in areas of limited statehood" (Risse 2013). The relative dependence or independence of hacking on law and policy can turn on a variety of factors. *Why Hackers Win* addresses cases where new laws on hacking have conflicted with both received policy traditions and emergent policy regimes and where hacking still occupies legal gray areas. Judicial review is not fully incorporated into many decision-making processes; broad categories of hacking remain the privilege of the state and therefore are exempted from the rule of law. Even hacking by private firms may be absolved by the state (such as when telecommunications carriers received retroactive immunity from illegal wiretapping violations).[5] Secrecy and self-regulation are the rule for states and firms, with little concern for values and norms for personal privacy.

Numerous national and international legal systems have categorized piracy and hacking as cybercrimes, which has intertwined their history and led us to consider them as distinct but related aspects of communicative social action. As with piracy, the conflicts surrounding trusted systems center on issues of ownership and control, based on the right to share private property or exclude others from access. It remains as unlikely today as it did in 2006, when we wrote *Digital Music Wars,* that a universal standard for digital-rights management will be adopted by even a single industry. But the reprising of digital-rights–management models for managing cybersecurity risks and the securitization of intellectual property in military cybersecurity policy suggest that guidelines for intellectual-property theft will dominate discourse over how to define and prioritize cyber threats. We also anticipate that enterprises dependent on trusted systems will employ technology practices, legal activities, and political lobbying to strengthen pecuniary rights at the expense of the public good. However unjust they may be, "consumption norms" already have gelled for trusted systems—along with their bases in surveillance and intellectual property (Burkart 2010, 2014). In the aggregate of digital dirty tricks and the attack vectors that enable them, we find an unfolding, alternative history of technological development and its impact on society. We conclude our study with a reflection on the overt and covert applications of hacking and cybersecurity by states and corporations and the importance of research and activist groups in drawing attention to these activities. Without their efforts the question of who is responsible for guarding the public interest in the Network Society seems to answer itself: no one. The development of hacking and its double star, cybersecurity, offers another example of how ostensibly resistant technologies and practices may be contained, controlled, and repurposed to suit the instrumental purposes of state and corporate power.

ACKNOWLEDGMENTS

Thanks go to the Department of Communication and College of Liberal Arts at Texas A&M University and the Department of Communication and Media Studies at Fordham University for institutional support. The Global Fusion consortium and NORDICOM also contributed in numerous ways. Allan Alford, Steve Bales, Göran Bolin, Sandra Braman, Stuart Brotman, James Caverlee, Barbara Cherry, Christian Christensen, Miyase Christensen, Jonathan Coopersmith, Gregory Donovan, Rob Drew, Cecilia Ferm-Almqvist, Johanna Jääsaari, Elaine R. Kahan, Emmett Krueger, Lucas V. Logan, Vincent Mosco, Jeffrey J. Radice, Brian Rose, Mary Savigar, Harmeet Sawhney, Dan Schiller, Lyn Uhl, Katja Valaskivi, and Peter Yu helped with motivation, conceptualization, research, editing, and publishing. Tom McCourt owes Jane Juliano a particular debt of gratitude for gently placing his hand back on the tiller.

CHAPTER ONE

On the Structures and Functions of Hacking

Individuals and groups may hack, or disrupt online systems as a means of causing mischief or creative destruction, while hacks by states and corporations may involve coordinated campaigns to gain political and economic advantage over rivals. Hacking, like espionage or an everyday ruse, is based on ingenuity and deception. It employs techniques to evade detection, redirect attention, and blur identities. We define "hacking" as changes made, without permission, to the confidentiality, integrity, and accessibility of computerized data or networks.[1] Jurisprudence typically regards hacking as unauthorized trespass, via the internet and networked devices, into trusted systems for purposes of surveillance and potential manipulation.[2] Hacks exploit "attack vectors," which are technical vulnerabilities providing points of entry by attackers into trusted systems. We discuss many of the most common attack vectors, including known vulnerabilities, phishing, malware attacks, and brute-force password hacking.

As much as a hack functions as a cultural and technological magic trick that illuminates its social milieu, it also represents an agonistic exercise of political, economic, and social power. A hack can be legally interpreted as malicious intent toward a targeted individual or institution, even if it is found to have been a wrong turn down the paths of a trusted system. A hack also may serve a symbolic function as speech, either as a discrete speech act or as part of a coordinated campaign. It may create a "ripple effect" that first influences interconnected socio-technical systems such as e-commerce and online banking and then ripples outward to political systems. Regardless of actor or intent, the apparent pervasiveness of cyberattacks today by intrusion software and distributed denial-of-service (DDoS) botnets ("botnet" is a portmanteau of "robot" and "network") suggests that surveillance, disruption, and loss of privacy are now basic costs of living with trusted systems both online and offline.[3] Trusted systems are essential for online commerce, banking, media entertainment, and a host of other activities. With promises of ever-greater "convenience," firms drive consumers to these systems, and the data that consumers wittingly and unwittingly contribute about themselves provides firms with increasingly granular user profiles and the ability to track and predict user behavior.

The closed nature of these networks is crucial to their legitimacy and engendering the trust of participants. Yet as more and more members of the public have their personal data collected, analyzed, and compiled into databases by third parties, these "data subjects" (in European Union parlance) increasingly are exposed to identity theft, financial disruptions, doxxing, and cyberbullying. Cloud computing already has introduced a new scale to the communicative effects of hacking (Mosco 2015). As a growing number of trusted systems connect "smart" devices like refrigerators, webcams, and digital video recorders to online services, the empirical bases for trust in these systems continues to erode even as these systems become ubiquitous. According to Gartner Research, the global number of "Internet of Things" devices has surged nearly 70 percent, to 6.4 billion, between 2014 and 2016. By 2020 the number will reach 20.8 billion (Lohr 2016, B3). Given that every thousand lines of software code has, on average, fifteen to twenty defects (Perlroth 2016c, F5), the Internet of Things promises a vast playground for hackers. For example, unsecured gadgets can be remotely commandeered to join in a network of robotically controlled botnets, which in turn can be converted into a targetable swarm cyber weapon (Limer 2016).

Hacks can employ many attack vectors to breach trusted systems, including printers, routers, USB drives, email attachments, infected web pages, and fake browser plugins. Once a system is breached and a "payload" (or recombinatory software code) is dropped, intrusion software can perform countless functions. It can take over a system for surveillance, destroying its data or holding it for ransom (i.e., "ransomware," which increasingly bedevils individuals and institutions through online extortion). Intrusion software can also exfiltrate ("exfil") or remove sensitive information from the network. Mass exfiltrations of account databases have leaked private data and personally identifiable information of millions of credit card users, subjecting them to possible identity theft. Email exfiltrations can lead to "doxxing," in which private information on individuals is released on the internet with malicious intent.[4] Intrusion software can also replicate in a botnet system, allowing a remote server to commandeer enslaved devices: "Cybercriminals use special Trojan viruses to breach the security of several users' computers, take control of each computer and organize all of the infected machines into a network of 'bots' that the criminal can remotely manage" (Kaspersky Lab 2018).[5]

Zero-day vulnerabilities—unknown or unaddressed holes in program or network security, so named because they are newly discovered, or zero days old—allow anyone with knowledge of these systems and a fluency in the appropriate coding language to penetrate trusted systems. These vulnerabilities increase the likelihood of an effective attack, as well as the attack remaining undetected by the recipient (Batey 2015). Furthermore, cyberattacks defy easy categorization. They may include espionage, terrorism, theft, vandalism, or protest; the lines between categories may be blurred, compounded by the difficulty of ascertaining perpetrators and motives. Hackers can employ encryption, virtual private networks, and pseudonyms to conceal their identities. They also can disguise the origin of their attacks: "If hackers in

Bucharest want to steal from a bank in Omaha, they might first penetrate a server in Kalamazoo, and from there one in Liverpool, and from there one in Perth, and so on, until their trail is thoroughly obscured.... A sophisticated hacker ... might hop as many as thirty times before unleashing an attack" (Schmidle 2018). Cyberattacks are relatively inexpensive and cost-effective. According to the chief technology officer of the cybersecurity firm Splunk, Snehan Antani, "The cost of cyberattacks is 1/10th to 1/100th the cost of cyber defense.... This is because attack tools are freely distributed, the computing resources are stolen, and because the labour costs in state-sponsored attacks are typically low" (qtd. in D. Williams 2016).

Since cyber warfare is based in code, it lacks the manufacturing, warehousing, and deployment costs associated with traditional weapons. The sole expense is the labor of coders, and this expense stands to fall with "cloud" sharing and mobile technologies. While criminal hacks may seek a quick financial return, state-based attacks may be more precisely targeted with a specific goal, such as gaining strategic or technical information that may later be employed for disruptive purposes. Yet intent may be as difficult to ascertain as origin: "When a Russian criminal group with ties to Russian intelligence was detected attacking U.S. banks in 2014, for instance, the security community debated whether it was regular old cybercrime, or an attack linked to Russian state interests, designed as a response to the sanctioning of the regime for its invasion of Ukraine. But even then, was the attack a retaliation that got caught? Or was it akin to a nuclear test in a crisis, a signal intended to be detected, a warning of greater consequences if the United States pushed further?" (Singer 2015).

Attacks are not necessarily waged between individual entities (such as single nation versus single nation), and both criminal and state hackers may use similar means and methods of attack, making them harder to differentiate. Reflecting the growing alliance of state and corporate actors, methods used by states may trickle down to private firms, while states may buy and stockpile exploits from hackers and brokers or employ cyber mercenaries. The difficulties of determining parties, motives, and responses is further complicated by the fact that revealing these factors also reveals how deeply state agencies (such as the National Security Agency) have penetrated their networks. A public response to a cyberattack may lead to escalation, while a covert response may not be viewed as proportional or serve as an effective deterrent.

Victims of massive hacking episodes and data breaches include Sony, Target, Anthem, Home Depot, J.P. Morgan, Chase Bank, T-Mobile, and Experian, as well as U.S. government agencies including the Internal Revenue Service, the Postal Service, and the Office of Personnel Management. The National Health Service in the United Kingdom also suffered a crippling cyberattack. By some estimates 90 percent of U.S. companies have been hacked. At a cybersecurity conference in 2012, then FBI director Robert Mueller claimed, "There are only two types of companies: those that have been hacked and those that will be" (Schmidle 2018). A computer user now must think like a network administrator: "Assume you're going to be hacked and try to catch it before it does too much damage" (Tynan 2016). Both of these guidelines promote thinking like a hacker.

Hacks are a technical application of force to affect communication systems. In one sense *hacking* is "only a modern term for bugging, eavesdropping, signals intercept, listening-in, tapping, monitoring," and other technical threats to electronic privacy (McMullan 2015). Force can also cause harm from data destruction. Tools for hacks (including "lawful intercepts" by police, intelligence services, and other government agencies) must—by law—be built into global communications networks through technical "back doors" and administrative controls. Yet these "official" back doors also may exploited by unauthorized and unknown users (Landau 2013, 12). Other hacking tools are based on the exploitation of mundane vulnerabilities like weak passwords or users' proclivity to open dodgy email attachments. A third vector for attacks is provided by the aforementioned zero-day exploits.[6] These exploits are collected and sold by a flotilla of established and ephemeral cybersecurity businesses, including stand-alone companies, divisions of defense companies and accounting agencies, and independent contractors. Much of this work on trusted-system vulnerabilities is treated as classified or proprietary research, further benefiting the bottom lines of stakeholders while further compromising the security of the public internet.

Since the turn of the twenty-first century, reports of hacking episodes have increased exponentially. Many go unreported, adding to the catalog of systemic risks we face in digital capitalism. Yet hacking, as an application of force to communication systems, is not new; it can be traced to an earlier, mechanical age. Kirkpatrick Sale's (1996) account of Luddite resistance in the early stages of the Industrial Revolution provides a prescient historical example. Hacking's antecedents also may be found in events surrounding the development of radio or "wireless telegraphy" at the turn of the twentieth century. Guglielmo Marconi, like Apple's Steve Jobs, employed extensive stagecraft when unveiling technology. Marconi's first public demonstration of wireless telegraphy, held in 1903 at the London Royal Institution's lecture theater, was preceded by extensive publicity. Much to his dismay Marconi's trusted system was subjected to a brute-force hack during the demo. The electrical system for the slide projector accompanying Marconi's lecture was remotely commandeered by a radio transmitter outside the theater, causing the projector to flicker in pulses, which were immediately recognized as Morse code (Marks 2011; Raboy 2016).[7] Marconi denounced the prank as "scientific hooliganism" (Marks 2011); the hacker was later identified as an envious magician and radio hobbyist.

"Scientific hooliganism" also provided an effective pretext for corporate and military interests to wrest control of the electromagnetic spectrum from "amateurs," whose number included hobbyists and bench scientists working alone or in early research labs. Competing claims to wireless innovations, and accusations of amateur "interference," led to the U.S. Radio Act of 1912, in which corporations and the military were awarded vast swaths of the electromagnetic spectrum, while amateurs were exiled to a sliver of the remaining accessible frequencies (Douglas 1987). The British-based Marconi operation quickly dominated the international market for wireless telegraphy. At the behest of the U.S. Navy in the interests of national security, American Telephone and Telegraph, General Electric, United Fruit Company, and Westinghouse formed the Radio Corporation of America in 1919. RCA gathered the necessary elements for end-to-end radio communications and further consolidated corporate control over the electromagnetic spectrum. It was the genesis of a trusted system for analog radio–frequency technology, including licensing and ownership regulations, for media and technology producers.

In the world of telephony, AT&T's switched telephone network and Western Electric devices comprised a trusted system that legally excluded access by rival wireline systems and devices and unsanctioned (or nonpaying) users. And hacking naturally followed: Phil Lapsley (2013) describes user "hacks" of the phone system in the mid-twentieth century, which inspired a loose social network of phone "phreaks" intent on subverting the monopolistic practices of AT&T and Western Electric. Phone phreaks breached analog switching systems to obtain dial tone and long-distance or conference calling without payment. In a 1971 article in *Esquire,* author Ron Rosenbaum vividly described how John Draper, aka Captain Crunch, demonstrated the global scope of the phone network's trusted system. Draper hacked into the Bell network and routed a toll-free call from his home through international switches to his own second telephone line. Specifically, Draper connected a single long-distance call from California through switching stations in Tokyo, India, Greece, South Africa, London, and New York and back to an adjacent phone in California, wrapping his call around the globe. "Needless to say I had to shout to hear myself. But the echo was far out. Fantastic. Delayed. It was delayed twenty seconds, but I could hear myself talk to myself," he stated (Rosenbaum 1971, 117). This demonstration proved network bypass was possible, and it became more popular until authorities responded, in the early phases of a "hacker crackdown" (Sterling 1992).

Eventually digital switching systems superannuated this type of bypass. Concurrently, engineers at MIT and other elite universities developed social and technical bonds through "hacking" (or breaching and programming) mainframe computers (S. Levy 1984). Much as radio amateurs found themselves at the sharp end of the stick from military and corporate interests, phone phreaks and mainframe hackers found their "disruption" contained and co-opted: they and kindred spirits migrated to the emergent cyber culture, developing interconnected email relays and operating online bulletin board services in the 1970s and 1980s, before commercial internet service providers came along. Later they were known for their affiliation with the Whole Earth 'Lectronic Link, Prodigy, and similar online services (Turner 2006; Markoff 2005).[8]

As with phone-system phreaking, software hacking came to symbolize technological craft and means of resistance, asserting individual and group agency over a world of increasingly abstract, complex, and interconnected technical systems that enabled new forms of social interaction.[9] The recursive or self-referential social shaping of information and communication technology has attracted the attention of social and political theorists to the field (Kelty 2008). Anthropological work on hackers in general, and on the "hacktivist" collective that calls itself "Anonymous" in particular (e.g., Coleman 2011, 2013), has provided insight into the motives, actions, and communicative effects of some high-profile hacking campaigns. We seek to build on this line of inquiry by addressing the impact of hacking on social complexity and communicative action.

Why Hackers Win examines the ways in which hacking illuminates the relationship between the technical codes of trusted systems, the legal codes in which they operate, and how these codes overlap and interact to shape our social reality. As Niklas Luhmann notes, economic, legal, and political systems require trust to function effectively. At the same time their structural and operational properties "may erode confidence and thereby undermine one of the essential conditions of trust" (2000, 103). Hacking can undermine trust by breaching interconnected social systems and challenging the expectations that accompany their use.

Given the Network Society's immense complexity and accompanying risks, state and corporate actors who rely on trust have incentive to promote their own trusted systems at the expense of rival systems. By detecting flaws, active hacking interventions create cybernetic feedback loops that provide opportunities for system learning as well as the ability to monitor and establish control in new networks. Particular hacks (such as "growth hacks") may even improve the effectiveness of trusted systems by staking their boundaries, seeking out their blind spots, and exposing risks in online activities.

Although hacks may provide useful knowledge, online risk cannot be eliminated from trusted systems due to structural flaws embedded in technical code. In early 2018 two major security flaws were discovered in microprocessors used by nearly all computers. Both "could allow hackers to steal the entire memory contents of computers, including mobile devices, personal computers and servers running in so-called cloud computer networks." Dubbed Meltdown, one flaw specific to virtually every Intel microprocessor would allow hackers to rent space on cloud systems and grab information such as user passwords.[10] Although cloud operators including Amazon, Google, and Microsoft patched the exploit, the patch potentially slowed computers by as much as 30 percent. While Meltdown was specific to Intel, Spectre affected virtually all microprocessors on the market. Researchers claimed the flaw was difficult to exploit yet noted that addressing it would require redesigning the processors rather than simply providing patches, a process that could keep the threat alive for decades. As one analyst noted, "There's been this desire from the industry to be as fast as possible and secure at the same time. Spectre shows that you cannot have both" (Metz and Perlroth 2018, B1).

UNTRUSTWORTHY SYSTEMS

By restricting public access, trusted systems centralize capital and power in corporate and government networks and intellectual-property portfolios. But building public trust in these systems is an ongoing, perhaps Sisyphean, task. It requires a growing part of the Network Society's capital and labor be invested in powerful surveillance systems that must comply with state authority as well as industry standards. At the same time the legal and empirical bases for trusting government and corporations with managing these systems abound with ambiguities and paradoxes. There is a long history of transposing property law from previous technological eras to the contemporary digital domain. Designating trespass and property theft as cybercrimes is but one example. These laws are critical to maintain trusted systems in our contemporary phase of networked digital capitalism. But their protections are reserved largely for the owners of trusted systems, not their clients or users, nor many of their researchers and developers.

Yahoo! and Equifax offer cases in point. In 2017 Yahoo! admitted it had lost control of personal account information for its three billion email users.[11] The admission came months after Verizon Communications acquired the firm for $4.85 billion. Yahoo! claimed that a "state sponsored actor" inflicted the hack, although evidence indicates the firm was extremely vulnerable to hacking.[12] To cut costs and attract a buyer, Yahoo! executives had denied new expenditures for security; "put off proactive security defenses, including intrusion-detection mechanisms for Yahoo's production systems"; and rejected an automatic reset of all user passwords "for fear that even something as simple as a password change would drive Yahoo's shrinking email users to other services" (Perlroth and Goel 2016, B1). Yahoo's remaining reservoir of user trust may have vaporized when it revealed, belatedly, that all of its users had been exposed to identity theft. Yet, at the time of this writing, neither Yahoo! nor its subsequent buyer (Verizon) are accountable for damages in the United States. Although forty-eight U.S. states have security breach–notification laws (NCSL 2017), the Federal Trade Commission has discretion—but isn't required—to take action and impose penalties for breaches. Federal laws require breach notification from banks and health-care firms, but there are no comprehensive federal standards for addressing claims from breaches.[13]

In 2016 hackers stole W-2 tax and salary data from Equifax, and in early 2017 tax records under the firm's purview again were hacked. Equifax failed to improve the security of its systems. On July 29, 2017, Equifax discovered it had been breached, again: hackers obtained personal information for 143 million U.S. consumers, including social security and driver's license numbers (Siegel Bernard et al. 2017, A1). While the July 2017 Equifax breach may have affected fewer people than the Yahoo! breach, it released more records with unique personal identifiers as well as financially sensitive information, potentially putting its victims at higher risk (see chapter 3). Unlike users who signed up for Yahoo! accounts, people with credit records held in the United States do not "opt in" or sign up for Equifax services (nor for those of its two major competitors, TransUnion and Experian). U.S. citizens do not control their personally identifiable information as they do in the European Union or in Canada, Argentina, Australia, Japan, or other countries (Solove 2008, 3). Instead, Equifax gathers these data from employment, credit, banking, licensing, and other public and private sources held in various electronic databases.

Although it lacked the protections required by banks, Equifax similarly was too big to fail:

> Experts said it was highly unlikely that any regulatory body would shut Equifax down over this breach. As one of the nation's three major credit-reporting agencies [Experian and TransUnion], which store and analyze consumers' financial history for credit decisions, it is likely to be considered too central to the American financial system; Equifax's demise would both reduce competition in the industry and make each of the two survivors a bigger target.... The more data a company has on us, the less likely it is that a breach will put the company in any real danger, because its very size protects it. (Manjoo 2017, B1)

As Massachusetts senator Elizabeth Warren pointed out in subsequent U.S. Senate judiciary hearings, Equifax stood to benefit financially from new sales of "anti-fraud" information (credit monitoring) and insurance to the very consumers whose accounts and identities it jeopardized.[14] As the public's risk to identity theft increases from Equifax's breach, the company's "potential costs are shockingly low. Consumers can sue the credit bureau, but it's historically not a lucrative route for recovery. It turns out the average restitution paid out for those that win a lawsuit is less than $2 per consumer" (Leonhardt 2017). Potential costs to businesses dropped further still when the U.S. Senate voted in 2017 to kill a bill protecting consumers from forced-arbitration clauses used by financial companies to thwart class-action lawsuits in cases like the Equifax breach.

Short of purchasing "cyber insurance" against hacking attacks and subsequent losses (see chapter 3), the public has few means to reduce the risk of losing control of their personally identifiable data. Although we may ritualistically shred paper bills and bank statements or actively seek to protect our privacy online, we cannot exert absolute control over our visibility or completely diminish the "data smog" we produce (Shenk 1997). As the Yahoo!, Equifax, and other megabreaches illustrate, individuals have very little influence over the security of corporately held information. For many categories of data, weak access controls do not yet provide cause for legal action in federal courts.[15] In addition, popular education and training in cybersecurity principles are scarce. While internet safety courses for children are spreading, they often do little more than address the timeless lessons of face-to-face interaction in public (such as "don't talk to strangers") or serve as corporate branding exercises.[16] Although this may be poised to change, computer-literacy training in schools is still oriented toward completing specific applications, platforms, and tasks and sharing information, generally without regard for enhancing the user's privacy or security. Industry public-relations campaigns may be repurposed as "public interest" campaigns: in the 2010s the recording industry and major movie studios developed "internet safety" curricula for public and private schools, based primarily on antipiracy messages ("Film Group" 2013). Many federal lawmakers partly responsible for the governance of trusted systems remain fundamentally ignorant of the internet's structure and functions and especially of the underlying "unity" of hacking and cybersecurity in engineering (Bratus et al. 2014, 7), even as they support the activities of intelligence services whose mission objectives include breaching trusted systems.

"EVEN THE GOVERNMENT DOES IT"

Intelligence services in the United States and elsewhere spend a lot of time hacking, though the public is rarely aware of it. Legal hacking by the state is designed for secrecy and is functionally indistinguishable from illegal hacking in some important ways. In the United States, illegal hacking by the state has undermined the normative basis for law and policy on hacking and cybersecurity. The Edward Snowden revelations (Greenwald 2014) exposed an astonishing array of National Security Agency (NSA) hacks, methods, techniques, and procedures, demonstrating that "the US government, with assistance from major telecommunications carriers including AT&T, has engaged in massive, illegal dragnet surveillance of the domestic communications and communications records of millions of ordinary Americans since at least 2001" (EFF 2015).[17] Snowden's exfiltration revealed the depth of AT&T's collusion with NSA from 2003 to 2013: in addition to assisting with the wiretapping of all internet communications at the United Nations headquarters in New York, in 2011 AT&T began handing over 1.1 billion domestic cell phone calling records per day to the NSA. At the time intelligence officials told reporters that records were restricted largely to landlines "for technical reasons." One exfiltrated document reminded NSA officials to be polite when visiting AT&T facilities, noting, "This is a partnership, not a contractual relationship" (Angwin et al. 2015, A1).[18]

The NSA's Boundless Informant program captured and analyzed millions of telephone and email records generated in the United States. In one month in 2013, NSA "collected data on more than three billion telephone calls and emails that passed through the US telecommunications system." AT&T was not alone in colluding with the NSA; it was revealed that "Verizon, AT&T, Facebook, Google, Microsoft and every other major internet company—nine in all—have been providing access to the personal communication of, potentially, every American—phone calls, e-mails, text messages, documents stored in the cloud—to the NSA secretly, and without a warrant, as a matter of course" (Halpern 2014). Through its Tailored Access Operations, the NSA has global access to potentially millions of trusted systems and produces intelligence on some of their "very hardest targets" at their sources of origin ("Documents Reveal" 2013).

In the United States, federal, state, and local governments also frequently employ independent spyware and hacking firms to supplement their police investigations. Companies like the publicly traded Harris Corporation, based in Melbourne, Florida, do a brisk business in technologies like cell phone tower simulators that intercept cell phone calls, texts, and emails. By 2015 the company had $5 billion in annual sales. The technologies are sold under names like StingRay and KingFish. Harris's clients must sign nondisclosure agreements before purchase, which gives the firm tremendous power to suppress what would otherwise be publicly available information about the program, creating a de facto control over public policy. According to Joe Simitian, a Santa Clara, California, county supervisor, "So, just to be clear, we are being asked to spend $500,000 of taxpayers' money and $42,000 a year thereafter for a product for the name brand which we are not sure of, a product we have not seen, a demonstration we don't have, and we have a nondisclosure requirement as a precondition. You want us to vote and spend money, [but] you can't tell us more about it" (Richtel 2015, B4). In addition to a lack of transparency, these nondisclosure agreements have an unintended consequence: since police are precluded from testifying about the role of StingRay in arrests, cases involving their operation may result in plea bargains or be dropped altogether.

At the local, national, and transnational levels, private cybersecurity and defense firms have formed a de facto "global security assemblage" with state intelligence and security agencies (Abrahamsen and Williams

2009; LeRiche 2017) that is invested with exceptional powers to manage political and economic uncertainty in the post-9/11 era. As these private players become more closely integrated with government security forces employed in transnational operations, they "undermine the monopoly on legitimate use of violence reserved for the state" (LeRiche 2017, 147). The work of these intermediaries is often supported by acquiescent technology vendors and service providers, who allow installation of back doors and provide other work-arounds to trusted systems. Code vendors have allied with mercenary security firms and private intelligence agencies, sometimes in partnerships with defense contractors. The shape-shifting alliances of cybersecurity-plus organizations insinuate themselves into top echelons of government power: Erik Prince, Blackwater founder and general-purpose mercenary, even lobbied U.S. president Donald Trump to create a private intelligence service for the new administration (Sciutto and Cohen 2017). Therefore, managing risk through hacking and cybersecurity markets can ultimately feed back into the political system as assertions of executive power and policy making by fiat.

GROWTH HACKS

The extent of corporate espionage (or "corporate intelligence") through hacking is unknown, although Fortune 500 companies use it to maintain defenses against IP theft (Bailey 2016).[19] As a byproduct of "digital capitalism" (Schiller 2000), hacking markets flourish at numerous levels (Burkart and McCourt 2017). In addition to markets for exploits and packaged cyber-defense tools, other "growth areas" include insurance against corporate hacking and identity theft (whether these insurance products add or reduce risk is another question). Markets for risk can diminish trust in social and sociotechnical systems, resulting in what Jürgen Habermas (1975) terms a "legitimation crisis." Although attempts to offload risk have worked for now, we can already see how legitimation problems in cybercrime law and policy are converging with escalating social risk toward catastrophe. As Ulrich Beck proposes, "risk is not synonymous with catastrophe. Risk means the anticipation of the catastrophe. Risks concern the possibility of future occurrences and developments; they make present a state of the world that does not (yet) exist. Whereas every catastrophe is spatially, temporally and socially determined, the anticipation of catastrophe lacks any spatio-temporal or social concreteness" (2009, 9). We address the institutional shaping of social norms in the next chapter.

Three cases, in which transnational corporations hacked trusted systems to engage in deceptive and anticompetitive behavior, illustrate the way in which "growth hacks"—a Silicon Valley euphemism "that describes breaking legal or moral rules in a quest for scale" (Roberts 2017)—have migrated from start-up culture to big business. We distinguish growth hacks from "deep hacks" (see chapter 2), which can emanate from outside the marketplace and which reverberate through the systems of technology, law, and society. The first example of a growth hack involves Uber Technologies, which secretly built the Greyball and Hell software tools into its drivers' smartphone app, enabling the company to operate in markets where its services had been restricted. Uber's Android rider app "phoned home" to send sensitive user data back to the company (Khandelwal 2014). News Corporation (News Corp) hacked voice-mail accounts and intercepted private communications to generate sensationalized stories for its *News of the World* tabloid newspaper—which it then tried to cover up. Finally, Volkswagen's software hack was created to mask excessive emissions by their diesel vehicles, in clear violation of environmental protection rules in the United States and abroad, even as the company sued researchers who had discovered a way to hack its vehicle's locks. These examples illustrate the ways in which corporations have relied on hacks of trusted systems as a standard business tactic while sometimes using antihacking law to slow discovery of vulnerabilities in their own systems.[20]

Uber has a particular "reputation for ruthlessness" (Estes 2017). Its business model, based on a trusted-system software platform shared by drivers and users, uses real-time surveillance to match rides more efficiently than taxicabs. To expand into areas where its operations were prohibited, in 2014 the company surreptitiously added the Greyball function to its smartphone app for riders. Greyball allowed Uber to identify and evade potential authorities through practices such as "geofencing," in which a digital map would locate city government offices and enable drivers to avoid riders from those areas. Besides deceiving regulators, Greyball also allowed Uber to survey social media and mine credit card databases to identify and flag potential government or police employees (Isaac 2017, A1). Another module on the driver app, known by Uber executives and engineers as "Hell," allowed the company "to track drivers using its biggest competitor in the US, Lyft, and to monitor which of Lyft's drivers also drove for Uber" (Cook and Price 2017). The Hell and Greyball programs exploited the surveillance features of smartphones on both sides of its platform—driver and rider—to seek anticompetitive advantage in labor markets for drivers and to evade government regulations.

Although these deceptive growth hacks contributed to Uber's business plan by adding scale to its overall market, they also added to a growing list of legal problems (including sexual harassment and anti-labor practices) attributed to Uber's former management. As of this writing, the company is under investigation by the U.S. Department of Justice for Greyball and by the FBI for both the Greyball and Hell initiatives. But Uber remains "unrepentant." The firm's response to getting caught deploying Greyball was to denigrate the public investigators and law enforcement who caught them, while at the same time implying that Uber was entitled to pursue hacking its employees' and customers' phones as a proprietary business strategy. It employed a classic hacking rationale to protect its trusted system (its private property) from trespass (theft): "This program denies ride requests to users who are violating our terms of service, whether that's people aiming to physically harm drivers, competitors looking to disrupt our operations, or opponents who collude with officials on secret 'stings' meant to entrap drivers," an Uber spokesperson stated (Estes 2017).

Uber was itself breached, as evidenced in May 2014, when two sellers on the anonymous Tor network offered thousands of Uber usernames and passwords that would allow buyers to log in and book rides (Gibbs 2015b). Uber first issued a denial, but in November 2017 the company admitted that it had hidden the breach, in which fifty-seven million driver and rider accounts were stolen from a third-party server, for over a year. After paying a $100,000 ransom, Uber tracked down the hackers and pushed them to sign nondisclosure agreements forbidding them to tell regulators or users that the information was stolen. The company then concealed the ransom by calling it a "bug bounty," in which hackers are hired to test the security of systems (Isaac, Benner, and Frenkel 2017, B1; Larson 2017b). Yet, as the *New York Times* noted, "The issue is not legally clear cut. Laws concerning bug bounties are ambiguous. The Justice Department weighed into bug disclosure programs for the first time in July and largely left it to organizations to decide what access they will authorize for hackers and what they can do with the data.... Breach disclosure laws also differ state to state. The state laws most relevant to Uber's case require disclosure if names are exposed in with driver's license numbers in a 'breach of security'" (Perlroth and Isaac 2018, A1).[21]

At News Corp illicit hacking teams appear to have operated regularly under the direction of its board of directors and subsidiaries, depending on the business needs of the day. To bolster readership of News Corp's well-known tabloids, its journalists have turned to innovative means of gathering information, including brute-force password hacking of voice-mail boxes to access and delete messages. One voice-mail box belonged to a teenage UK girl at the center of a missing person's case, who was later discovered murdered; others belonged to victims of 9/11. A former *News of the World* employee (Paul McMullan, deputy features editor) offered a wildly bent rationale for his team's illegal phone hacking. He claimed that surveillance and privacy violations are necessary to acquire exclusive sources for any story: "Phone hacking is a perfectly acceptable tool, given the sacrifices we make, if all we're trying to do is get to the truth.... Privacy is for pedos" (qtd. in Lyall 2011). By 2017 News Corp's newspapers had settled with more than a thousand phone-hacking victims (Ruddick 2017). That same year News Corp's News Group apologized in court to a former British intelligence official whose computer had been infected with eBlaster spyware by a "private investigations" firm operating under News Group's direction (2017a).

The legal record strongly suggests that hacking for business advantage is normal operation in News Corp's TV distribution division as well. Although the company claims to have disproved all allegations of illegal hacks, their extensive computer hacking, including that in the service of "predatory piracy" (Sauer and Tepper 2008), has been traced to roughly 1997. Four separate lawsuits, accusing News Corp firms of hacking copy-protection schemes, revealed a News Corp team dedicated specifically to developing such "black ops" in support of its DirecTV operations. Following a 2011 shareholder action against the company, a court found News Corp's subsidiary NDS guilty of hacking Vivendi and Echostar TV smart cards and recruiting hackers to distribute counterfeit NagraStar cards to pirate Dish Network signals, beginning in 1997. Specifically, NDS "was accused by satellite company EchoStar of illegally extracting software code from competitors' cards and posting the information online, allowing hackers to create counterfeit cards that could be used to intercept television programming. A federal jury found that NDS's practices were illegal and the court subsequently granted EchoStar an injunction preventing NDS from intercepting its satellite signal" (Pilkington 2011). NDS won on appeal to the U.S. Ninth Circuit Court in 2010 and eventually collected $18 million from EchoStar. But in the testimony a witness claimed to have been paid more than $20,000 in cash concealed in CD and DVD players from HarperCollins (a News Corp division) to "develop a pirating program to make DirecTV more secure, not to sabotage rival systems" (Zetter 2008).

Researchers have noted that News Corp's News America Marketing division "has been the subject of five lawsuits alleging anti-competitive behavior... [forcing] the company to pay out more than $650 million in settlements to three competitors" (Longstreth and Hals 2011). One suit involving a competitor, Floorgraphics, claimed that "on at least eleven separate occasions between October 2003 and January 2004, News intentionally, knowingly and without authorization breached FGI's secure computer system and repeatedly accessed, viewed, took and obtained [Floorgraphics'] most sensitive and private information concerning its past and upcoming advertising and marketing programs" (Edwards 2009).[22] News America Marketing settled the lawsuit by purchasing Floorgraphics' contracts midtrial, before the company had finished presenting its case. The claims involving News Corp cluster around breaches of trusted systems, for corporate espionage (theft of intellectual property), hacking news makers and public officials, and circumventing digital-rights management (conditional access controls for competitors' satellite TV channels). Their pattern begins with News Corp–owned (or majority-owned) companies instigating hacks against competitors, continues with defensive litigation, and typically resolves with a corporate takeover, settlement, or (in the case of *News of the World*) restructuring.[23] As UK regulators evaluate the Murdoch dynasty as "fit and proper" in News Corp's bid for total ownership of Sky (Sweney 2017), its hacking victims have undermined News Corp's claims that its standards and practices are, to use British military parlance, tickety-boo.

Volkswagen's software hack enabled cars marketed as "clean diesel" vehicles to "pass" emissions tests despite dirty exhausts, and its discovery triggered international regulatory reforms for car emissions. Installed inside the car, Volkswagen's defeat device informed the emissions-testing computer when a testing cycle was activated and changed the vehicle's emissions accordingly. Researchers at West Virginia University discovered cars with hacked chips emitted pollutants almost forty times what was allowed by U.S. regulations (Glinton 2015). After pleading guilty to federal fraud and conspiracy charges, Volkswagen paid $15 billion in fines for software installed in cars made from 2009 to 2015 (McCarthy

2017). It also agreed to compensate individual owners and repair all affected models. An engineer pled guilty to participating in the scheme and was sentenced to a forty-month prison sentence in 2016. New York and Massachusetts attorneys general have pursued a civil case against Volkswagen, claiming that "this was a widespread conspiracy involving many, many people," including the company's CEO, who resigned when the scandal went public (Isidore 2016). At the time of this writing, German authorities arrested and held the CEO of Volkswagen's Audi branch for over three months in an ongoing criminal investigation into emissions-test cheating.

With the discovery of its "defeat devices," Volkswagen found itself on the wrong side of its own hack. But Volkswagen was not charged with creating and deploying defeat devices; it was instead charged with conspiracy to defraud the United States and its customers and to violate the Clean Air Act. However, two years prior to the emissions-hack revelations, Volkswagen sued Flavio Garcia, a computer science security researcher at the University of Birmingham (and his team), to prevent disclosure of a vulnerability in the antitheft system of some Volkswagen vehicles, including high-end sports cars. In this case Volkswagen asked the UK government to censor research findings that the wireless auto-ignition system was easily hackable by thieves or others with criminal intent. The lawsuit prevented Garcia and his team from presenting their findings at the USENIX Security Conference in Washington, DC, in August 2013 (Trotman 2013).[24]

Publication of the research (Garcia, Verdult, and Ege 2013) was delayed two years by the suit but was soon followed by a new paper, whose findings were even more serious (Garcia et al. 2016): "Volkswagen left not only its ignition vulnerable but the keyless entry system that unlocks the vehicle's doors, too. And this time, they say, the flaw applies to practically every car Volkswagen has sold since 1995." These cars numbered about a hundred million units. With Volkswagen's security system disclosed as a potential attack vector, the company faces extensive recalls and repairs and possibly other large expenditures related to the vulnerability (although none are reported at the time of this writing). The hack used a cheap, off-the-shelf microcomputer kit (called an Arduino). The suit against the Birmingham researchers raised concerns that the company may have known about the security vulnerability for years. The chip manufacturer that served Volkswagen and other companies noted that VW's chip uses "a legacy security algorithm, introduced 18 years ago. . . . Our customers are aware" (Greenberg 2016). The UK court's 2013 order against Flavio Garcia's team quashed the news of the vulnerabilities and placed an embargo on their publication. The ruling reduced VW's short-term financial risk in the conflict but potentially increased security risks to the public through vulnerabilities that were known but unfixed for at least two years.

These three cases of corporate "growth hacks" are known through their failures; we must ask how many other cases –successful or not— have gone undiscovered and unreported. Each company has offered a unique response to its resulting public-relations nightmare. Volkswagen launched advertisements titled, "Keeping Your Promises" with the tagline, "It's more than just a car. It's keeping your promises" (Slater 2016), a campaign seemingly designed to exploit audience ignorance or short-term memory loss. News Corp's Rupert Murdoch (sort of) apologized to the family of the dead thirteen-year-old girl whose voice mail was hacked: "As the founder of the company, I was appalled to find out what happened" ("Murdoch Begins" 2011). Uber claimed to have deployed Greyball in charity, "because it was 'deeply concerned that its driver-partners would be penalized financially' or otherwise for their driving" ("Uber Faces" 2017). The cases of Uber, News Corp, and Volkswagen share a corporate realpolitik: turnabout is fair play when hacking is part of corporate strategy. Hack your customers, your employees, your competitors, your regulators, and, if expeditious, retaliate if you're hacked. Deny, disclaim, or even cover up as needed, and offer a counternarrative for plausible deniability. Use antihacking law to your advantage if others find bugs in your trusted systems. None of these cases demonstrates negligence as clearly as they demonstrate hubristic anticompetitiveness. As giant corporations caught abusing trust, their growth hacks add social risk, complexity, and extra layers of secrecy and suspicion to the economy, politics, and the law. They signify the impetus to manipulate trusted systems, a form of "soft power," to compete for advantage.

A hacker's successful exploit of a trusted system is not the sort of news willingly shared by a company whose reputation and business depends on that system. News of hacking cases bubbles up from industry trade magazines, hacker forums, security email listservs, and other sources removed from the business pages of newspapers and magazines.

Hacking tools and techniques allow states and corporations to manipulate sociotechnical systems for advantage, sometimes illegally through outright fraud but more commonly through legal "gray zones." Nurtured by legal fictions, aporias, and other vagaries, hacking can blur the boundaries between military and corporate intelligence programs, between national and international legal systems, and between corporations and clients. Hacking can catalyze changes in multiple domains and across related subsystems, often in a "cascading" fashion that can escalate the scale of their effects (Landau 2013, 160). Since interconnected networks increasingly are essential to the state's political and economic functions, they are considered to be among the state's strategic defense interests. Yet national legal regimes are riddled with inconsistencies that reduce their effectiveness in coordinating social systems and may even exacerbate social risks of hacking.

THE VAGARIES OF LAW AND POLICY

State and federal agencies in the United States (especially the Department of Justice) typically initiate new cases for prosecution but have wide discretion in doing so; they are criticized both for overprosecuting and underprosecuting under the Computer Fraud and Abuse Act (CFAA), which was codified in 1984 (Mishkin 2016). Online intruders, fraudsters, snoops, and thieves typically "exceed authorized access" (in the CFAA's famously vague phrase) in the course of committing other crimes. Yet law in general, and the CFAA in particular, is only selectively applied, particularly in cases with international jurisdiction.[25] As operating law, the CFAA assumes fraudulent intent for all prosecutions rather than requiring that fraudulent intent be demonstrated. This assumption removes unintentionality as a defense against a charge of hacking and has created precedents that muddy the already messy demonstrations of intentionality in the unlawful use of a computer to access a trusted system. Data breaches go unprosecuted while seemingly innocent activities that may trespass a trusted system can be ensnared in the law. For example, great confusion arose following a 2016 legal decision involving trade secret theft and economic espionage *(United States v. Nosal)*. Netflix password sharing was widely reported to have become a federal crime under the CFAA, although the Ninth Circuit majority who decided the case did not fully consider the broad consequences of their decision.[26] If a law intended to outlaw criminal hacking can be targeted at legally naive or "clueless" users of streaming movie or music services, then its value in reducing insecurity and risk from malicious hacking of trusted systems is dramatically diminished. The Netflix example shows how maladapted law and policy has exacerbated uncertainty in those media markets most dependent on trusted systems.

It seems likely that effective regulations of invasive software will remain a "pipe dream" both domestically and abroad (Segal and Waxman 2011). International agreements leave up to half of the world's population largely ungoverned by treaty-based law on hacking and trade in cyber weapons (made of malware or invasive software). The Council of Europe's Convention on Cybercrime (the Budapest Convention) presently harmonizes the international legal regime for forty-seven countries, including the United States. Although it has noted weaknesses (Akdeniz 2008), the Budapest Convention nonetheless "has the widest coverage of any international agreement dealing with cybercrime (estimated to cover one-third of current internet users)" (Harley 2010). The U.S. Senate ratified the Convention on Cybercrime with the European Union in 2006, adjusting national law to incorporate measures that criminalized "offenses against the confidentiality, integrity and availability of computer data and systems" (Council of Europe 2018).[27] The United States also committed to mutual assistance in pursuing cases, including intercepting and sharing traffic and content data from service providers in real time, as well as extradition. The convention requires signatory states to adopt laws to punish offenders "by effective, proportionate and dissuasive sanctions, which include deprivation of liberty" (art. 3, sec. 1). The United States has adapted federal law to fit the convention in its various updates to the antiquated CFAA. But India, China, Russia, and Brazil have declined to join the convention. Consequently, a majority of the world's internet users live outside the rules.[28]

States have not adopted a Geneva convention for cyber weapons or cyber warfare, despite principles of jurisprudence developed in the *Tallinn Manual* beginning in 2009 (Schmitt 2013). On top of the Budapest Convention, there are overlays of state coalitions and circles of "trust" that pertain to surveillance and cybersecurity. These include Five Eyes (the United States, the United Kingdom, Canada, Australia, and New Zealand); Nine Eyes (adding Denmark, France, the Netherlands, and Norway), and Fourteen Eyes (adding Germany, Belgium, Italy, Spain, and Sweden) (Schneier 2015). Sweden has an official policy of international neutrality (it is not a North Atlantic Treaty Organization [NATO] member) and a long-standing record of human-rights advocacy. Yet in 2008 the Swedish government authorized the Försvarets Radioanstalt (FRA; National Defense Radio Establishment) to monitor all communication traveling over fiber-optic lines in and out of Sweden, including emails, texts, and phone calls. The FRA began sharing data with NSA in 2011 and partnered with the NSA and Britain's Government Communications Headquarters on the Quantum hacking operation, intended to hack into foreign computers and networks. In a quid pro quo arrangement, the Swedish FRA was allowed access to the NSA's most powerful analytic tool, XKeyscore. According to NSA documents, the tool provides real-time observation of web activity and enables the retrieval of "nearly everything a user does on the Internet" (Eakin 2017, 56).

These transnational circles of trust are permeable and shifting. One-off partnerships between rivals, such as when the United States tracked Chechen separatists and Russia warned the United States about the Boston Marathon bomber, are similar to these honor agreements ("Russia Warned" 2014). Such arrangements also may include provisos in which a state grants access to another state on the condition that it doesn't gather information on resident citizens. All parties involved presume the unenforceability of these agreements. Members routinely hack one another for surveillance purposes, as evidenced by the NSA's purported monitoring of German chancellor Angela Merkel's encrypted mobile phone (Traynor, Oltermann, and Lewis 2013). It was reported in 2017 that "the German security agency BND had used almost 4,000 keywords in internal surveillance databases that related to American targets from 1998 to 2006. These included White House email addresses as well as phone and fax numbers, as well as the US Department of State and Treasury" (Lowe 2017). Nevertheless, BND has used the NSA's XKeyscore surveillance tool since at least 2013. Nonpariah states are legally immune from responsibility for such invasive campaigns, which further blurs the boundaries between hostile hacking campaigns by military agencies and intelligence gathering between allies.

CONCLUSION

Our basic premise, then, is that hacking is best understood as an embedded function, rather than disruption, of the Network Society. As the trusted systems that increasingly define our online interactions become more complex and diffuse, they require greater monitoring to function effectively, with corresponding implications for the social totality. This introductory chapter has established our focus on hacking trusted systems. Chapter 2 further explores issues of risk and presents a communication-based theory of hacking and cybersecurity using cybernetic social systems theory. We focus on how the conflicted domains of hacking and cybersecurity accelerate each other's development. Chapter 3 identifies the levels or layers of the markets for hacking insecurity, including those for hacking tools (especially malware and botnets) and commercially available cybersecurity products and insurance. Chapter 4 examines the law and policy domain pertaining to hacking and cybersecurity, including the difficulties in maintaining a transnational or global regime for regulating hacking as cybercrime and the attendant use of intellectual-property law for recodifying hacking law and policy. Chapter 5 provides a summary of the contemporary situation and discusses possibilities for greater transparency and accountability in the global legal regime. In an environment of legal uncertainty, hacking reflects a growing trend in which corporations act as state proxies, underscoring the ways in which state policy is increasingly determined outside the bounds of public debate and accountability—with profound implications for the polity and civil society.

CHAPTER TWO

Hacking and Risk to Systems

In the first chapter we argued that the Network Society's management of risk and uncertainty hinges on a fundamental paradox. To engage in commerce and access culture, members of the public increasingly are drawn into trusted networked systems that require verification of users. These systems in turn are "entrusted" to provide continual feedback to decision makers. But their basis in digital technology also renders them vulnerable to hacking, which undermines trust in their use (Camp 2001). Hacking disrupts online systems; the field of information security (or cybersecurity for short) addresses the disruptions and in the process further impacts these systems. The need for states, corporations, and other social systems to protect assets through cybersecurity also heightens the need for hacking as a means to gain advantage over their competitors. Hacking and cybersecurity therefore operate reciprocally, reinforcing each other in a positive feedback loop. In their agonistic to-and-fro, hacking and cybersecurity provide cybernetic self-knowledge by testing subsystem boundaries. They also enable state and private entities to influence social systems outside of public discourse or accountability. Our analysis is grounded in critical studies of information law and policy and seeks to reveal major sources of reification and disenfranchisement in the Network Society (Fischer-Lescano 2012,

3–4). Political economy provides a useful perspective on systems theory and sociology and has been incorporated into second-generation Frankfurt School critical theory through Jürgen Habermas's (1984, 1987) theory of communicative action.[1]

Hacking and cybersecurity operate as varieties of instrumental power to "get business done." A hacker may seek unauthorized entry into a vulnerable machine to deploy malware for "business" objectives including surveilling, deleting or "exfiltrating" (stealing) data, identity spoofing, or performing other surreptitious operations. Malware can also be used to add the machine to a remotely commandeered "botnet," to join in distributed denial-of-service (DDoS) attacks. A responding business objective involves providing forward defenses to promote network and computer security. A growing cadre of cybersecurity elites is in the business of planting digital tripwires or depth charges inside networks to detect or prevent "the primary 'threat' of the Internet . . . , the potential for systems 'crash,' loss, theft or corruption of data, and interruption of information flows" (Deibert 2002, 131). The encoding of "trust" in trusted systems also serves ideological purposes. Since it is based in social convention, rather than on demonstrated proof, the security of trusted systems is at least partly a construct of powerful social actors. For example, since the Stuxnet malware relied on a spoofed Microsoft security certificate, its deployment risked public trust in the security of all of Microsoft's products, which supposedly take only authenticated and secure updates from the internet (Klimburg 2017, 183).

Trusted systems are naturally degraded through everyday use. The populations that rely on trusted systems for their electricity, telephone, email, online payments, health care, voting, transportation, and so forth frequently are the weakest links in the chain, as they provide reliable attack vectors for malware infections. As the software embedded in network-connected devices and services approaches its end of life, whether through the "planned obsolescence" of operating systems or the disposability of devices, it decreases in quality and reliability and is increasingly exposed to vulnerabilities. Signaling System 7 (SS7) was created in 1975 to allow phone users to transfer networks as they traveled. SS7 was an integral part of 2G cellular systems, which are still maintained globally. In 2017 hackers exploited SS7 weaknesses to intercept text messages containing one-time passwords for bank customers in Germany. The hackers then used the passwords to steal money from the victims' accounts (Quintin 2018, A19).[2] Even those who ordinarily should "know better" can fall into a trap. The 2016 hack of the Democratic National Committee's email database and its subsequent data exfiltration originated from a targeted "spear-phishing" expedition. John Podesta and Colin Powell were lured to a spoofed Gmail site, where both changed their log-in credentials. Hackers then used these credentials to dox Podesta and Powell ("John Podesta Emails" 2016; Murnane 2016; Franceschi-Bicchierai 2016b).[3] The doxxed emails are widely believed to have helped tip the balance of the 2016 U.S. presidential election, together with other important factors (including FBI director James Comey's investigation of Hillary Clinton's email security and an information war attributed by U.S. agencies to Russia). A lingering lesson from the omnishambles of the 2016 U.S. elections may be that when trusted systems used by political and social organizations are hacked and doxxed, their secrets can spill into the public domain and sow disruption, creating new "political opportunity structures" (Tarrow 1999, 75) for social movements and other actors.

The global banking system, which has been instrumental to the rise of "digital capitalism" (Schiller 2000), is particularly vulnerable to risk arising from problems with trusted systems. In February 2016 $81 million was stolen from the central bank of Bangladesh through a hack of the Society for Worldwide Interbank Financial Telecommunication (SWIFT) payments transfer system, which is used by banks to move funds globally. Hackers repeatedly breached a secured trusted system and manipulated messages guiding money flows between banks; according to SWIFT, "the thieves somehow got their hands on legitimate network credentials, initiated the fraudulent transfers and installed malware on bank computers to disguise their movements" (Corkery 2016). The SWIFT episode illustrates the function of a hack as a "steering medium": when a hack breaches a boundary within a trusted system, this in turn affects power dynamics within interconnected social systems such as financial institutions. A rogue actor was enriched; more significantly, the boundaries required to authenticate and distribute funds within a system broke down, blurring the lines (in this case) between client and criminal. The SWIFT hack "rocked faith in the system whose messages had, until then, been accepted at face value" ("SWIFT Banking" 2016).

Other hacks affecting global banking and finance include the Paradise Papers and the Panama Papers, which exposed the secret bank accounts of politicians and other elites from 2014 to 2017. In the case of the Paradise Papers, a law office specializing in offshore investments for well-heeled clients—Appleby Global Group Services—was hacked and doxxed. An Appleby spokesperson protested the hack was not an "inside job": "Our systems were accessed by an intruder who deployed the tactics of a professional hacker and covered his/her tracks to the extent that a forensic investigation by a leading international Cyber & Threats team concluded that there was no definitive evidence that any data had left our systems. This was not the work of anybody who works at Appleby" ("Appleby Reaction" 2017). The Panama Papers doxxing episode—targeting Mossack Fonseca, a giant "offshore law firm"—exfiltrated 11.5 million records. Victims included "twelve national leaders among 143 politicians, their families, and close associates from around the world known to have been using offshore tax havens" (Harding 2016). An "SQL injection flaw" (a database exploit) on one of the firm's corporate systems provided the attack vector (Infosec Institute 2016). The political fallout from the Panama and Paradise breaches was profound and ongoing, as it has implicated elites in secret business arrangements around the world (ICIJ 2017).

DEEP HACKS AND SOCIAL SYSTEMS

The work of German social theorist Ulrich Beck can be used to conceptualize law and policy questions in terms of contingency and risk to entire social systems. Beck's studies of risk management (1996, 2006; Beck et al. 2013) emerged from European discourses concerning post–Cold War globalization and the beginning of the telecommunications and computing boom of the 1980s and 1990s. By reenvisioning Europe as part of a new world system, in which the focus of geopolitical gamesmanship shifted from the military-industrial complex to international trade-related advantage, "the distinctions and boundaries between internal and external, national and international, local and global, ourselves and others grow more confused or hybridized, [. . . and] the units, issues and basic concepts in each of the social sciences tend to become more contingent [and] the premises and boundaries defining those units fall apart" (Beck 2004, 132).

Stated another way, the harnessing and taming of risk through the manipulation of system boundaries increasingly offers opportunities to exercise power. A hacking incident or campaign may effectively "hack through" layered systems for health, public safety, finance, and education, whose interconnection and mutual dependence may become apparent only after they are hacked. Since networked trusted systems pass information to one another, a hack of one system has the potential to affect related systems at a deeper level than hacks of analog telephone or television systems (Berke 2015). At the infrastructure level, for example, telecom outages can lead to loss of internet connectivity for servers and loss of telephone systems, with subsequent losses of access to data and personnel. Banking and finance are especially important to interconnected economies. Since they are at least partly automated, they are particularly vulnerable to cyberattacks. Depending on the nature of the organization, the effects of hacks can reverberate through entire social institutions, including political systems. The Bangladesh Bank heist using the SWIFT transfer system further strained the country's financial and political systems, which already were dealing with an influx of Rohingya refugees driven from neighboring Burma. The WannaCry cyberattacks on Britain's National Health Service had "potentially serious implications for the NHS and its ability to provide care" (National

Audit Office 2017) and "propel[led] health funding to [the] center" of the British election campaign (Faulconbridge and Holden 2018).[4] Accusations of hacking campaigns and information warfare have become de rigueur in this era of geopolitical conflict.[5] Ukraine, Estonia, and Georgia provide researched case studies, while observers from countries in Western Europe wonder if they also are becoming object lessons (Branford 2017).

These events provide examples of "deep hacks," in which a hack can exploit a political or economic opportunity and, in the process, potentially redraw social, political, and legal relationships in ways that were unforeseen and unintended—perhaps even by the perpetrators themselves. By hacking these loops, deep hacks steer communicative action within and across social systems to redraw or alter existing boundaries in novel ways. As exercises of power, they may have political characteristics; used as leverage in markets, deep hacks can exert economic power comparable to that of money. Therefore, deep hacks serve as a distinct class of communicative "non-linguistic steering media," similar to money and power, as described by Habermas in *Theory of Communicative Action* (1984; 1987, 1, 171, 261–97, 332–85). The communicative effects of a deep hack are detectable only after the fact. A deep hack shapes the opportunities for strategic action, even if its origins and motives are not known.

On the other side of the hack, defenders likewise reshape social reality through active defense strategies intended to reduce the risk of incoming hacks. Both offensive and defensive hacks serve as forms of strategic action that can be partly, but not entirely, characterized through their communicative effects. There is also another important communicative dimension of the hack—the performative dimension. A hack may be viewed as a speech act freighted with meanings. In delivering the message the hacker fulfills at least one adversarial social role—as trickster, deceiver, prophet, denouncer, and so forth. Weaponized computer code can operate at the symbolic layer of social reality, contributing to social change through messaging that is disruptive or destructive to organizations and entire institutions. Guccifer 2.0 is credited with playing this role for a Russian military-intelligence unit by hacking and doxxing Podesta; news media have referred to the persona as a "cutout" or agent providing a pass-through for communications. Other examples include the DDoS attacks attributed to "Anonymous" against Scientology's web servers and a campaign against online payment systems withholding contributor payments to WikiLeaks—an action dubbed "Operation Payback" (Coleman 2011). These hacks arguably contributed more to heightening cultural conflicts than to disrupting organizational structures. Yet they demonstrated social solidarity in communication practices that, on separate occasions, derailed Scientology's highly managed public-relations campaigns and disrupted financial transactions of trusted online payment systems.[6]

THE DEBORDERING OF STATE SURVEILLANCE

Hackers may include criminals, mercenaries, paramilitary groups, and activist groups acting alone or in combination with state agents. Hard distinctions between state, military, and nonstate agents are often elusive.[7] The problem of specifically attributing the causes and effects of hacking further complicates the ability to determine responsibility and provides ample cover for plausible deniability (Lucas 2017, 54n23). Hacking impacts military, political, and economic systems; similarly, the institutional response to hacking, cybersecurity, is a hybrid domain shared by military, political, and market systems. The U.S. government in particular seeks to tighten linkages with corporate partners in planning for "net centric war" (Schiller 2014b, 273) as concerns over territory, authority, and rights lead to "debordering" of state authority (Sassen 2006, 408–11). The military-industrial complex has developed a high-tech entrepreneurial sheen since Eisenhower's day: government cybersecurity is based on a "revolving door," which circulates elites among political, corporate consulting, and military-intelligence roles and contexts. The financial and political rewards for firms and state agencies that develop and sell cyber weapons such as intrusive malware and zero-day exploits (with legal protections in many cases) helps ensure their permanence in cyberspace. In the United States, "commercial actors like Lockheed Martin, Boeing, and BAE Systems have all launched cyber-security divisions. Traditional defense contractors, such as Northrop Grumman, Raytheon and ManTech International now invest heavily in information security products and services.... High profile members of US presidential administrations, who have gone back and forth between government service and the private sector [in cybersecurity] include Mike McConnell, formerly National Security Agency chief and Booz Allen Hamilton vice president, and Richard A. Clarke, formerly special advisor to several presidents on cyber security and currently the chairman of two corporate risk management firms." As Kristin Bergtora Sandvik notes, the threat-framing techniques and the politics of fear cultivated in discourses of "cyber warfare" and "cyber terrorism" build demand for cybersecurity firms and their products. This rhetoric "co-constitutes the reality which it is describing" (2016, 179) and helps keep the revolving door spinning between the military and private sectors.[8]

Internationally, cybersecurity currently is governed through overlapping initiatives by public and private stakeholders, with the intent of "bringing state and non-state actors together to cooperate under indirect state rule" (Muller 2016, 132). The Budapest Convention on Cybercrime provided a basis for harmonizing hacking and cybersecurity laws among EU member states, focusing on "criminal acts relating to the (mis)use of hardware and software, stealing and destruction of information for financial gain, to destroy competition, or to gain a strategic advantage" (Sandvik 2016, 177). The convention boosted regional investment, research, and development of cybersecurity software. The overall cybersecurity market in the European Union in 2015 was about $26 billion (Siudak 2017, 6). An EU-based Computer Emergency Response Team (CERT) now provides cybersecurity for EU government agencies, as well as information sharing and advisory services to the CERTs of member states. Despite taking a stricter approach to electronic privacy than the United States, EU member states produce and export a number of products designed to "lawfully" intercept and analyze internet traffic.[9] EU member states are prohibited by law from using these surveillance technologies on their own citizens, and sometimes the export of surveillance tools to countries suspected of abusing human rights is restricted. But enforcement is lax, and Syrian intelligence agents have already combined Area Spa (Italy), Qosmos (France), and Utimaco (Germany) into a system for tracking the locations and communications of opponents to the al-Assad regime, in real time (Elgin and Silver 2011).

U.S. citizens also have been surveilled en masse. Private firms monitor location data, contacts, communications, and preferences through customer phone apps that enable their online activities to be tracked. The government surveils citizens in ways that sometimes necessitate hacking trusted systems; more often, this can be accomplished through means that are pro forma and legal. In the United States, cybersecurity governance increasingly is framed in terms of national security. This displacement of holistic internet governance by state security concerns in policy-making discourse threatens the internationally harmonized approach to governing distributed and cross-border networks, raising the possibility of a newly balkanized regime and increasing social risks. This reversal ignores the "inadequacy of national responses" to threats from "difficult-to-trace actors and distributed actors and attacks that easily cross national borders" (Mueller 2017, 423).

Yet since 9/11 significant security threats have been linked to the policies and practices of the U.S. government itself, many of which have been found by courts to be illegal. We are especially interested in the expansion of online surveillance through "legal hacking" and some illegal hacking by state agencies or their proxies. Collection and analysis techniques formerly reserved for foreign targets have been duplicated and repurposed for mass domestic surveillance of trusted communication systems. On behalf of the government, wiretapping techniques have been applied to software back doors for all telephone and internet communications (Landau 2013). The statutes for issuing "National Security Letters" provide FBI field agents with subpoena power for "at a minimum, every Web site a particular person has accessed, as well as the recipient addresses and subject line of every e-mail sent through the provider in question" (Nieland 2007, 1214). Warrantless surveillance of bulk metadata continues under the 2018 reauthorization of the USA Patriot Act's section 215. The web of surveillance extends as it deepens: in addition to expanding its nonterritorial powers, the US-CERT now coordinates information exchanges about "threat indicators" from "all levels of government, industry, academia, and international partners" (Mueller and Kuehn 2013, 20).

In 2002 the U.S. government created a cabinet-level mega-agency from twenty-two different federal departments and agencies: the Department of Homeland Security. A key player, DHS developed programs, known as Einstein One and Einstein Two, that featured intrusive, deep-packet inspection to shield federal computers from malware and allow domestic wiretapping by the National Security Agency.[10] The latter capability marked a "significant change in NSA's role, which was supposed to be confined to foreign targets" (Mueller and Kuehn 2013, 13). These programs are now available partly through the private sector, with a predicted market value of $1.8 billion annually by 2024 (Market Research Media 2018). In 2013 a White House executive order and a presidential policy directive authorized Lockheed Martin, Raytheon, Northrup Grumman, SAIC, AT&T, and CenturyLink to become the first of more than two hundred "defense industrial base" companies to participate in DHS deep-packet inspection programs providing "enhanced cybersecurity" (Mueller and Kuehn 2013, 17). Military equipment has been repurposed, enabling federal and state law-enforcement agencies to launch warrantless surveillance campaigns using cellular phone tower "spoofing" equipment (the aforementioned StingRay). The NSA shared information obtained through "warrantless wiretaps" with the Drug Enforcement Administration and the

Internal Revenue Service, and other federal agencies have shared information from StingRay with police agencies throughout the United States. As the *Washington Post* noted, "It's all another sobering reminder that any powers we grant to the federal government for the purpose of national security will inevitably be used just about everywhere else. And extraordinary powers we grant government in wartime rarely go away once the war is over. And, of course, the nifty thing for government agencies about a 'war on terrorism' is that it's a war that will never formally end (Balko 2016).[11]

In a primary example of "debordering" within the state, the NSA increasingly focuses on domestic affairs rather than the foreign intelligence that is its raison d'être. As of 2014 NSA had sixty thousand civilian contractor employees and thirty thousand agency employees, many with "confidential" and "top secret" clearances (Halpern 2014). Nicholas Schmidle (2018) notes that "the N.S.A.'s recruiting strategy relies, in part, on appeals to mischievousness: at conferences, agency representatives often pitch prospective applicants by promising work that might otherwise land them in jail." Following 9/11, intelligence and criminal investigators were allowed to share information about suspects. Prior to this such exchange was prohibited because intelligence investigations use lower evidentiary standards than criminal inquiries. According to documents released through the Edward Snowden exfiltration, the Obama administration developed a new cybersecurity policy in May 2009 that included the creation of Cyber Command at the Department of Defense.[12] This policy indicated that the United States intended to use the internet for offensive purposes and further blurred the line between a terrorist and any other cybercriminal. In a classified appendix to a policy report, the White House National Security Council stated, "Reliance on legal authorities that make theoretical distinctions between armed attacks, terrorism and criminal activity may prove impractical." In addition, "About that time, the documents show, the N.S.A.—whose mission includes protecting military and intelligence networks against intruders—proposed using the warrantless surveillance program for cybersecurity purposes. The agency received 'guidance on targeting using the signatures' from the Foreign Intelligence Surveillance Court, according to an internal newsletter" (Savage et al. 2015, A1).

The Snowden exfiltration of classified documents further revealed that in mid-2012 the Obama administration expanded NSA's warrantless wiretapping of international internet traffic involving U.S. citizens for evidence of malicious computer hacking, "including traffic that flows to suspicious Internet addresses or contains malware." That same year, according to a 2012 NSA document, the FBI began using the NSA's system to monitor internet traffic through "chokepoints operated by US providers through which international communications enter and leave the United States." As Charlie Savage and colleagues note, "The disclosure that the N.S.A. and the F.B.I. have expanded their cybersurveillance adds a dimension to a recurring debate over the post-Sept. 11 expansion of government spying powers: Information about Americans sometimes gets swept up incidentally when foreigners are targeted, and prosecutors can use that information in criminal cases" (2015, A1). The Snowden exfiltration also revealed that the NSA developed the ability to match targets with facial-recognition technology across numerous databases, including video teleconferences, airline passenger data, and photo IDs from foreign countries. By 2010 the NSA intercepted about fifty-five thousand "facial recognition quality images" per day, with no express protection for facial-recognition data (Risen and Poitras 2014, A1).[13]

While courts must ostensibly approve the use of facial-recognition imagery of U.S. citizens, cross-border communication is exempt. Under section 702 of the 2018 Foreign Intelligence Surveillance Act, the emails and other private messages of U.S. citizens in contact with foreign targets can be collected without a warrant, empowering the NSA to monitor non–U.S. citizens and everyone with whom they communicate. Although the NSA claims to capture only metadata, the fact remains that this *is* data, and particularly useful data when aggregated (Halpern 2014). The NSA has also been working with the CIA and Department of State on the Pisces program, which collects biometric data on border crossings from numerous countries. Underscoring the private-public connection, "the N.S.A. relies in part on commercially available facial recognition technology, including from PittPatt, a small company owned by Google, the documents show" (Risen and Poitras 2014, A1).

Once these actions were revealed, the NSA's legal authority to hack phone and internet records in warrantless dragnet operations was challenged domestically and abroad. But attempts at reigning in the NSA have been stunted at best. In May 2014 "the House of Representatives passed an NSA reform bill, the USA Freedom Act, that had become so diluted that a number of its original sponsors refused to support it" (Halpern 2014). Although the act eventually passed in 2015 and formally rescinded the secret program to collect U.S. domestic phone logs in bulk, the NSA collected more than 534 million records of phone calls and text messages from U.S. telecommunications providers like AT&T and Verizon in 2017—more than three times the number it collected the preceding year. Although NSA obtained permission to target only forty-two people in 2016, and forty the following year, a staggering number of messages were collected, including texts and calls from everyone with whom the targets had contact. A report obtained by the *New York Times* listed several other notable statistics about surveillance activities: "For example, it showed that the number of people whom the surveillance court granted approval to target with wiretaps for national-security purposes dropped somewhat, from 1,687 in 2016 to 1,337 last year. By contrast, the number of targets for the N.S.A.'s warrantless surveillance program—noncitizens abroad whose communications are collected from American companies like Google—grew significantly, from 106,469 in 2016 to 129,080 last year" (Savage 2018, A11).

Since 9/11 Congress and the Federal Communications Commission have expanded the category of "lawful hacking" by U.S. law-enforcement agencies to include internet voice and text messaging. They seek a further expansion via the Communications Assistance for Law Enforcement Act, which already provides legal back doors to law enforcement to access unencrypted voice calls. A joint 2010 proposal by the FBI, the

Department of Justice, the NSA, the White House, and other agencies asked Congress "to require all services that enable communications—including encrypted email transmitters like BlackBerry, social networking websites like Facebook, and software that allows direct 'peer to peer' messaging like Skype—to be technically capable of complying if served with a wiretap order. The mandate would include being able to intercept and unscramble encrypted messages" (Savage 2010, A1). The proposed revisions have engendered fierce opposition from privacy advocates and security researchers. The implications of point-and-click wiretapping for online social media and messaging applications are obvious. Electronic privacy advocates repeatedly have sounded alarms over the expansion of back-door access to telecommunications networks, even for applications restricted to "lawful wiretapping," for fear that these back doors would expand illegal access by police, the military, or criminals. Examples of abuse of "lawful wiretaps" and point-and-click wiretaps using back-door access have already emerged in Greece (Lee 2013) and Italy (Wilkinson 2005).

Needless to say, such state-led hacking and wiretapping programs skirt the edges of wiretapping laws in ways which are being challenged at court ("Street Level Surveillance," n.d.). The invasive searching and sorting of "threat indicators," often in automated processes, effectively ignores the rights of those individuals whose private communications in trusted systems are targeted. The spillover effects of public surveillance also jeopardize the rights of "innocent bystanders" whose personal data and privacy may be compromised in the course of these searches. The ratcheting up of invasive warrantless surveillance by authorities targeting all communications demonstrates the normalization of hacking by military and law-enforcement regimes that have global scope and access. The consequences of accepting continual surveillance in "post-privacy" life have been examined from the standpoint of media piracy (Burkart and Andersson Schwarz 2014) but need renewed examination in the context of "legal hacking" by military and police surveillance organizations.

THE NORMALIZATION OF "PWNING"

For Beck (1992b) and for Niklas Luhmann (1983, 1995), systems are frequently characterized by vague and often overlapping authority structures. In the context of hacking and cybersecurity, the risk of a catastrophic failure of interconnected trusted systems grows through the accumulation of innumerable smaller risks, as we rely on these systems for commerce and communication. Cybersecurity research can enhance trust in trusted systems by performing an auditing function. But the NSA, and perhaps other government agencies, have units working to discover and stockpile zero-day bugs, as we learned from their appearance in stolen source code used for ransomware attacks (Goodin 2017). "Zero-day" bugs are fresh bugs that are as yet unpatched and therefore still potent. Many companies already employ invasive software and hacking as business practices. Indeed, these practices are frequently part of shared surveillance campaigns with quasi-military agencies like the Department of Homeland Security: "The United States has already backed into a de facto system of 'public-private cybersecurity'" (Eichensehr 2017, 470). This system is characterized by the growing quasi-governmental role of the private sector on key cybersecurity issues, in which the federal government acts more like a market participant than a traditional regulator. At the same time researchers and ordinary computer and internet users alike confront an ambiguous and frequently unintelligible legal landscape that can ensnare the unsuspecting into legal culpability.

Numerous studies document the expansion of panoptic surveillance in public and private trusted systems.[14] Such "all-seeing" surveillance is crucial to the increasingly automated profiling and classification of communications, credit, retail spending, travel, health, and other activities traditionally regarded by consumers as private. The rapid development of these surveillance systems raises the question of what is a "reasonable expectation of privacy" amid the continual gathering, sorting, and distributing of intimate information (Nissenbaum 2004b, 101). Based on concepts drawn from Michael Walzer's (2008) political theory, "contextual integrity" may be used to evaluate claims about new kinds of privacy violations arising from "smart" surveillance: "Contextual integrity ties adequate protection for privacy to norms of specific contexts, demanding that information-gathering and dissemination be appropriate to that context and obey the governing norms of distribution within it" (Nissenbaum 2004b, 101). This is all well and good for those with the ability to opt in and out of everyday surveillance practices—yet their ranks are few, as more and more members of the public rely on trusted systems.

Aside from the legal and technical vagaries that confront users of trusted systems, both sociological studies of surveillance and the political theory of contextual integrity fail to consider the repercussions of "mass" data breaches. The number of computer or smartphone users whose personal information and privacy has been compromised by theft or fraud, stemming from hacks of banks, employers, schools, or other agencies, continues to grow. What is a reasonable expectation of privacy for consumers whose employer or bank gets hacked? What is a reasonable expectation of privacy for individuals who are not customers of a certain firm, but whose personal information is gathered by that firm and then stolen in a cyber exploit? It is likely that well over half of the U.S. population's household information has been hacked, stolen, shared, or sold through the "dark web." But even as markets for exfiltrated personal data grow, the companies that operate trusted networks have been held relatively unaccountable to their clients.

After the large-scale data breaches at Target, J.P. Morgan Chase Bank, Home Depot, and Neiman Marcus Group, the U.S. Congress failed to pass the Personal Data Protection and Breach Accountability Act of 2014. The proposed act would have imposed fines and jail time for failure to protect customer information, notify affected parties in a timely manner, correct discovered problems, and follow privacy and security policies. Even after some tough talk by U.S. senators following Equifax's massive breach and delayed reporting of the problem, no criminal penalties can be levied on the company at the time of this writing. In 2017–18 the Trump administration even dismantled a federal agency set up to protect consumers from some consequences of such breaches. The diminution of available class-action protections during the same period renders victims legally atomized and estranged.

The lack of legal remedies for victims of breaches in the United States stems from a political system that largely overlooks the public interest in online privacy, a point that public advocacy groups have argued for years. In particular, companies whose economic interests are grounded in surveillance may sustain the legal impasse for personal or group protections. And if the common public response to intensive electronic surveillance is indifference or only slight unease (Turow 2017), then a public resignation to the insecurity of trusted systems should be expected to follow. The entrenchment of these responses would further guarantee a persistent threat environment with a telos oriented toward escalation. The situation in the European Union, however, is now very different with new enforcement of the General Data Protection Regulation (GDPR), which gives "data subjects" the right to claim compensation for "material or non-material" damage as a result of a GDPR breach (General Data Protection Regulation 2016).

Back online, "active defense" campaigns by private and public network administrators are intended to preempt suspected attacks with forward-positioned countermeasures, thereby potentially reducing risk. In both the military and private cybersecurity sectors, the risks and rewards of active defense measures are currently being debated, recalling earlier debates about antiballistic missile systems such as Star Wars (Graham 1986).[15] But in the cyber domain, active defense combines the intrusiveness of offensive measures with a response that may or may not be apparent to the target, to authorities, or to researchers. Strategies for active defense include the use of "white worms" (also called "righteous malware") for persistent scans and virus disinfection; "honeypots," or decoy servers, meant to lure possible hackers for study; and "hack backs," which involve

> analyzing an intrusion to identify perpetrators and technology sources responsible for a cyber-attack and hacking them in return to neutralize their efforts. The attackers' own tools are being used against them but, crucially, this takes place in their systems and networks. This technique enables the neutralization of malware, the identification and prosecution of perpetrators and the impairment or destruction of malicious networks.... If a cyber-attack is identified and is ongoing, a defender can use hack-back techniques not just to take action against the opponent in real time, but also scan that opponent's network, examine how they interact with the defenders' systems and understand the target set of the attack. (Dewar 2017, 8)

Hack-backs are attractive for several reasons. P. W. Singer (2015) notes, "This rhetoric of Cold War deterrence by retaliation is appealing not just in its simplicity, but also because it seemingly demonstrates strength and resolve." Yet hacking back is rife with difficulties. Hannah Kuchler (2015) cites Howard Schmidt, former White House cybersecurity adviser to former presidents Barack Obama and George W. Bush: "There is a 'big discussion' on whether companies should be able to hack back. 'There's a tremendous amount of frustration.' If a person has their car stolen and finds it abandoned, they are legally allowed to get back in it, he says. 'In cyber it doesn't work that way. It is a felony to do that. You need a body that will do it for you.'" Attributing responsibility for the originating hack remains an epistemological problem for analysts, even as those accused of hacking look for plausible deniability. Delivering a revenge attack could endanger many underlying public networks and damage users' data as collateral damage. "Striking back" immediately may not be an effective deterrent, as hack-back victims may quickly assess damage and retaliate in kind, leading to an escalation of the conflict. A breach may not be discovered for years, which befogs the effective time frame for a hack-back. In addition, perceived offensive capability may not deter hack-backs, as the asymmetry of cyber warfare mitigates power imbalances. Hack-backs are probably illegal in most cases and expose defenders to new liabilities; the most risk-averse private corporations may avoid hack-backs to avoid creating new claims of liability for harm.[16]

Some corporations suffering losses from cyberattacks nevertheless have sought to have hack-backs treated as a variety of "lawful hacking," which includes surveillance by law-enforcement agencies. The Active Cyber Defense Certainty Bill (ACDC) would have amended the Computer Fraud and Abuse Act (CFAA) to allow victims of cybercrimes (companies and private citizens) to hack back, which the bill describes as "limited defensive measures that exceed the boundaries of one's network" to block or deter would-be hackers (Kumar 2017). The bill was introduced into the U.S. House of Representatives in October 2016 by Kyrsten Sinema (D-AZ) and Ted Graves (R-GA), the chair of the Financial Services and General Government Subcommittee of the House Appropriations Committee and a member of the House Appropriations Subcommittee on Defense. The ACDC bill would allow private firms to operate outside their network's boundaries to determine the source of an attack, disrupt an attack in progress, and conduct surveillance on hackers who had previously penetrated their systems or were allegedly planning attacks. Firms also could use "dye packets" akin to those used by banks: if a file is stolen, code embedded in a file would be triggered, rendering all the data unusable (Schmidle 2018). Although they would be allowed to roam outside their networks, firms would have to notify the FBI National Cyber Investigative Joint Task Force before taking action and would be prohibited from destroying anything other than their own stolen files (Uchill 2017a).

After it was introduced, the bill gained seven additional Democratic and Republican sponsors, including Trey Gowdy (R-SC), who sat on the House Permanent Select Committee on Intelligence. Essentially using the rationale that more guns make for a safer overall environment, the bill would legalize private hacking, authorizing the private sector to militarize and possibly initiate a cyber war. Despite overall administration support, President Trump's former top cybersecurity adviser Rob Joyce criticized the bill for allowing "digital vigilantism": "Even if hacking back were to be authorized 'in a prescribed way, with finite-edge cases,' you're still going to have unqualified actors bringing risk to themselves, their targets, and their governments." Former NSA deputy director Richard Ledgett added, "Attribution is really hard. Companies have come to me with what they *thought* was solid attribution, and they were wrong.... [Legalizing private hacking would be] an epically stupid idea" (Schmidle 2018).[17]

THE INTRINSICALLY CONFLICTED CHARACTER OF HACKING AND CYBERSECURITY

The field of cybersecurity reflects the power dynamics, indeterminacies, and risks facing networks and their administrators and owners. The boundaries between civilian and military cybersecurity campaigns, and the private and public interests they serve, are vague and in flux, owing in part to the dual-use nature of cybersecurity products themselves.[18] Software sold to target external threats or criminal activity online (including unauthorized access) can also be used to track private citizens domestically whose communications are protected by law. At the same time some of the basic activities of accessing, sharing, and consuming digital content fall into uncertain legal territory of unauthorized access, owing to the double duty of antihacking laws serving the interests of antipiracy campaigns. The concept of "dual use" was grounded in Cold War–era trade restrictions on products with military applications. Today dual use also characterizes technologies like invasive software, which may be deployed in military and business networks for both defensive and offensive campaigns. The international markets for buying and selling zero-day exploits, rootkits, and malware are not unlike those for small arms and light weapons: despite "sales valued at billions of dollars per year, little international regulation exists to control these sales," and the markets themselves are secretive and hard to detect (Salton 2013, 407).[19] The transnational nature of these markets, criminal networks, and hacking cases poses additional problems for enforcement.

The scrambled nature of dual use is further exacerbated by the "black hat" and "white hat" distinctions used by hackers and cybersecurity engineers themselves. Since researchers typically test, discover, demonstrate, and fix vulnerabilities and bugs when developing software, "black" and "white" distinctions essentially are moot from an engineering standpoint: "an exploit, a rootkit, and a defensive module that inserts itself into a piece of software are all likely to use the same technique of reliably composing their own code with the target's" (Bratus et al. 2014, 7). Where commercial digital media are concerned, cybersecurity research is fraught with legal landmines left over from the antipiracy wars of the 1990s, such as the anticircumvention provision of the Digital Millennium Copyright Act (DMCA). In the case of computer-security professor Edward Felten against the Recording Industry Association of America (EFF, n.d.), the recording industry's trade group, the RIAA, used an anticircumvention claim under the DMCA to try to squelch the publication of research that detailed how the Secure Digital Music Initiative (SDMI) copy-protection scheme was cracked.

Black and white hat actors, military and civilian technology domains, public and private responsibilities for security—while ostensibly separate domains, the bleeding of these binaries into one another has led to a lack of clarity in law and policy regarding computer hacking and cybersecurity research. We believe this ambiguity points to changes in the geopolitical footing of world actors, an ascendant security assemblage of hybrid state-mercenary forces, and a de facto reliance on older antipiracy principles regarding noncircumvention of secure or trusted systems. These changes have consequences for security research. The criminalization of digital media sharing and legalization of intrusive surveillance for digital-rights management (DRM) systems set the precedent for developing hacking and cybersecurity law and policies, with the objective of punishing violations of intellectual property, principally copyright. In fact, the legal protections for trusted systems and their content are already codified in legislation such as the Digital Millennium Copyright Act of 1998 for DRM systems and the Economic Espionage Act of 1996, which criminalizes theft of proprietary information. Such deceptive transferal of changes in one legal domain to another under the cover of legislation has been criticized as "policy laundering" (Sarikakis and Rodriguez-Amat 2014). Indeed, the domains of intellectual-property rights are likely to become extended and deepened through corporate and military cybersecurity and cyber-warfare partnerships and accompanying circulation of personnel through corporations and the military. This process will be abetted by the U.S. government's reorientation toward protecting intellectual property as a national-security priority (see chapter 4).

Antipiracy campaigns by the recording industry have borrowed hackers' techniques, in practices such as releasing CD ROM rootkits, enjoining internet service providers (ISPs) in packet-sniffing operations, and seeding peer-to-peer file systems with fake file downloads. The media industries' years of practice with dirty tricks played among competing firms—not to mention by firms on their customers—provides a historical backdrop for the battle to shape U.S. and global cybersecurity. Sony provides a case in point. The so-called hack of the century against Sony Pictures Entertainment in 2014 garnered news headlines across the globe (Elkind 2015). The hack of the century featured a long period of undetected hacks of its user database, followed by hacker penetration and surveillance of Sony Pictures' servers, a gradual data exfiltration, and a denouement that featured massive data dumps of Sony financial information, salaries, internal emails, computer source code, user passwords, and credit card–account information. The malware finally formatted the hard drives of tens of thousands of Sony computers, but not before the hack campaign released Sony digital assets such as feature films onto file-sharing services (Frizell 2014).[20]

The media framed the Sony hack as a contest of wills between Hollywood movie moguls and North Korea's strongman, Kim Jong Un, with Sony paying a price for not withdrawing its film *The Interview*. What news reports frequently overlooked in their coverage of the hack of the century was that "Sony is a company that hackers have loved to hate for 10 years" (Bruce Schneier, qtd. in Elkind 2015). In 2005, a decade prior to the hack of the century, it was revealed that, in an ill-informed attempt to force digital-rights management on its customers, Sony BMG introduced a rootkit "Trojan horse" program that hacked the trusted systems on users' computers, disabled CD ripping, "phoned home" to Sony every time an affected disc was played, and provided a back door to other malicious software (Burkart and McCourt 2006). The company settled subsequent hacking lawsuits without admitting guilt. In 2011 Sony went on the offensive against its PlayStation 3 users who learned to "jailbreak," or circumvent, Sony's digital-rights–management software, suing hacker George Hotz and others for criminal federal violations of the CFAA, DMCA, copyright infringement, and trespass. In 2011, in what observers have interpreted as retaliation (and what may have presaged the Sony hack of the century), hackers breached a company database and released "personal information for 77 million customers and credit card records for 10 million of them" (Elkind 2015) onto the internet. After both incidents federal agencies such as the FBI and Department of Homeland Security worked with Sony and its cybersecurity vendor, FireEye, to share information about Sony's cyber conflicts.[21]

The hack of the century showed that Sony's insufficient cybersecurity defenses jeopardized its global commodity chains for online gaming and film distribution. At the same time companies such as Sony manage their own hacking operations as "skunkworks," an ongoing cost of maintaining networked enterprises. After the fact Sony employed a classic hacking technique (DDoS) to hack back and sabotage servers providing access to its data (Gibbs 2014). Hacking back in such a fashion probably breached legal boundaries, as it was shown to have done when Sony BMG distributed Trojan "rootkits" on its music CDs (Burkart and McCourt 2006). The case of Sony Pictures Entertainment exemplifies the ways in which hacks have intervened into political and economic domains through targeting powerful corporate agents. Following the hack of the century, the U.S. Congress made a renewed push for sharing information about threat indicators, in real time, for joint cybersecurity campaigns.

As the Sony cases illustrate, protecting intellectual property from "theft" by customers drawn into proprietary networks and other trusted systems has displaced other legal priorities in the Network Society, including customers' online information security and their rights to fair use of media. In an analog age circulating cassette mix tapes among friends and family once raised the ire of the recording industry. Later the "shared" online folders of Napster users led to a new set of legal defenses for intellectual property, notably the DMCA. Today the sharing of Netflix or Hulu passwords may generate a "nasty lawyer letter" alleging hacking violations under the CFAA. The headline of a 2016 *Fortune* magazine article provided a sobering example: "Sharing Passwords Can Now Be a Federal Crime, Appeals Court Rules." The CFAA was too vague to be applied in *United States v. Nosal* (described in chapter 1), and other statutory laws failed to clarify protections for shared household access to subscription television. The CFAA has also created uncertainty for university archivists:

> Though CFAA is often understood to be an anti-hacking law, that clause in particular has been applied to many cases that fall far short of actual systems tampering. CFAA has, for instance, been used to prosecute violation of Terms of Service agreements (which are themselves a contested practice). Most notoriously, the law was used to pursue Aaron Swartz, the young programmer who committed suicide after being charged with mass-downloading research papers from an MIT database, in violation of its terms of service—despite the fact that he was then a research fellow at MIT, with authorized access to the involved database (Morris 2016).

We will return to the riot of legal contradictions in the Swartz case, arising from prosecutors' mashup of hacking-and-piracy claims, in chapter 4. Still other paradoxes emerge as laws protecting intellectual property come into conflict with antihacking law. For example, Miranda Rodriguez (2016) observes that, the CFAA notwithstanding, U.S. law not only fails to criminalize the creation of malware containing rootkits but may actually offer intellectual-property rights (including patent and copyright protection) to malware developers, thereby legitimating the market. Virus exchangers can keep a toehold in the sanctioned world of intellectual-property rights, although many remain anonymous and insist on nonattribution for their work when exchanging or publishing their code.

In sum, U.S. law may protect the intellectual-property rights of those who create cyber weapons, while depriving researchers and developers of the right to discover flaws and vulnerabilities of existing trusted systems.[22] This confusion is a fundamental flaw in the CFAA and implicates the "lawmakers [who] do not see their unity" (Bratus 2014, 7). To worsen matters the CFAA automatically adds fraudulent intent onto any alleged computer crime, stacking claims of criminal fraud on top of hacking claims. The lack of a "patch" for this serious flaw in legal code helps ensure that the CFAA will continue to conflate cybercriminals and cybersecurity researchers, leading to a chilling effect on research (Rodriguez 2016, 672–73). Even the U.S. Department of Defense "must provide additional reassurances in the form of nonattribution and anonymity" to contractors invited to "hack a government system without threat of being prosecuted under state and federal law" (Panton et al. 2014, 476). These paradoxes contribute to social conflicts that pervade the law and policy of cybersecurity in dual-use contexts.

CYBERCRIME AND THE LIMITS OF STATE ACTION

Following Luhmann (1983), we view the social world as a taxonomy of subsystems that constitute a total system; following Beck, we can conceive of social systems and subsystems in terms of the kinds of risks they manage. For example, industrial capitalism managed the risks of revolutionary change through the implementation of "scientific management" to promote efficiency and the provision of welfare "safety nets" to address inequality. Politically organized institutions such as the United Nations have managed the attendant risks of the "hazards of the nuclear and chemical age," including the increasing probabilities for the occurrence of "normal catastrophes" (Beck 1992a, 1992b, 104). In an era of heightened global uncertainty, strong states increasingly follow exceptionalist or extralegal rules. The rapid dismantling of transatlantic and regional multilateralism and the growth of unilateral or binational rules for engagement mark a historical break with postwar Western systems for globalized finance and defense (like the World Trade Organization [WTO] and North Atlantic Treaty Organization [NATO]). The rationales for state-led surveillance have expanded from policing and national security to include intervention into illegal global markets for branded intellectual property. In particular, the 1998 Napster scare led to new internet surveillance systems for IP "leakage" around the world, as well as the "three strikes" or "graduated response" policies of ISPs. These policies mandated continual surveillance of millions of internet users for illegal file sharing and, in some cases, led to corporate hacks of customers' computers. Internationally, these trade measures tend to bypass national political systems, where political challenges to "bad laws" can occur.[23]

As noted earlier, piracy and hacking are often treated as filial threats to international business, law, and order. One may assume that they are equally prohibited, but a stark contrast exists between international law on piracy and that on hacking. The emergence of mass digital piracy, especially of the peer-to-peer variety, quickly galvanized transnational companies to crack down on rogue players and lobby for new intellectual-property protections in international free-trade agreements. In contrast, information law and policy dealing with computer hacking is quite thin and brittle, with significant gaps and breaches between national regimes. Increasingly entangled legal initiatives prosecute the two together as criminal fraud and conspiracy (as the examples of Aaron Swartz's EBSCO access, Andrew Auernheimer's AT&T hack, and Matthew Keys's *LA Times* website defacement show).[24] Yet the legal system countenances the production of hacks and tools used for surveillance, provided that the players have influence within the system through market power, participate in the revolving door with the military, or are successful in their lobbying activities.

The boundaries of networked social systems are often ill-defined, and state action to circumscribe and codify cybercrime is continual. But it is possible to observe a tendency for the state to "solve" for the aforementioned paradoxes of cybersecurity by tailoring policy objectives to suit the needs of the military as well as the industries dependent on revenues from royalties. The former pushes expanded surveillance capabilities over the internet as a priority, while the latter has long promoted surveillance for digital-rights management. The push for online cybersecurity coincided with the push for DRM prior to 9/11 and led to the invasive tracking systems that now riddle the internet with customer-relationship-management personalized surveillance that collects information on customers and tailors sales messages accordingly. The watershed "Internet Christmas" of 1999 diffused computer media hardware and software into the consumer marketplace and normalized peer-to-peer access to digital content. Later a rush to recover from the September 2001 attacks in the United States inspired overreaching online policing laws such as the USA Patriot Act and its successors. The Patriot Act redefined any attempted hack of any device interconnected with a "protected computer" managed by the government as a potential act of terrorism. What 9/11 did for the militarization of the internet is not entirely dissimilar to what Napster's 1999 release did for authoritarian antipiracy law and enforcement. Both occurred within the same approximate time frame.

The conflation of hacking and piracy in law and policy serves a strategic purpose in an era of globalization still partly dominated by U.S. media exports. But it is unclear that companies with major intellectual-property assets would prefer to see hacking jurisprudence cleaned up or consistent worldwide. The lack of shared regulations and "the failure to establish an international definition of either 'piracy' or 'cyber attack'" (Shackelford and Russell 2015, 8) may actually favor the interests of these industries, which have made a concerted effort to keep the cybercrime waters muddied. Trade groups have generated white papers and official reports linking online piracy with malware and scams, and cybersecurity plans with antipiracy programs ("Pirate Sites" 2014; "MPAA Links" 2015). Some legal historians see the development of antiterrorism law and cybercrime law intertwined in the context of U.S. Department of Homeland Security surveillance centers (data "fusion centers") and the explosion of private information brokers such as Axciom and Experian.[25] Bernard E. Harcourt (2018), for example, has described long-term "domestication of counterinsurgency" programs in the United States built around surveillance and targeting of political threats by the police and military. The security of cyberspace is also comanaged by private telecommunications firms (ISPs and telephone, cable, and satellite companies).

Private cybersecurity firms increasingly serve as state proxies for monitoring and policing networks. Outsourcing of intelligence and security operations by the United States since the George W. Bush administration has externalized many state security roles and campaigns to private companies (including the notorious Blackwater USA). These developments undermine the pragmatic "rational actor" perspective on state action, characteristic of "Westphalian" models of the state, in favor of an emergent "global private security-industrial complex" (LeRiche 2017, 154) that remaps the threat environment to primarily benefit private actors.[26] The result is a quasi-governmental network of "cyber mercenaries," in which various private firms hired by the United States and other governments play defensive and offensive operations interchangeably. These firms feed exploits and opportunities to one another in a morphing system of network security and governance. The handoff of internet security to a secretive cadre of private security professionals is consistent with what is occurring in police and military organizations and "represent[s] the depoliticization and marketization of security.... The effect of the commodification of security is to delink it from local issues of justice and politics, making it a commodity that can be bought and sold on the free market and a technique that is universally acceptable everywhere" (148). Hived off from public policy making, privatized security practices generate governance that is far removed from democratic deliberation and accountability, potentially undermining trust in the first responsibility of state.

CONCLUSION

To sum up: as hacking is drawn increasingly into the ambit of U.S. antiterrorism law, antiterrorist programs and policies address threats to the entirety of the network by applying their exceptional powers to any part of the network, including all "protected" machines and those interconnected with protected machines. Ad hoc governance in response to perceived risks from "terrorism" leaves little room for fixing social problems related to the legal vagaries of the CFAA, DMCA, and other laws and policies for cybercrime. Resolving conflicts through policy making and through public participation and accountability in determining cybersecurity standards and practices diminishes in proportion to the rapid advance of the domain's militarization and privatization.[27] Some European laws offer encouraging prospects for consumer privacy and protection from hacking. These treaty-based laws, such as the previously mentioned GDPR, include new legal responsibilities for public and private entities whose customer information is stolen or leaked to the public. The European Union's Directives on Cybersecurity and Network and Information Systems also seek to consolidate transnational security standards. But these and other efforts are countered by attempts to frame harms and remedies in terms of intellectual-property rights rather than network security.

Chapter 4, on law and policy, delves into these clashing principles and operations in more detail and offers a critique of the current legal system. The next chapter reviews the economic side of the creation, trade, and use of invasive software such as malware and botnets. International political economy places the activity of commodification, or creating markets, as the engine of capitalist exchange (Mosco 1996). As state and corporate organizations seek to privatize wealth, they socialize risk; if unable to do so "behind our backs," they then commodify risk using insurance and financial instruments and may also seek state subsidies or agencies to cover the costs of managing risk.

The markets for cybersecurity products and services are proliferating and deepening, exploiting the divergences between "law in action" and "law in the books" and turning up still more legal paradoxes with profound social implications. Trust and privacy are increasingly in tension, yet both are necessary to "legitimate" trusted systems. Helen Nissenbaum's situational framework (2004a) is useful for assessing individual privacy violations, while George R. Lucas (2017) finds that global norms concerning "morally permissible" hacking of trusted systems for espionage and surveillance, such as informed consent, are developing. Even so, social norms regarding new technology practices involving hacking and surveillance are developing in a legal vacuum. As it stands, cybersecurity is a conflicted concept and practice in the hands of powerful companies, and the U.S. policies of warrantless surveillance of its own citizens has undermined "the public's trust in the security agencies of its government" (154–55). Legal hacking has validated panspectric surveillance as public policy and business model. Without guarantees that this access will be constrained by legal review, we face an era of inherently "treacherous computing" (Stallman 2002). As systemic risk is being embedded into the deepest infrastructures of the Network Society, very little effort has been made to place the activities, technologies, and interests that are generating such developments under effective legal and democratic control.

CHAPTER THREE

The Political Economy of the Hack

In the last chapter we identified some of the ways in which deep hacks can steer communicative action and shape boundaries in social systems as they bypass the rules and resources encoded in these systems.[1] Cyberattacks propagate insecurity and risk (of privacy and property loss) throughout networks; the results can ripple through the entire social system. Corporate, state, and military enterprises all now ride the knife's edge of network security and insecurity. Costs to private businesses for cyber intrusions and cyberattacks include loss of reputation and heightened customer turnover. In 2015 the costs of cyberattacks averaged $6.5 million for large U.S. companies and $3.79 million for large companies, globally (Mandel 2017, 13). At the same time these attacks create markets for analyzing and repelling them. The hacking and cybersecurity dynamic therefore can enrich the firms that convert the risks of data breaches, network intrusions, malware infections, and other cyberattacks into sales of services such as hacking insurance and products such as software firewalls, antivirus programs, and other defensive measures. In these ways the commodification of risk serves to reshape social reality.

While cybersecurity software ostensibly is designed to test flaws in computer networks and enhance their security, its filial relation, spyware, offers powerful potentials for harassing journalists and political dissidents as well as compromising the privacy of untargeted "innocent bystanders" on the internet. We argue the markets for hacking and cybersecurity are connected for several reasons. At a code level the software can be indistinguishable: "the software used by malicious, criminal attackers to exploit vulnerabilities can … be very difficult to meaningfully distinguish from mainstream, legitimate security research and testing tools," and "the security research community depends on the open availability of software tools that can test and analyze software vulnerabilities" (Bellovin et al. 2014, 63). Cyberattacks and cybersecurity respond reflexively to each other in escalating threats.

This chapter looks at the ways in which communications, software code, labor, and law contribute to markets for vulnerabilities and exploits as well as related industries that promote cybersecurity to enhance trust. They can run the gamut from antivirus makers to "pen testing" (penetration testing) software vendors to companies offering spyware and "cybersecurity-plus" arrangements. Software, like digital media and business services, is bought and sold internationally in markets characterized by little or no regulation or political oversight—aside from intellectual-property–rights law and export control regulation—since the end of the U.S. "crypto wars" of the 1990s.[2] Given the growing demand for vulnerabilities and lawful intercept technologies, a thriving market in globally circulated cyber commodities like malware, rootkits, and botnets makes selective use of the law. As an illustration, we offer a case study of the Hacking Team, whose spyware has been sold and put to use in espionage campaigns by repressive political regimes against political targets.

Spyware is sold as lawful intercept software or cybersecurity software and the terms of use, and of market access and sales, are typically negotiated in secret. In addition, it can trespass or steal data in ways that legally "exceed authorized access" (Tuma 2011) by the standards of the U.S. Computer Fraud and Abuse Act (CFAA). Given the malleable nature (or dearth) of international laws and controls, however, the specific terms for "authorized access" to a target's trusted system (typically a computer or smartphone) are often legally indeterminate and ultimately defined by the customers for cybersecurity software. Regionally, the European Union and the United States set restrictions on exports of "intrusion software" based on the Wassenaar Arrangement (2017), a nonbinding honor agreement among member states intended to create greater transparency and control over the export and transfer of certain weapons and dual-use technologies. Members are admitted by unanimous vote, with signatories including the United States and forty other countries, but not China or Iran. The group meets annually and sets general guidelines by consensus; all information exchanged among members is kept secret. A particular Wassenaar objective is to prevent member states from exporting hacking or cybersecurity software to "pariah" nations such as Iran, Iraq, Libya, and North Korea (Durscht 1997, 1109–13). In 2013 the agreement was amended to include controls for surveillance software of the sort sold by the Hacking Team, Gamma, NSO, and other vendors. A subsequent loosening of "intrusion software" definitions in 2017 not only eased some of the concerns of the security vendors and their supporting researchers and developers (Hinck 2018) but also won support from the Israeli government, which has links to NSO and had remained a holdout. But the activities of cyber-mercenary firms such as the Hacking Team, NSO, and others revealed that these guidelines have been challenged repeatedly. The global market for hacking-based surveillance software poses new and significant privacy risks to the public, especially those engaged in activism, journalism, politics, and other sensitive work.[3]

Ironically, more transparency and legal accountability may increase "systemic" risk to the entire security-insecurity market: international agreements seeking to regulate malware and intrusion software are likely to expand the black markets for these tools. Creators and brokers find the least restrictive routes for their sale or lease, use technical means to evade regulators, or bribe government officials charged with regulating them (Mandel 2017, 54). Even if they could effectively regulate the primary markets for vulnerabilities, licensing schemes and export controls likely would create market failures that carry their own unknown risks. U.S. elected officials have frequently sparred with cybersecurity experts in industry and defense over how much of a free market in cyber weapons should be allowed to flourish. In both the United States and European Union, industry players such as Symantec, IBM, McAfee, Northrop Grumman, Booz Allen Hamilton, and Computer Sciences Corporation (CSC) have preferred a "light touch" regulatory approach so that their cybersecurity divisions can continue to develop new products. The director of the Center for Cyber and Homeland Security has called the resulting international market for spyware, rootkits, and Trojan horse programs an "arms bazaar of cyber weapons" (16).

In 2014 the private online surveillance industry generated more than $5 billion in profits (Sankin 2015). Concerns about abusive surveillance practices are particularly acute in authoritarian political systems, especially those with unstable or divided political support. Such concerns were amplified in the United States by the end of the Obama era, with the erosion of safeguards against politically motivated (including algorithmically generated) mass surveillance and the strengthening of the executive branch's power. The same is true of other Western countries as well (Greenwald 2016). The Department of Commerce's willingness to update its export regulations, based on inclusion of "invasive software" in the Wassenaar Arrangement, partly reflects concerns about abuses in politically unstable and authoritarian countries.

The international marketplace for "lawful interception" technology is estimated to reach $1.3 billion by 2019. These technologies are showcased in global trade shows featuring large corporate subsidiaries; independent firms that sell spyware and malware to state security and law-enforcement entities; and third parties, akin to traditional gunrunners, that link independent firms to states and police. The Intelligence Support Systems World Americas conference, nicknamed the "Wiretappers Ball," is one of several conferences organized by TeleStrategies, a Virginia-based firm, that are held around the world each year (Risen

2015). These conferences are closed to media and members of the public. A Washington-based surveillance and privacy expert told the *Guardian* about concerns raised by these private markets:

> When there are five or six conferences held in closed locations every year, where telecommunications companies, surveillance companies, and government ministers meet in secret to cut deals, buy equipment, and discuss the latest methods to intercept their citizens' communications—that I think meets the level of concern. . . . They say that they are doing it with the best of intentions. And they say that they are doing it in a way that they have checks and balances and controls to make sure that these technologies are not being abused. But decades of history show that surveillance powers are abused—usually for political purposes. (Gallagher 2011)

We turn our attention now to the trade in software and tools for lawful interception, spyware, and other products based on vulnerabilities.

THE HACKING TEAM CASE

The parameters of a multibillion-dollar industry—what Reporters without Borders terms "digital mercenaries" (Kushner 2016)—have come into focus. The WikiLeaks Hacking Team archives reveal an industry of firms for hire that sell cyber armaments such as zero-day exploits and coordinate targeted attacks on corporations, governments, and individuals. While state agencies rationalize the application of these dual-use tools in the name of countering terrorism or criminal activity, it appears that these applications frequently are used for performing domestic surveillance and targeting journalists and political dissidents. In particular, these firms feed exploits into political systems with corrupt and authoritarian governance. Dozens of firms compete for clients; industry leaders are the Gamma Group (owned by a shell corporation in the British Virgin Islands and whose spyware is marketed through Germany), Israel's NSO, and the Milan-based Hacking Team (Perlroth 2016a). As of October 2015, intelligence and law-enforcement agencies in at least fifty countries have purchased off-the-shelf spyware and contractor services for purposes of international and domestic surveillance (Paletta, Yadron, and Valentino-DeVries 2015, A1). Although functionally stateless, these cyber mercenaries often have benefited from de facto state support and export controls designed for previous eras of conflict.

Hailed as the "Blackwater of surveillance," the Milan-based Hacking Team (HT) has been a fixture at Intelligence Support Systems shows (Kushner 2016). In 2001 Italian programmers Alberto Ornaghi and Marco Valleri wrote Ettercap, a free and open-source program for detecting passwords, eavesdropping, and remotely manipulating target computers. In 2003 Ornaghi and Valleri added David Vincenzetti as CEO and formally incorporated as HT. Under Vincenzetti's direction, the company focused on developing malware and other offensive capabilities, releasing Remote Control System (RCS, or Da Vinci) in 2003. Promotional literature touted RCS as enabling authorities to break into hardware such as computers and smartphones and control microphones and webcams to monitor subjects through surreptitious recordings and screen captures. RCS also allows authorities to remotely upload files and retrieve information such as emails, passwords, and documents from targets.

An RCS program could scale from one to hundreds of thousands of targets. RCS could be physically installed via a USB stick (if authorities could directly access the computer) or remotely through email attachments or spear-phishing scams as well as "network injectors" (physical devices housed with internet service providers that enable authorities to intercept ordinary web traffic, such as streaming video, and infect it with malicious code). HT claimed that RCS could also emulate or spoof access points, pretending to be a free Wi-Fi hotspot to which targets had previously connected (Currier and Marquis-Boire 2014). This "man in the middle" surveillance technique is particularly useful for connected devices. RCS functions also could be uploaded onto phones and track users via GPS. By 2013 HT counted thirty-five employees, with offices in Milan, Annapolis, Maryland, and Singapore.[4] HT's revenues were $17.5 million in 2015; HT's clients have paid between

$50,000 and $2 million annually for RCS, depending on the number of targets and platforms (Kushner 2016). Hacking Team's website boasted "total control over your targets. Log everything you need. Always. Anywhere they are" (Silver 2012). Other promotional material advertised, "Hack into your targets with the most advanced infection vectors available. Enter his wireless network and tackle tactical operations with ad-hoc equipment designed to operate while on the move.... Remote Control System: the hacking suite for governmental interception. Right at your fingertips" (Hern 2015a). HT and other cyber mercenaries rely extensively on outside vendors for zero-day exploits. HT began working with vendors in 2009, as the company shifted its focus from information security to surveillance. Although HT sought to develop in-house talent and established new contacts with developers toward this goal, it met with mixed success. Since many established vendors and brokers preferred to sell exclusively to governments rather than private companies, HT's suppliers were often small or marginal concerns, and obtaining exclusivity rights was difficult (WikiLeaks 2015a).

HT was first linked directly to attacks on political dissidents in 2012. Hisham Almiraat was editor and cofounder of Mamfakinch, a Moroccan prodemocracy website created during the Arab Spring. On July 13, 2012, Almiraat and his colleagues received an email with "Denunciation" in the subject line. "Please do not mention my name or anything. I do not want any trouble," wrote the sender. A website link directed them to a document labeled "Scandal," which, once downloaded, was blank. Morgan Marquis-Boire, who worked in Google security and volunteered for the Citizen Lab research group based at the University of Toronto's Munk School of Global Affairs, examined the email and found that anyone who opened it had been infected with spyware. This spyware originated from an IP address linked to Morocco's Supreme Council of National Defense, which operated the country's security agencies and was thereby implicated in the attack. A few lines of source code unwittingly left in the Scandal document are reported to have led directly to HT (Kushner 2016).

In March 2013 Reporters without Borders included HT on its annual Corporate Enemies of the Internet list and warned that online surveillance posed a "growing danger for journalists, bloggers, citizen-journalists, and human rights defenders" (Kushner 2016). The list also included Gamma (whose FinFisher system was sold to Bahrain, Turkmenistan, Ethiopia, and South Africa, among others) and Blue Coat Systems, a U.S.-based firm that has sold monitoring systems to Iran, Syria, and Sudan. Claiming that "one person's activist is another person's terrorist" (Brewster 2013), HT spokesperson Eric Rabe countered that "the software we provide is essential for law enforcement and for the safety of all in an age when terrorists, drug dealers and sex traffickers and other criminals routinely use the Internet and mobile communications to carry out their crimes" (*USA Today* 2014).

As journalists raised alarms about the proliferation of its software, HT claimed that the company's checks and balances included an external board of lawyers and engineers who vetted potential clients, with the power to "veto any sale" (Gilbert 2013). HT has also stated that its license prohibited users from passing along technology to third parties (although how this was enforced is unclear, aside from claims that its "audit tool" could trace how software is used). Bruce Schneier stated, "They just need plausible deniability because . . . morally it's like selling [electro]shock batons to South Africa in the 1960s" (qtd. in Worrall 2013, 6). Although HT insisted it took extensive precautions to limit potentials for abuse, in late 2013 Citizen Lab reported that clients in the United Arab Emirates, Bahrain, Morocco, Ethiopia, Vietnam, and Turkmenistan were using HT malware to target and harass political activists and dissidents, human rights workers, and journalists. HT declined to confirm or deny the identities of its licensees on the grounds that such "information could jeopardize legitimate investigations" (Timberg 2014).

In 2013 the Saudi Arabian government came close to buying a controlling interest in HT. Safinvest, an investment company owned by Wafic Said (a Syrian-born businessman based in the United Kingdom who was close to the Saudi royal family), would have purchased HT for 37 million euros. The sale also involved Ronald Spogli, a venture capitalist and former U.S. ambassador to Italy who serves on the board of trustees at Stanford University. Spogli owned a 10 percent stake in an investment company, Innogest, which in turn controlled 26 percent of HT. Then HT would (imaginatively) have been rechristened Halo, and Vincenzetti wrote an associate that "the newco should be away from countries adhering to the new, forthcoming export regulations on 'offensive technologies' which will [be] dictated by the recent Wassenaar Arrangement. We would like the newco to be in a country which will not impair the export of our technology." As Italian journalist Marco Lillo noted, "It's paradoxical that [HT] couldn't sell its software to Saudi Arabia but it could sell them the entire company" (Kushner 2016).

Vincenzetti's focus on selling the company, rather than developing its software, further heightened tensions within the firm. Alberto Pelliccione, a senior developer, resigned from HT in March 2014, expressing dissatisfaction with the company's growing focus on malware and surveillance. Pelliccione stated that sales to repressive governments were the subject of internal debate at HT, leading to the separation of the developer unit and the sales team (Brewster 2015a). Claiming that employees working on aspects of the same platform would not communicate with one another, Pelliccione added, "We were really being compartmentalized, didn't like the way things were going with the management" (Farivar 2015). Pelliccione was soon joined by Serge Woon, who was HT's Singapore-based representative, and Alex Velasco, CEO of Hacking Team reseller Cicom. Others followed. When HT employee Guido Landi gave notice, Vincenzetti told him that it wasn't new information, implying that employees were under surveillance as well. "We accepted this," Pelliccione said. "They know where you are and where you go" (Kushner 2016). These departures helped scotch HT's sale to Saudi Arabia, and the deal collapsed in early 2014, when Prince Bandar bin Sultan was removed as head of the Saudi intelligence service. Bin Sultan, a former Saudi ambassador to the United States, had backed the purchase, but it was rejected by his replacement (Willan 2015). Declassified sections of the U.S. government's report on 9/11 revealed an indirect link between bin Sultan and the Al Qaeda organization (Staufenberg 2016).

THE HACKING TEAM HACKED

According to lore, on August 6, 2014, hacktivist Phineas Fisher (a play on Gamma's FinFisher spyware suite) leaked four hundred gigabytes of marketing and technical information from HT rival Gamma online. Eleven months later, on July 5, 2015, Fisher hijacked HT's Twitter account. He changed the account's name to the Hacked Team; altered the bio to "Developing ineffective, easy-to-pwn offensive technology to compromise the operations of the worldwide law enforcement and intelligence communities"; and posted a message that read, "Since we have nothing to hide, we're publishing all our emails, files, and source code" (Goodin 2015).[5] A BitTorrent link was included, which allowed access to the company's most sensitive business data (including passwords, internal emails, and exchanges with clients) as well as 80 percent of the company's source code, including the zero-day exploits that were in its arsenal (Lemos 2015a). Fisher apparently had gained access to an HT engineer's computer while it was logged into the network. The engineer's password was Password (Greene 2015).[6]

WikiLeaks created a searchable archive of HT emails culled from the online data dump, including a spreadsheet that listed HT's active and inactive clients at the end of 2014. In addition to the countries listed by Citizen Lab, the spreadsheet revealed that HT clients also included law-enforcement and security agencies in Egypt, Nigeria, Oman, Lebanon, Bahrain, India, Mexico, Ecuador, Thailand, South Korea, Russia, Italy, Hungary, and Switzerland. Mexico provided the largest revenues to HT, followed by Italy and Morocco (Hern 2015a).[7] U.S. clients included the Florida Metropolitan Bureau of Investigation, which paid HT more than $400,000 (Smith 2015); the Drug Enforcement Administration, which paid HT $2.4 million for RCS in August 2012 to spy on seventeen "foreign-based drug traffickers and money launderers" (Kushner 2016); and the FBI, which paid HT more than $773,000 since 2011 (Goodin 2015).

Although the FBI had developed malware in 2001 known as Magic Lantern, which could take over a computer, log its users' keystrokes, and bypass encryption (Currier and Marquis-Boire 2014), the agency likely was hedging its bets by monitoring technological developments and potential competitors and adversaries. So was the Russian government. Exfiltrated documents revealed that HT sold RCS to KVANT, a Russian-owned military research and development firm that works with Russia's secret police, the Federal Security Service (FSB). KVANT established a relationship with FSB through Neptune Intelligence Computer Engineering (NICE), an Israeli company that specialized in surveillance and data security and acted as a reseller for HT's tools (Brewster 2015b). The WikiLeaks archive indicates that there were extensive negotiations with third-party partners in India and Pakistan. It also revealed that HT specifically targeted Bitcoin and other cryptocurrencies to allow governments to exploit vulnerabilities in Bitcoin anonymity protections and "follow the money" trails (Lemos 2015b).

The HT doxxing event pulled the curtain back on other intrigues. Receipts indicated that South Korea's 5163 Army Division had purchased RCS in January 2012 and made subsequent maintenance payments for the remainder of the year (Marczak and McKune 2015). But South Korea has no such army division; the name was probably used by the South Korean intelligence agency to disguise foreign operations. A Citizen Lab report claimed that HT sold programs to Ethiopia to target journalists: "Later correspondences confirmed the country was dropped due to Citizen Lab's report, but not because of the allegedly unethical spying; it was cut due to its 'incompetent use' of the product that caused it to get caught. But according to leaked emails, the firm ended up offering to reinstate Ethiopia about two months later, with strict conditions and a bigger bill" (Lou 2015). Other leaked comments vividly contrasted HT's public-relations rhetoric and internal practices. In one email Vincenzetti characterized human-rights activists as "idiots ... good at manipulating companies and people" (Savides 2015). In another email, less than a month before Phineas Fisher's HT hack, he boasted to colleagues, "Imagine this: a leak of WikiLeaks showing YOU explaining the evilest technology on earth!:-) You would be demonized by our dearest friends the activists, and normal people would point their fingers at you" (Goodin 2015).

The posted documents revealed that, contrary to the company's claims, HT undertook only the most pro forma and superficial vetting of clients and contractors and cultivated extensive negotiations with police and state security agencies accused of human-rights violations. Along with Russia's KVANT, leaked internal documents listed Sudan's National Intelligence Security Service as "not officially supported" by HT, rather than as having "active" or "expired" status as a client (Hern 2015b). Although HT denied it had ever done business with Sudan, which was under a UN arms embargo, a June 2012 invoice for 480,000 euros to the Sudanese security service was posted (Auchard and Menn 2015). HT claimed that its programs were sold in Sudan before dual-use technologies were regulated. "If one sells sandwiches to Sudan, he is not subject, as far as my knowledge goes, to the law. HT should be treated like a sandwich vendor," the firm's legal counsel argued (Kushner 2016).

Shortly after the online document dump, HT's Christian Pozzi tweeted, "A lot of what the attackers are claiming regarding our company is not true. Please stop spreading false lies about the services we offer" (Hern 2015b). Pozzi's feed was itself hacked shortly thereafter, and the user account was later deleted. After initially blaming an unspecified government or governments for the hack, Vincenzetti speculated that it could have been an "inside job" by six former employees (Gibbs 2015a). Although Italian authorities have not yet brought charges against anyone, Pelliccione, whose resignation in early 2014 triggered a mass defection from HT, claimed that he was one of the six employees under investigation for the hack (Brewster 2015b). According to Vincenzetti, HT lost 20 percent of its customers following the leak, including its U.S. clients, but the company still reported $14 million in revenue for 2015. HT rewrote its software from scratch for three months after the breach, resulting in what Vincenzetti trumpeted as a "much better" product (Kushner 2016). But Italy implemented the Wassenaar Arrangement on January 1, 2015, which meant the Italian government would now vet HT's clients. In early April 2016 the Italian Ministry of Economic Development revoked HT's global license, with subsequent licenses for clients outside of Europe to be obtained on a case-by-case basis. Although it lost its global export license, HT still has approval to sell to countries within the European Union (Brewster 2016).

CYBER-MERCENARY STRUGGLES FOR MARKET DOMINANCE

The market for commercial spyware suites is flourishing. Gamma and NSO Group are HT's major competitors, and Gamma offers a particular insight into the tangled web of international cyber surveillance. The firm is owned by William Louthean Nelson through a shell corporation in the British Virgin Islands (Leigh, Frayman, and Ball 2012). Its spyware suite, FinFisher, is marketed through a Munich-based branch, Gamma International, as well as Gamma International in Andover, England. Other cyber-mercenary firms include the following:

- South Africa's VASTech provided the technology that enabled Muammar Gadaffi to monitor all telephone calls going in and out of Libya. VASTech was underwritten by a 4 million Rand grant from the South African government.
- Blue Coat, a U.S.-based firm, has sold monitoring systems to Iran, Syria, and Sudan, despite U.S. embargoes. Blue Coat has claimed that it didn't sell these systems directly; instead, they were obtained through intermediaries.

- Nokia subsidiary Trovicor provided Iran with the capability to block international radio and television broadcasts, as well as censor social media sites like Twitter and Facebook.
- Boeing subsidiary Narus "sold deep-packet inspection technology to filter content and track users on the network of Egypt Telecom during the Arab Spring." Narus also sold systems to the government of Saudi Arabia to block VoIP traffic as a means of protecting the national telephone operator from competition and also to block access to websites the Saudi government deems dangerous (Sankin 2015).

Since the Hacking Team's decline, NSO has garnered the largest international reputation for dirty tricks. Headquartered in Herzliya, Israel, NSO Group Technologies was founded in 2009 by Shalev Hulio and Omri Lavie and sells primarily to government agencies; it claims to "make the world a safe place" as its corporate mission statement (Perlroth 2016c, F5). The NSO Pegasus system is touted for its ability to

> extract text messages, contact lists, calendar records, emails, instant messages and GPS locations. One capability that the NSO Group calls "room tap" can gather sounds in and around the room, using the phone's own microphone. Pegasus can use the camera to take snapshots or screen grabs. It can deny the phone access to certain websites and applications, and it can grab search histories or anything viewed with the phone's web browser. And all of the data can be sent back to the agency's server in real time. In its commercial proposals, the NSO Group asserts that its tracking software and hardware can install itself in any number of ways, including "over the air stealth installation," tailored text messages and emails, through public Wi-Fi hot spots rigged to secretly install NSO Group software, or the old-fashioned way, by spies in person. (2016a, B5)

Pegasus's bag of tricks commands a premium price. After a $500,000 setup fee, NSO charges $300,000 to spy on five Symbian users or $500,000 for five BlackBerry users; the cost for ten iPhone users or ten Android users is $650,000, with a sliding scale for additional targets.[8]

NSO charges an annual system-maintenance fee of 17 percent of the total price every year after the initial purchase.

In 2014 NSO sold a controlling stake to San Francisco–based private equity firm Francisco Partners for $120 million (McMillan 2016). Within a year Francisco was trying to sell NSO for ten times that amount (Perlroth 2016a). In mid-July 2017 the Blackstone Group engaged in advanced talks to buy a 40 percent share of NSO for $400 million. The talks fell apart a month later, in part because of protests by activist groups such as Citizen Lab and Access Now, who pointed to widespread deployment of NSO's Pegasus software in Mexico and elsewhere. Citizen Lab's John Scott-Railton noted that "NSO's spyware has a documented abuse potential, and the list of cases continues to grow. Serious investors who have done their due diligence may be thinking twice about just how problematic this category of investments could be to their image and their bottom line" (Finkle 2017). A $1 billion merger deal with Verint Systems was shelved in 2018.[9]

According to Citizen Lab, Mexico is unrivaled in the scale and scope of its surveillance operations (Ahmed 2017, A1). Mexico was the Hacking Team's largest client, with over $6.3 million in contracts between 2010 and 2015, and at least three Mexican federal agencies have purchased a total of $80 million of NSO spyware since 2011. In August 2016 three vocal proponents of Mexico's 2014 soda tax found they had been targeted by NSO malware. The national soda tax, the first public health reform of its kind, was "aimed at reducing consumption of sugary drinks in Mexico, where weight-related diseases kill more people every year than violent crime" (Perlroth 2017, A1). The attack coincided with efforts to double the tax, which had stalled in November 2016. In 2015 NSO spyware was found on the phone of Mexican journalist Rafael Cabrera, who reported that a home built for then president Enrique Peña Nieto was owned by a Chinese company that had received government contracts worth hundreds of millions of dollars. Former Panamanian president Ricardo Martinelli also employed NSO to spy on his rivals. In July 2018 Martinelli was extradited to Panama from the United

States to face charges of embezzlement and espionage on political opponents. According to court filings, Martinelli spent nearly $13.5 million on NSO's Pegasus spyware (Brewster 2018a).

Gulf monarchies have been steady customers for NSO, reflecting Israel's priorities in the Saudi-Iranian Middle Eastern endgame. Although the United Arab Emirates does not officially recognize Israel, researchers uncovered widespread use of NSO spyware by the United Arab Emirates after Citizen Lab and Amnesty International developed a "fingerprint" for NSO attacks. The distinctive anonymizing techniques employed in Pegasus essentially blew NSO's cover and allowed researchers to positively identify their targets (Brewster 2018a), once the targets became suspicious of NSO phishing attempts. On August 11, 2016, UAE activist Ahmed Mansoor received text messages on his iPhone promising "new secrets" about detainees tortured in UAE jails if he clicked on an included link. Instead, Mansoor sent the messages to Citizen Lab researchers. Citizen Lab recognized the links as belonging to an exploit infrastructure connected to the Israeli NSO Group. Their report claimed, "The high cost of iPhone zero-days, the apparent use of NSO Group's government-exclusive Pegasus product, and prior known targeting of Mansoor by the UAE government provide indicators that point to the UAE government as the likely operator behind the targeting." Mansoor had won the spyware trifecta: in addition to harassment by NSO, he was targeted by HT's RCS spyware in 2012 and FinFisher's FinSpy spyware in 2011 (Marczak and Scott-Railton 2016). UAE targets also included Saudi prince Mutaib bin Abdullah, who was a rival to Crown Prince Mohammed bin Salman. Prince Mutaib was later removed from serving as minister of the Saudi national guard and temporarily detained on corruption charges. In late 2018 Omar Abdulaziz, a Montreal-based Saudi dissident, filed a lawsuit in Israel against NSO alleging that the company assisted the Saudi government in implanting spyware to monitor his communication with journalist Jamal Kashoggi before the latter was believed to have been murdered and dismembered at the Saudi embassy in Turkey (Kirkpatrick 2018, A9).

On behalf of victims of FinFisher software, Privacy International and Bytes for All filed unlawful surveillance complaints and privacy lawsuits against the Bahraini and Pakistani governments, respectively (Singh 2015). The Electronic Frontier Foundation brought suit in the United States against HT on behalf of an Ethiopian opposition party member who had been targeted with spyware by the Ethiopian government in 2011 (Goyett 2015). NSO was targeted by two lawsuits brought by Mexican journalists and activists as well as a Qatari citizen in 2018. Leaked emails belied NSO's claims that it is not responsible for illegal uses by governments that purchase its software; instead, NSO affiliates actively hacked and spied on dissidents, journalists, and government officials at their customers' request: "For the U.A.E., documents show, an affiliate of the NSO Group specifically suggested language for the corrupting [phishing] text messages. Many were tailored for the Persian Gulf with seemingly innocuous invitations like 'Ramadan is near—incredible discounts' and 'keep your car tires from exploding in the heat.' Leaked technical documents included in the lawsuits also show that the company helped its clients by transmitting the data gained through surveillance through an elaborate computer network" (Kirkpatrick and Ahmed 2018, A7). In late July 2018 Amnesty International reported that one of its employees in Saudi Arabia had been targeted by NSO, bringing the number of people identified as subjected to NSO spyware to 174 (Brewster 2018a).

NSO has operated under different names; as OSY Technologies, it paid Michael Flynn, President Trump's former national-security adviser, more than $40,000 to serve on its advisory board from May 2016 until January 2017 (Ahmed and Perlroth 2017). While NSO claims that it sells spyware to help governments fight terrorists, drug cartels, and other criminal groups, the firm adds that it cannot determine who is behind specific hacking attempts. These claims ring hollow, as software updates could include a latent disabling code or kill switch. In addition, NSO could withhold new software patches, features, and updates. Despite widespread application of NSO spyware against human-rights activists, journalists, and anticorruption groups and individuals, the firm has not condemned, much less acknowledged, any abuse. Yet what goes around comes around: as NSO was in merger talks with Verint, an indictment filed by Israel's attorney general revealed that an NSO programmer had stolen the company's code and offered it on the Tor network for $50 million in cryptocurrency. The lawsuit was not triggered by pangs of conscience on the part of the Israeli government. Rather, they were concerned that "the actions of the suspect could've jeopardized the security of the state. That harm came from the fact that the NSO tools were used by Israel's armed forces, the indictment revealed" (Brewster 2018b).

The cases of HT and NSO reveal the growing demand for software exploits, which is only a part of the burgeoning overall market for cyber weapons. Just as traditional arms manufacturers offer "defensive" capabilities while providing features useful for offense, these firms are primarily engaged in developing offensive measures: "None of their software will help clients avoid cyberattacks, tighten up their internal networks, or patch flaws in their software. [Their] main business is offensive hacking … [selling] software to law enforcement and national security agencies around the world, letting them hack into targets' computers and mobile devices, install backdoors, and monitor them with ease" (Hern 2015a). In addition to cyber weapons, the market also generates antivirus software, firewalls, and other passive (rather than invasive) products developed and used for protecting networks and their trusted systems. We now turn to commercial cybersecurity markets and their products. The stack of these markets, ranging from raw hacks to antivirus software and cyber insurance, feeds information about social risk back to the market and legal system.

THE DIFFERENTIATION OF CYBERSECURITY MARKETS

Hacks are produced at industrial scale and stockpiled like arms in a military-industrial complex. In 2015 the compound annual growth rate of the $100 billion–plus global cybersecurity market was over 9 percent ("Cyber Security Markets" 2017). The market enjoys a substantial public subsidy from U.S. taxpayers, although its total size is unknown because of its partial inclusion in "black budgets" for defense needs. At the time of this writing, in 2018–19, the U.S. government is the cybersecurity market's biggest customer, spending about $20 billion per year. Other leading customers include the banking and finance, health care, energy, and information and communications technology industries (Commonwealth of Australia 2016).

The U.S. government is also one of the most widely recognized producers of hacks: "By the end of 2016, the CIA's hacking division, which formally falls under the agency's Center for Cyber Intelligence (CCI), had over 5,000 registered users and had produced more than a thousand hacking systems, trojans, viruses, and other 'weaponized' malware. Such is the scale of the CIA's undertaking that by 2016, its hackers had utilized more code than that used to run Facebook" (WikiLeaks 2017). The National Security Agency also "apparently regularly engineers, discovers, or purchases 'zero-day' vulnerabilities … and then stores them for use in its own offensive cyberattacks" (Mandel 2017, 37). The NSA also leaks its own tools and malware, known as "implants," and analysts await their reemergence in the internet "wild" as components of new exploits: "The crown jewel of the implant collection," now residing on the open internet, "appears to be a program named FUZZBUNCH, which essentially automates the deployment of NSA malware, and would allow a member of the agency's Tailored Access Operations group to more easily infect a target from their desk" (Biddle 2017). Evidence of repurposed Fuzzbunch code in new malware appeared in 2018.

Private cybersecurity markets developed before the year 2000, as IBM, Microsoft, Cisco Systems, and other information technology companies began marketing services to outside firms. By 1998 accounting firms such as Price Waterhouse, Coopers & Lybrand, and Ernst & Young offered "swat teams" to clients; between the end of 1996 and March 1998, Price Waterhouse alone tripled their cybersecurity business (DiDio

1998). In 1998 Microsoft established an internal hacking team (the 24-7 Security Problem Response Team) and formed partnerships with a host of private companies and public agencies, such as the Computer Emergency Response Team at Carnegie Mellon University and the Computer Incident Advisory Capability (CIAC) at the U.S. Department of Energy (Burns 1998). Higher education also contributes to technology transfer and labor for the sector. Hackathons, university professional degree programs, and "capture the flag" and "red-team/blue-team" hacking contests also serve as campus venues for cybersecurity research and development. "Hacking schools" operate at the University of Tulsa and Carnegie Mellon in Pittsburgh (Nakashima and Soltani 2014).

The NSA has long served as an incubator for startups in computer and network security. For example, Trusted Information Systems, a Glenwood, Maryland–based computer-security firm, was founded in 1983 by a former NSA and Department of Defense researcher (Chandrasekaran 1998). The company focused on four primary areas: firewalls, antivirus software, VPNs (virtual private networks), and intrusion-detection software against "insider" hacks. Its success led to its purchase by Santa Clara–based Network Associates for $307 million in 1998 (McIntosh 2000). The post-9/11 "gold rush" in computer and network security accelerated the revolving door between government-intelligence agencies such as Government Communications Headquarters (GCHQ) and NSA and private industry. Former CIA director R. James Woolsey and many NSA veterans have sat on the board of directors of Invicta Networks, founded by Soviet-defector Victor Sheymov (Risen 2000). General Keith Alexander, former U.S. Cyber Command and NSA head, attracted "seven-figure consulting fees for his IronNet Cybersecurity firm. This after Alexander left the NSA under a cloud . . . over [Edward] Snowden's revelations of NSA bulk surveillance and warrantless wire-tapping" (Moroney 2014).

The raw exploits that can become the transformational code underlying an intrusive hack, or a passive cyber-defense mechanism, are the first link in the value chain for cybersecurity products. These bugs hold greater value for cybersecurity companies than they do for the software companies that produce them in the first place: "Companies in the market, such as Acton [and] Netragard Inc., pay bug hunters more for the information than the makers of the flawed software themselves. Netragard CEO Adriel Desautels says that while the software industry might pay a few thousand dollars for vulnerabilities to patch systems and better protect customers, his company sometimes pays $100,000 or more for an exploit of an unknown flaw" (Silver 2012). Yahoo! initially paid researchers who discovered vulnerabilities with an online voucher for a T-shirt, while Apple offered no payment at all—despite revenues of $182 billion in 2014 (Batey 2015). Beginning in 2008 an exploit in Apple's iTunes enabled third parties to install unauthorized programs in online updates of the program. At security trade shows a Gamma demo showed prospective clients how to install FinFisher on users' computers using iTunes's update procedures. Remarkably, Apple did not patch the flaw until November 2011 (C. Williams 2011). Disclosing zero-day vulnerabilities to cybersecurity enterprises rather than to the originating software vendors encourages these organizations to stockpile them against potential adversaries instead of reporting them as bugs. But, as we shall see, the longer the zero day exists, the more likely it is to escape into "the wild," leaving the public exposed and the network as a whole devalued by increased risk.

Labor markets for the cybersecurity industry are tight, so hackers may be given security clearances to enable firms to perform vulnerability assessments for government agencies. Computer Sciences Corporation "emphasizes that CSC doesn't hire reformed hackers—cyber-outlaws who crossed the law in the past but who've had a conversion. 'Some of those hackers have turned totally ethical, but there have been some cases where they haven't,'" according to a spokesperson (Wingfield 2002). The University of Tulsa's hacking school claimed that students are screened for security clearances and must "promise" to work for the National Security Agency, Central Intelligence Agency, or another government agency upon graduation (Nakashima and Soltani 2014). The ironies

TABLE 1
Security software and vendor revenue, worldwide (millions of dollars)

Company	2015 revenue	2015 market share (%)	2014 revenue	2014–15 revenue growth (%)
Symantec	3,352	15	3,574	−6.21
Intel	1,751	8	1,825	−4.05
IBM	1,450	7	1,415	2.47
Trend Micro	990	4	1,052	−5.89
EMC	756	3	798	−5.26
Others	13,773	63	12,611	9.21
Total	22,072		21,275	

SOURCE: Gartner Research (2017). Tabulation errors on totals were corrected.

abound in trusting hackers to defend trusted systems. These ironies are characteristic of a field based on the dual-use characteristics of exploits and the ambiguous legal distinction between "use" of and "intent" to access a device in a way that "exceeds authorized access" (in CFAA language; "Fraud and Related Activity," n.d.).

In the broader market for cybersecurity software, as of 2018 the top five firms control less than 40 percent of the market. Symantec dominates global sales of security software, with double the revenues of its next two competitors, Intel and IBM (see table 1). Four of the top five companies are headquartered in the United States (the outlier is Japan's Trend Micro); these top players also offer diverse products besides security software. Other leading firms include Cisco Systems, FireEye, Hewlett Packard, and Rapid7 (all based in the United States) and Sophos (United Kingdom) ("Cyber Security Markets" 2017).

LEAKS IN THE "VULNERABILITY MARKET"

Evidence for a black market for vulnerabilities was tested and supported in 2007 (Radianti, Rich, and Gonzalez 2007). Since then spyware has become increasingly available and easy to use: "For example, today hackers can buy BlackEnergy or NetBot Attacker—cyberattack tools made by Russian and Chinese hackers, respectively—for less than $100 apiece" (Mandel 2017, 47). Depending on the quality, freshness, scarcity, and breadth of application, prices for exploits may range from the low thousands to over a million dollars: the greater the platform's sophistication (such as Apple's iPhone), the higher the price of the exploit. Bradley C. Panton and colleagues (2014, 476) provide a pricing guide for zero-day vulnerabilities for all major operating systems and applications for mobile devices and desktop computers. Prices range from $5,000 for Adobe Reader to up to $250,000 for iOS (the Apple operating system).

The commodity chain for custom-configured spyware spans international labor and currency markets and free-trade regimes. But spyware production is complex and fraught with uncertainties. Vulnerability information (such as zero-day exploits) is time-sensitive; pricing is not transparent, and the value of the exploit cannot be demonstrated without risk of loss. The utility and market value of an exploit drops when it is discovered: "Because cyber weapons are computer programs that operate by stealth and deception, once one is discovered, the programming innovations it employs quickly become ineffective.... The nature of the deception will have become apparent to information technologists, so that all security teams and operators will be on the lookout for it.... Cyber weapons are by and large 'one and done' when it comes to their effectiveness" (Lucas 2017, 59–60). Of the various factors affecting the market for vulnerabilities, reverse (Dutch) auctions can reflect the declining value of these cyber commodities better than other approaches such as bug challenges, bounties, and traditional auctions (Panton et al. 2014). Continual updates are required to maintain effectiveness as holes in code are discovered and patched. Spyware vendors frequently use a subscription model, as it allows buyers to minimize risk by parceling out payments over time and terminating these payments if a given vulnerability is patched before the subscription expires (Tsyrklevich 2015). As with other markets for media, subscriptions also allow the company to book revenues up front and potentially retain more customers after an initial purchase.

The vulnerabilities market is further complicated by other factors of "tradecraft": the fact that buyers and sellers may have difficulties finding each other, that exclusive rights cannot be guaranteed, and that buyers' intentions may be malicious (Miller 2007), all of which undermine trust in business transactions. Even if markets can find buyers and sellers, all parties still run the risk of being cheated in a deal. As markets for vulnerabilities skirt numerous legal risks, legal or even extralegal remedies are negligible at best. As previously discussed, a raw hack may be legally saleable intellectual property, but in the event of a dispute, the incentives may not exist for a court petition by an aggrieved buyer or seller.

In an effort to preserve the capital required to collect them and also as a hedge against uncertainty, bugs are often hoarded after discovery. Lucian Constantin (2017) notes that "numerous hacker groups have used zero-day exploits in their attacks over the years, some so frequently that they probably have large stockpiles of unpatched flaws. There are also private brokers that pay huge sums of money to acquire such exploits and then resell them to their customers, which includes law enforcement and intelligence agencies." These agencies themselves hoard vulnerabilities: "Since the CIA's hackers require unpatched vulnerabilities to penetrate systems and devices, the CIA routinely 'hoarded' those vulnerabilities by discovering them but not reporting them to the hardware and software manufacturers" (WikiLeaks 2017).

The deep hack of Britain's National Health Service (mentioned in chapter 2) owes its effects to the stockpiled exploits leaked from the NSA. In August 2016 Harold T. Martin III, an employee of NSA's premier hacking unit, Tailored Access Operations, was arrested on charges of theft of government property and mishandling classified information.[10] Martin, who worked at Booz Allen Hamilton from 2009 to 2015, was accused of stealing "many terabytes of data," an amount much larger than the data involved in the Snowden or Panama Papers exfiltrations. The NSA tools were subsequently leaked by "ShadowBrokers" (Shane, Apuzzo, and Becker 2016, A1). In early May 2017 a massive ransomware attack via phishing emails infected two hundred thousand computers in more than 150 countries. Users were locked out via encryption until ransom was paid. The victims included "FedEx in the United States, the Spanish telecom giant Telefónica, the French automaker Renault, universities in China, Germany's federal railway system and Russia's Interior Ministry. The most disruptive attacks infected Britain's public health system, where surgeries had to be rescheduled and some patients were turned away from emergency rooms" (Sanger, Chan, and Scott 2017, A1).

Hackers (believed to be based in eastern Europe) used ransomware "cobbled together from many places and sources," making traceability more difficult. The hacking tool, Eternal Blue, affected vulnerability in Microsoft Windows servers in 2016. Finger-pointing ensued, as Microsoft "even offered to provide NSA exploits to paid monthly subscribers" (Perlroth and Sanger 2017a, A1). While NSA indicated that it had informed Microsoft after the theft, and Microsoft claimed that it had patched the vulnerability earlier, the patches were not automatically installed and previous iterations of Windows weren't covered: "Privacy activists said if that were the case, the government would be to blame for the fact that so many companies were left vulnerable to [the] attacks. It takes time for companies to roll out system-wide patches, and by notifying Microsoft of the hole only after the N.S.A.'s hacking tool was stolen, activists say the government would have left many hospitals, businesses and governments susceptible" (2017b, A1). The release of the hoarded NSA bugs was widely considered to "far [exceed] the harm to American intelligence done by Edward J. Snowden, the former N.S.A. contractor who fled with four laptops of classified material in 2013" (Shane, Perlroth, and Sanger 2017, A1).

Another leak occurred in 2017, when code was exfiltrated by an NSA employee (Harold Martin, a former contractor for Booz Allen) and taken home to a computer running Kaspersky Lab antivirus software.

Russian hackers were believed to have exploited the Kaspersky software to steal classified documents (Shane and Goldman 2017). The Martin case is wending its way through the courts; in January 2018 Martin pled guilty to one count of willful retention of national defense information, based on his taking home a single classified NSA document. He still faces charges involving nineteen other documents (twelve from NSA, five from the military's Cyber Command, and one each from the CIA and the National Reconnaissance Office). Martin, whose lawyers described him as a "compulsive hoarder," squirreled away classified documents on paper, hard drives, and flash drives in his car, home, and a shed in his yard. But prosecutors have been unable to directly connect Martin with Shadow Brokers (Shane 2018). While a "smoking gun" linking leaked NSA exploits to myriad cyberattacks has not been found, the field is littered with spent cartridges. The U.S. government's largest producer of, and client for, vulnerabilities unsurprisingly contributes to the underlying insecurity of the very systems it is charged to defend.

THE HACKING VALUE CHAIN

Given the perishable, ephemeral, and spotty market for exploits, the production of hack-based commodities is bolstered in a variety of ways. In addition to markets for raw exploits (or vulnerabilities), standardized or custom ("bespoke") software solutions and platforms may be offered as products and services. Smaller markets feed demand for toolkits (antisecurity programs) and other components, and a burgeoning "piecework" market for products and services is developing in both customized and off-the-shelf packages (such as CloudFlare and Symantec).[11] Risk also is commodified through markets for identity protection for individuals and cyber insurance for businesses, as well as the proliferation of advertising-based and subscription-based cybersecurity products (like free antivirus). These "mediatized" representations of systemic risk inform decision making in firms and agencies and also send price signals to the market. The stock offerings of publicly traded cybersecurity firms, as well as exchange traded funds that bunde holdings of those firms' stock, represent another form of hacking's commodification. Rather than serving only as a sink for economic value, the industries bolstered by hacking and cybersecurity create value through the commercialization of risk, intellectual-property rights, and news media. Each market also provides feedback to the overall system by signaling its risk state at specific times and places.

While some code for intrusive malware, Trojans, and other hacks is created and circulated on forums for free, most is written by "only a small percentage of hacker members [who] possess a high level of skill in creating and disseminating malicious assets" (Samtani et al. 2017, 1026). The overall market value of hacker labor is high because it is skilled and scarce, although automation and global piecework may reduce costs. Software coding, like other labor-intensive industries, is symptomatic of "Baumol's disease," in which labor costs rise without corresponding gains in productivity. For enterprises this means that quality Trojan horse viruses will probably become more expensive to acquire over time. Less skilled coders can simply package together collections of toolkits for distribution through online illicit markets (toolkits facilitate the building and deployment of invasive or malicious software with a minimum of software coding skills). Their widening distribution "prolongs malware lifecycles and assists or outright enables potential attackers to gain entry to vulnerable systems" (Macdonald and Frank 2017, 50).

Hundreds of web forums, only partly visible to observers, draw hackers from the United States, Russia, China, and other countries with industrial-scale malware production. These forums publish tens of millions of messages related to the financialization of data breaches and cyber warfare. Sagar Samtani and colleagues estimate that "tens of thousands of malicious assets" are associated with these posts, which are created by "millions of hackers." Notwithstanding the high level of "noise" in these forums, they provide knowledge and know-how for both hackers and cybersecurity vendors. They educate "the majority of forum participants [who] are unskilled" in both technical knowledge and cultural tacit knowledge. In addition to free assets such as Structured Query Language injections, banking vulnerabilities, and variants of the same Trojan rootkit (Zeus), researchers have found that forums offer payloads, full services, and credit card information for sale (2017, 1025–26).

As the overall market grows, forums have differentiated into particular sharing communities and specialties. Moreover, traffic in the special topic areas of these forums spikes with corresponding threat events: "In 2009, for example, the popular website builder WordPress.com received widespread attention for being vulnerable to backdoors. Additionally, there was a surge in real keylogging exploitations between 2008 and 2010. More recently in the forum, crypters have received slightly more attention, possibly because they are the foundation for the robust cyber weapon Ransomware (a tool that encrypts a user's files as ransom for payment), one of the most malicious tools known to date. Such an increase in forum assets correlates and is validated with the growing amount of actual exploits conducted with crypters and Ransomware during the same time period" (Samtani et. al. 2017, 1039). Hacker forums provide wellsprings of innovations, gossip, and culture to the cybersecurity industry's commodification. The cybersecurity value chain resembles other value-chain models in the software and media industries, beginning with finance capital, intellectual property, packaging, distribution, and marketing. In the next section we see how tiers of products have emerged that are roughly tied to these links in the value chain.

OTHER ROUTES FOR COMMODIFICATION

Table 2 offers an overview of the markets that develop around hacking and cybersecurity, their business domains, and their nearest industries. Each successive market is dependent on underlying markets and represented by layers, or tiers, of accumulated value. In the first tier business is tied to the exchange value of zero-day exploits, dump files,

TABLE 2

Tiers of commodification in cyber markets

Tier	Business	Industry
Tier 1	Exchanges of techne and raw hacks (e.g., zero days, dump files, Trojans)	Consulting
Tier 2	Repackaging and exchanges of malware suites	Consulting
Tier 3	Repackaging and sales of cybersecurity suites (including CTI)	Software and business services
Tier 4	Sales of corporate cybersecurity equities	Financial
	Sales of enterprise cybersecurity news and research	Media
Tier 5	Sales of cyber insurance for firms and individuals	Financial

and intrusive malware like Trojans. The second tier includes more widely distributable packages of malware, including toolkits. The third tier produces commercial products for customers of software and business services and includes companies like the Hacking Team and its spyware competitors. In the fourth tier, information about security markets is commodified in two ways: through exchange traded funds, or stocks for individual cybersecurity companies that are bundled (like a mutual fund) for public trading like regular stocks; and through media offering "business intelligence" to the security industry and its clients. The fifth tier provides insurance products for security theft, cyber theft, and other damages from hacking.

We already have presented the tier 1 order of the value chain closest to the producers of vulnerabilities, who may or may not also publish or otherwise distribute them in a second tier. In a third tier of the market, packaged and custom-made software "solutions" include defensive, offensive, and mixed measures. Defensive measures, such as cyber-threat intelligence (CTI), are reactive rather than proactive, as they are based on data from prior attacks. Some products claim to offer "comprehensive and proactive CTI" by mining data collected "from the online hacker community" and identifying threats in progress (Samtani et al. 2017).[12] Thus CTI capabilities, which are provided by firms such as FireEye and Cyveillance, are migrating to "active defense." Many custom cyber-defense products are uniquely tailored to the organizations that develop them. Other commercial products are then spun off, including variations of the originals licensed to other organizations.

Cybersecurity vendors fall under more specific industry classifications. In 2018 the top four vendors of "computer peripheral equipment," catering exclusively to markets for network and content security, were (from largest to smallest) Palo Alto Networks, Fortinet, FireEye, and ForeScout (Nasdaq.com). Older companies, such as Xerox, are also entering the market. "Security information and event management" firms offer software that provides basic security monitoring; advanced threat detection; and cyber-incident (event) identification, investigation, and response. Leaders in this field include LogRhythm, Splunk, and McAfee, with MicroFocus, ArcSight, and Dell subsidiary RSA as challengers. IBM is an integrated company offering services built into their own products (Gartner Research 2017). The future development of CTI into "active defense" would introduce new growth opportunities for the cybersecurity sector but may require a more acquiescent legal system. While the law has not, in fact, constrained the reflex to hack back at cyberattackers, it vacillates between permissiveness and light touch regulation (as the next chapter demonstrates).

At the fourth level in our model, we find financial equities derived from the underlying value of hacks. Venture-capital influx into cybersecurity companies leaped from $1.1 billion in 166 deals in 2011 to $3.8 billion in 332 deals in 2015 (Acohido 2016). In the retail financial markets, "very few tech sectors raise more than $2.5 billion in a year," but global cybersecurity investments were $1.7 billion in 2013 and $2.5 billion in 2014 ("Cyber Security Investment" 2015). In 2016 nearly $3.5 billion was invested in cybersecurity firms, up 6 percent from 2015, and four startups in the new cohort each raised at least $100 million in new venture-capital funding. CrowdStrike raised a total of $250 million, with the company valued at nearly $1 billion (de la Merced 2017).[13] Adding to the froth in the market is the PureFunds ISE Cyber Security ETF, traded under the ticker symbol of "HACK." This tier also features publishing and advertising media surrounding these securities and underlying markets. As the gold rush in enterprise software generates winners and losers, a throng of analysts provides consulting, news and commentary, gossip, and statistics about the fortunes of vendors and their clients. Consulting firms may produce original data and software for clients, while publishing firms collect and repackage information for clients and the general public.[14]

In a fifth tier, insurance serves as a "kind of security pact against industrially produced dangers and hazards," in an age when nuclear, chemical, and genetic technology undermines the "calculus of risks by which modern societies have developed a consensus on progress" (Elliott 2002, 296). This working consensus about addressing systemic risk is the underlying thesis of Ulrich Beck's risk sociology, in which the handoff of social insurance policies from political systems to the private sector transfers risk to economic and financial systems. Consistent with the dynamics of Beck's risk society, the cyber-insurance market flourishes as the threat of hacking and potential damages increases.[15] The pricing of insurance is derived from, and also contributes to, pricing in adjacent and ancillary markets, including reinsurance, banking and finance, computer hardware and software, and business valuations. Besides the use of pricing to signal between systems, these markets also manage systemic risk by externalizing the costs of hacking from public programs to private parties, in which policyholders are typically corporations and individuals.

This fifth-order commodification begins when hacking risk is calculated into actuarial insurance tables, with data derived from CTI and other sources, and then used to sell insurance against the risk of being hacked or victimized by a cyberattack. The growth in markets for such cyber-insurance policies is reflected in the fact that "U.S. cyber premiums hit $1.84 billion in 2017, a 37 percent increase compared to the previous year" as cyber-insurance products are becoming bundled with other policy packages ("Cyber Insurance Market" 2018).

In addition, cyberattacks have prompted insurers to massively hike cyber premiums and deductibles for companies perceived to be high risk: "In some cases [insurers limit] ... the amount of coverage to $100 million, leaving many potentially exposed to big losses from hacks that can cost more than twice that" (Finkle 2015). To Evgeny Morozov (2017a) the insurance market is worse than extortionate, thriving without the benefit of any promised deliverables:

> In essence, cyber-insurance—like any other form of insurance—is a domain of rentiers who are keen to extract a regular premium payment from those needing their services. The truly innovative element here is that the risk that creates this new class of rentiers exists partly—and, one could even say, mostly—because of government activity.... Imagine if the government regularly dispatched a group of well-paid and well-educated saboteurs to weaken the anti-flood or anti-earthquake defenses of our houses, leaving us no option but to turn to the private sector for security, either in the form of better defenses or better insurance. This is the situation we are in right now; the only difference is that cyber-security disasters are almost entirely human-made and thus avoidable.

At these upper-tier markets for hacks, artificial intelligence and robotic automation are seemingly natural applications for cybersecurity products. Like other markets for analytic services, CTI and enterprise risk management are becoming increasingly automated as they assume more complex and continuous tasks. Artificial-intelligence software is becoming integrated into cybersecurity platforms, to provide "continuous feedback loops" for companies seeking to ascertain risk and possible breaches at any given moment. Artificial intelligence contributes directly to autopoiesis when coupled with cybersecurity in these cases. In the process this software can "support behavioral analytics to identify undesirable patterns of behavior by individuals or groups" (High 2017). As with soothsaying aspirants in other fields of business analytics, the vendors' "solutions" offer a modicum of predictive power, albeit with the standard caveat: your mileage may vary.

PWNERSHIP AND THE RISKS OF IDENTITY THEFT

Popular communication on the subject of the dark web and other hacker environments suggests giant but unknown exchanges where the hacked personal information of data subjects is circulated and brokered for sale. Financial companies use the threatening "dark web" term to induce paranoia and promote their financial products, witnessed by a web ad from Experian: "Get a free dark web scan to see if your SSN, email, or phone number have been compromised." Experian, LifeLock, and their competitors currently charge around twenty dollars per month for identity-theft detection and notification services, using news reports of database breaches and other data spills to drum up new business. Table 3 shows data spills, and table 4 shows data breaches.

Personally identifiable data from these breaches are often sold in lists known as "dumps." These lists are purchased for spamming and phishing campaigns, which botnets can conduct on a massive scale. While more than 80 percent of U.S. companies have reported breaches (High 2017), and attack vectors multiply along with targets of opportunity for hackers, table 4 dispels the illusion of an ever-cresting tsunami of cyberattacks causing data breaches. Although the number of qualifying data breaches did indeed quadruple between 2005 and 2014, the number of exposed records per year stayed relatively stable. Some of those records, moreover, may not have been newly exposed; data breaches may have reexposed records or exposed old records, which nonetheless added to a growing cumulative number of exposures. Breaches leading to exposure began to spike in 2013–14, but this spike may be correlated to increased observation and news coverage of cybercrime and cyber warfare. Nonetheless, as accounts of hacked and leaked databases grew in number (often reported long after the fact), hundreds of millions of U.S. resi-

TABLE 3

Selected data spills (United States)

Year	Target	User accounts	Source
2005	CardSystems Solutions	40 million	Evers (2005)
2006	AOL	20 million	Arrington (2006)
2007	TJ Maxx	50 million	Espiner (2007)
2008	Myspace	360 million	Franceschi-Bicchierai (2016a)
2009	Heartland Payment Systems	10 million	Lewis (2015)
2010	Netflix	100 million	Singel (2010)
2011	Valve/Steam	40 million	"Valve's Online" (2011)
2012	LinkedIn	20 million	Hunt (2016)
2013	Yahoo!	3,000 million	Larson (2017a)
2013	Adobe	40 million	Ducklin (2013)
2014	eBay	150 million	Peterson (2014)
2015	Anthem	80 million	Greene (2015)
2016	FriendFinder	40 million	Whitaker (2016)
2016	Dropbox	70 million	Cox (2016)
2017	Equifax	140 million	Irby (2019)
Total		4,160 million	

Note: These private-sector cases are the largest reported breaches of personally identifiable information from user accounts in each year. The overlap of affected users and accounts is unknown.

dents had their data exposed and were put at much greater risk of identity theft and fraud. Contributing to the vulnerability is the fact that, as of 2016, fewer than one-half of companies in fourteen sectors and eleven countries used encryption across their operations (Preimesberger 2016). Reliable figures are scant for average costs of identity theft for consumers, but trade-press articles routinely put the costs for data breaches of businesses in the millions or tens of millions of dollars.

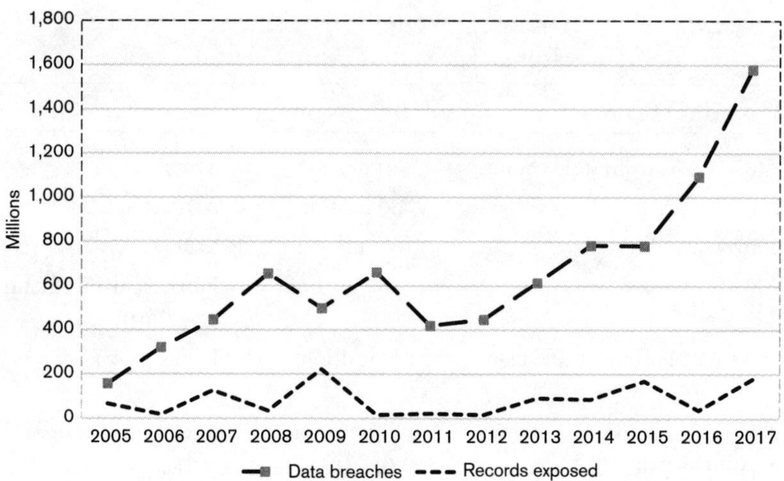

Year	Data breaches	Records exposed
2005	157	66.90
2006	321	19.10
2007	446	127.70
2008	656	35.70
2009	498	222.50
2010	662	16.20
2011	419	22.90
2012	447	17.30
2013	614	91.98
2014	783	85.61
2015	781	169.07
2016	1,093	36.60
2017	1,579	178.96

SOURCE: Statista (2018).

Figure 1. Data breaches and records exposure.

The threat of cybercrime is often abstract and difficult to communicate to the public. Identity theft has made it a more salient concern. As it pursued antipiracy campaigns twenty years ago, the royalties industry faced major challenges in convincing the public of digital piracy's ostensible harms, in part because the intangibility of digital content undermines its perceived value and because copyright theft was broadly perceived to be a victimless crime. Today cybersecurity firms have had less difficulty communicating real harms of hacking to their current or potential customers facing years of low-level but recognizable risk from identity theft. The fear of identity theft helps stoke the growth of the cyber-insurance industry.

While anxiety about the risks of hacking is not misplaced, risks are also exaggerated by journalists and research analysts who report hacking campaigns and data breaches as jarring intrusions and disruptions to everyday life. A study conducted between 2009 and 2014 found that "only a tiny number of people exposed by leaks end up paying any costs, and for the victims who do, the average cost has actually been falling steadily" (Popper 2015, BU-6). The average price of a stolen credit card number for a hacker to buy was only $7.65 per card, according to one 2016 study ("Darknet Site" 2016), and under $10 for a stolen medical record.[16] Banks and merchants must bear losses related to credit card hacking. The low prices for stolen records on the black market partly reflect an oversupply of exploitable records and may have contributed to a migration among online fraudsters to ransomware attacks that offer higher yields (Korolov 2016).

But such information does not suit the self-interest of insurance companies; hyping what is still a manageable risk can help them generate a lucrative business in new consumer insurance protection. "One of the most memorable statistics on identity fraud comes from advertisements that say a new victim is created every two seconds. That figure, which comes from Javelin Strategy and Research, is largely attributable to standard credit card fraud, in which criminals use a stolen credit card number to buy goods—not the sort of thing most people imagine when they think of identity fraud. The more troubling identity theft, in which new accounts are opened in an unsuspecting person's name, make up only 5 percent of the total figure given by Javelin" (Popper 2015, BU-6). Sorting out the layers and levels of risk from data dumps, identity theft, and ransomware is beyond the ken of hundreds of millions of people dependent on trusted systems to navigate everyday life. Instead, they must, in Dan Tynan's (2016) words, "assume you're going to be hacked." As a result, cybernetic risk assessment for individuals, firms, and households has been handed off to sprawling markets to conduct. In the process it foreshadows the crisis of legitimacy in postprivacy social norms.

CONCLUSION

At present Symantec and McAfee dominate the overall commercial market tracked by financial firms, with many smaller and private firms also competing for licit and illicit market share. These privately held firms operate at a remove from analysts and the public. The market structure for cybersecurity is changing, with the big two losing market share to competitors like CrowdStrike. The value of the overall security market is on track to reach $202.4 billion by 2021, up from $122.5 billion in 2016 (Kuranda 2017). This figure is likely be conservative, as it may not include all costs in enterprises with many divisions. Valuations aside, this market carries outsized influence in the social world—perhaps offering a clue about the characteristics of the cybernetic work it performs. It mediates interaction between various social systems and provides something like a social "difference engine" that processes various systemic risks. The commercial availability of hacks may be somewhat modulated by national and international regulations, but overall the global marketplace for exploit-based software operates relatively freely. This situation owes in part to the intangibility of the commodities, the secrecy of the trade, and high levels of competition in cybersecurity software and related markets. Buyers and sellers in the markets most directly linked to the malicious code base that forms their technology are able to operate at a much higher level of secrecy than firms buying and selling packaged and repackaged hacks or cybersecurity companies offering publicly tradable stock.

The laws governing the creation and sale of hacking tools and cyber weapons are not unified or consistent. But the *use* of these tools and weapons is criminal, barring exceptional reasons of state (which is frequently claimed by intelligence or police agencies). We have referred to this as the market for legal hacking. This distinction between creation and use allows raw hacks to be sold in primary markets and for spyware and cybersecurity firms to legally serve "legitimate" customers. Lawmakers in the United States have pushed aggressively against the creation, distribution, and use of cyber tools in fraud and intellectual-property theft cases; as we have seen, they have begun to promote hack-back legislation for some corporate targets of hackers. In addition to "legitimate" databases, personally identifiable information also is commodified in illegal markets, and forensic analyses of the breaches that yield them can form the bases for additional cyber commodities such as cyber insurance and evolving CTI and enterprise risk-management products. U.S. federal law is largely devoid of basic electronic privacy protections, leaving a patchwork of state laws to protect consumer rights and offer legal remedies to those affected. As previously mentioned, the Consumer Financial Protection Bureau's capture by the industries it should be regulating (Chait 2017) is symbolized by the federal government's partial release of claims against Equifax following its 2017 data breach, although the Federal Trade Commission and some states continue to pursue cases against the company.

In the next chapter we elaborate on the legal underpinnings that enable the business practices discussed so far. Specifically, we assess how intellectual-property matters—including trade secrets, patents, and designs—are merging piracy and hacking concerns into a new cybersecurity policy regime. The industry narrative supporting this new blended regime frequently alleges that corporate intellectual property lost or exposed in data breaches has passed a threshold and now qualifies the problem as a national-security risk. According to CrowdSource executive Dmitri Alperovitch, "What we have witnessed over the past five to six years has been nothing short of a historically unprecedented transfer of wealth—closely guarded national secrets . . . , source code, bug databases, email archives, negotiation plans and exploration details for new oil and gas field auctions, document stores, legal contracts, supervisory control and data acquisition (SCADA) configurations, design schematics, and much more has 'fallen off the truck' of numerous, mostly Western companies and disappeared in the ever-growing electronic archives of dogged adversaries" (Mandel 2017, 22–23). To industry executives and their clients, theft or loss of intellectual property appears as a "wealth transfer" to an adversary rather than as inventory "shrinkage" in traditional accounting terms or as a geopolitical trade-off for conducting business. Historically, antipiracy initiatives (including the Stop Online Piracy Act and PIPA) invoked similar "dogged adversaries." But characterizing this aspect of cybercrime as a countersystemic force misses the bigger picture. IP theft or loss at the hands of hackers is only part of the political economic equation. It is counterbalanced by profitable cyber-defense work, private insurance, and other forms of wealth creation that begin in the discovery and stockpiling of new exploits.

In the hottest financial markets for cybersecurity software, industry players are hedging their bets and playing more than one side in a game to lock down risk markets for hacking and cybersecurity. Markets for cyberattack tools are flourishing alongside the markets for defending against them. We have written this story before, in *Digital Music Wars*. The technical and legal infrastructure for digital media coalesced around customer relationship management, digital-rights management, and antipiracy law and policy. Antipiracy grew from an industry reflex into an industry strategy, culminating in the contemporary online model of individual and exclusive access to intellectual property. As was the case with piracy in the final decade of the twentieth century, computer fraud and abuse (broadly construed as hacking or cyberattack) now provides a central impetus for monitoring our information environment.

CHAPTER FOUR

Antihacking Law and Policy

Despite the scope of its financial, political, and social influence, the global commodity chain for hacking products and services has evaded comprehensive, or even substantial, regulation to date. Instead, a jumble of Budapest Convention guidelines, EU directives, U.S. federal and state laws, and international honor agreements sustains the growth and confluence of industry and military interests in the cyber arena. "Cyberattacks" and "malware" are not defined in the national or international laws governing cybercrime and cybersecurity, and they also defy easy categorization for prosecutors, forensic analysts, chief security officers, and others charged with improving the security of trusted systems. Hacking motives may include espionage, terrorism, theft, and vandalism, and perpetrators may be difficult to ascertain. The cornerstone of U.S. law on cybercrime, the Computer Fraud and Abuse Act (CFAA), ignores intent; all charges of "exceeding authorized access" to a protected system are prosecuted as fraud. In social systems theory, law coordinates social action through strict binaries of legal and illegal activity. In contrast, the market coordinates social action through economic transactions—which leads the latter into areas ill-defined by law. Although the global entertainment and communications industries successfully deployed cybercrime law against piracy in the 1980s and

1990s, a harmonized international legal system for contemporary cybersecurity law and policy has not developed.

Information sharing, both military and civilian, has been the contemporary Western approach to state security and risk management. Other approaches to state network security have been territorial firewalls (China and Iran), bans on the export of certain encryption technologies (United States), and censorship (Singapore and others) (Deibert 2002). Some transnational frameworks, like the Budapest Convention, the European Union's Network and Information Security Directive, and GPRS (digital privacy law), aspire to promote network security at a global level.[1] Starting with the rights of the individual "data subject," they may scale to include the household, firm, agency, and country. But these legal agreements differ from those governing exchanges of military information and other resources, such as the North Atlantic Treaty Organization (NATO) cybersecurity system. Also, as treaty-based arrangements, they differ from the honor agreement underlying Wassenaar, which remains subject to change from country to country. In the current geopolitical flux, some observers of global internet policy see China and the European Union taking control of the law and policy agenda for cyberspace (Geller 2018). While the United States currently is retreating in many global-policy domains, it retains advantages accumulated from an era in which it exercised nearly hegemonic power—particularly in its military cyber operations.[2]

INTERNATIONAL TRADE POLICY AS CONTROLLED ANARCHY

In the Cold War era, the Allied powers established a legal system for arms embargoes on Eastern Bloc countries. The United States developed export controls in response to changing geopolitics and security needs; the Coordinating Committee for Multilateral Export Controls (COCOM), for example, responded to "events such as the Berlin Crisis, the Communist takeover in China, and the development of nuclear arms in the Soviet Union" (Dursht 1997, 1098n127). COCOM served as a forum for Western countries and allies to hash out the aforementioned "crypto wars" in the 1990s. It became superannuated by the Wassenaar Arrangement, which imposes political conditions on technology trade that would otherwise be handled by the markets. As a "soft law," or honor agreement, Wassenaar lacks the status of an enforceable treaty (Hoelscher and Wolffgang 1998, 54–55) but generates information sharing and feedback about international trade in products built for hacking and cybersecurity. Specifically, Wassenaar calls on member states to "notify transfers and denials" (Wassenaar Arrangement Secretariat 2016, 11). Rather than mandating rigid controls, Wassenaar was designed to promote licensing, greater transparency, and information exchange in combination with diplomacy (Dursht 1997, 1116). Christoph Hoelscher and Hans-Michael Wolffgang note that individual member states retain the privilege of deciding cases of special concern:

> The Wassenaar Arrangement differentiates between the exchange of information on dual use goods and the exchange of information on arms. Information on license denials with respect to exports in non-member countries is supposed to be transferred twice a year. In the case of sensitive and extremely sensitive goods, there should be individual notification, most likely within 30 days and at least within 60 days after the denial of a license. As far as transactions involving extremely sensitive goods are concerned, member countries are allowed to apply stricter standards and national criteria. With respect to arms, information exchange should also happen every six months. The information should include data on quantity, destination and specifications of models. (1998, 54)

From "sensitive" to "extremely sensitive goods" to "national criteria," Wassenaar remains purposefully vague to encourage its adoption. In the European Union export licenses are issued on a country-by-country basis, with wide national discretion (although Italy did impose export restrictions on the Hacking Team after disclosures of the company's business activities). In the United Kingdom the Export Control Organisation licenses exports of weapons and cybersecurity products on an "advisory basis" (UK-DIT 2018). But "virtual weapons don't sit in packing crates ready to be examined by customs officers; they may be being developed and sold globally without the ECO ever knowing they exist" (Batey 2011). Moreover, countries pursuing economic growth through exports and foreign investment are hesitant to overregulate a high-growth segment of the software market (obviously, militaries might have reasons for some firms to avoid certain exports). What may be euphemistically termed "software development activities" receive some special tax waivers in Romania, an EU member state, and countries including China and the United States have created free-trade zones and tax incentives for software research and development.

Unlike the Wassenaar's honor agreement, the Budapest Convention on Cybercrime regulates the proliferation of spyware or military-grade cyber weapons through treaty law. Ratified in 2001, the Budapest Convention is the only multilateral treaty outside of the EU legal system to harmonize national laws regarding hacking; it has "the widest coverage of any international agreement dealing with cybercrime" (Harley 2010). In addition to harmonizing national laws for its forty-eight members, the convention offers a template for other states to update their own criminal laws. Article 6 of the convention requires its signatories to criminalize the "production, sale, procurement for use, import, distribution or otherwise making available of . . . a device, including a computer program, designed or adapted primarily for the purpose of committing any of the offences" it establishes as criminal. Germany and the United Kingdom have enacted laws targeting "hacking tools" (Bratus et al. 2014, 6). Signatory states must punish offenders "by effective, proportionate and dissuasive sanctions, which include deprivation of liberty" (Council of Europe 2001, art. 3, sec. 1). Articles 2–13 of the convention provide a broad definition of cybercrime, which includes violating the confidentiality, integrity, and availability of computer data and systems through unauthorized access, interception, and misuse of devices; computer-related offenses related to forgery and fraud; content-related offenses, such as trafficking in child pornography; and infringements of copyrights and related rights, as well as aiding and abetting these offenses (Haase 2015, 3).[3]

The U.S. Senate ratified the Budapest Convention in 2006, but few additional countries are expected to join. As Adrian Haase notes, "The Council of Europe is, despite its universal approach, a regional organization. Hence, it did not integrate significant countries beyond the western hemisphere in the drafting process or even invite them to participate as consultants" (2015, 3–4). As of 2016, its forty-eight signatory states did not include China, Russia, or Brazil. Over half of the world's population remains excluded from the Budapest Convention, as are many countries with active cybercultures and powerful hacking traditions. A principal reason authoritarian states such as Russia and China have refused to join the convention is that it "permits the digital equivalent of hot pursuit: A police force investigating a cybercrime can access networks in other jurisdictions without first seeking permission" (Bennhold and Scott 2017, A6).

When codifying cybercrime norms, political representation is difficult to achieve. It involves a welter of existing and overlapping initiatives, operating in conjunction with vaguely defined and shifting categories of actors and actions. Elected officials have few or no roles among these categories, and lines of responsibility are not clearly drawn. Different actors seek different ends, which further hampers coordination. Participants in the Budapest Convention include "the EU, the UN (especially the ITU as a specialized agency of the UN), Interpol, Europol," and others, demonstrating that not only states but also quasi-governmental organizations are involved: "Although the Council of Europe claims that more than 100 countries have used the Convention in some way to update their cybercrime law, various other institutions with regional or thematic expertise in cybercrime legislation are willing to lay down universal rules for the harmonization of substantive and procedural cybercrime law as well as for international cooperation during the prosecution process." Finally, the Budapest Convention has been criticized for defining cybercrime in overly broad terms. In 2006 the convention was extended beyond copyright violations and child pornography to cover racist and xenophobic material, yet basic definitions are vague or nonexistent.[4] As Haase notes, "the label 'cybercrime' seems rather arbitrary as long as the only common denominator is the involvement of a computer (system) in any possible way. The criminal law in potentially acceding countries would have to be harmonized in various sections to fully comply with the Convention's requirements. Therefore, countries solely interested in parts of the Convention's provisions, namely the core cybercrimes, cannot ratify the Convention" (2015, 3–4).

As mentioned previously, the United States and the European Union have incommensurate data-breach laws. In the United States federal law does not require companies to report data breaches that result in mass exfiltration or publication of personally identifying information, outside of health and educational records. Companies therefore have incentives to suppress timely information about hacks. The absence of a federal breach-notification law (besides what is required by the Health Insurance Portability and Accountability Act, or HIPAA) increases the risk that these breaches are discovered late, add to commercial losses and recovery costs, and reduce the chances of legal remedies. In contrast, EU laws, which member states must transpose into their national laws, specifically require firms to report breaches. One example is Directive 2009/136/EC, which is designed to protect user data handled by electronic communications service providers. The directive requires providers to report breach information to authorities and, under specific circumstances, also contact affected individuals.[5] The European Union can fine firms for noncompliance, and individual member nations can also impose additional reporting requirements. The growing split between the United States and the European Union regarding the legal rights for data subjects indicates long-term conflicts over the legal disposition of private trusted systems that share personal data across the Atlantic.

In 2007 botnets attributed to the Russian military engaged in waves of distributed denial-of-service (DDoS) attacks on strategic networks in

Estonia. Following these attacks, in the 2010 Lisbon Summit Declaration, NATO identified cyber threats as demanding urgent attention. In 2014 NATO declared that cyberattacks on one or all members should be considered an attack on all allies, "in accordance with the Wales Summit Declaration... based on the provisions for 'collective defense' in NATO Article 5" (Lee and Lim 2016, 860). Military security relies on sharing threat indicators in real time, and NATO has begun coordinating threat intelligence through its cybersecurity headquarters in Tallinn, Estonia. Other alliances seek to harmonize cybersecurity standards. The European Union is currently implementing the Directive on Network and Information Security, modeled on the 2013 Cybersecurity Strategy, which planned for an "open, safe and secure cyberspace" (European Commission 2013). In addition, the Europol police agency launched the Europol Cybercrime Center in 2013. Based in The Hague, Netherlands, the center is intended "to act as a European focal-point in fighting cybercrime, to merge information and to inform Member States about impending threats of attacks against information systems" (Březinová 2017, 8). The European Union and NATO also have "discussed the potential for cooperation in response to Russia's hybrid warfare, which includes cyberattacks" (Lee and Lim 2016, 860).

NATO's melding of state-corporate network security, as described by Tony Morbin (2015), illustrates how states, corporations, and civil society interact to create system boundaries; how these boundaries disclose the complex and adaptive nature of these systems; and how they can mutate, merge, or disappear. When cyberattack risks are heightened, these boundaries handle the trip switches to contain crises that otherwise could cascade through the defense, financial, and infrastructural sectors of member countries. The Charter of the United Nations already authorizes national self-defense while prohibiting most uses of force involving aggression and armed attack. Chapter 1, article 2(4), of the charter states, "All Members shall refrain in their international relations from the threat or use of force against the territorial integrity or political independence of any state, or in any other manner inconsistent with the Purposes of the United Nations." Yet chapter 7, article 51, ensures that "nothing in the present Charter shall impair the inherent right of individual or collective self-defense if an armed attack occurs against a Member of the United Nations, until the Security Council has taken measures necessary to maintain international peace and security" (United Nations 1945). While the charter does not address hacking or cyber warfare, scholars have been tasked with spelling out rules of engagement on the model of the Geneva conventions. Their ongoing work on the *Tallinn Manual on the International Law Applicable to Cyber Warfare* is based on the Charter of the United Nations and associated treaties. The *Tallinn Manual* (Schmitt 2013) may provide a framework for a multilateral or plurilateral treaty governing hacking, but the odds are not favorable at present. In 2011, when plurilateralism was at its height in Western defense policy, the U.S. Council of Foreign Relations regarded a global and treaty-based regime for cybersecurity as a "pipe dream" (Segal and Waxman 2011).

To match U.S. export regulations with the Wassenaar Arrangement, the U.S. Department of Commerce issued a proposal in 2015 that would have added new licensing requirements to export "intrusion software." The proposal was designed to address spyware exports in response to reports that "linked exports of Western surveillance technologies to human rights abuses in countries such as Bahrain and the UAE, Turkmenistan, and Libya" (Galperin and Cardozo 2015). (We have addressed these products and vendors in chapter 3.) But the Department of Commerce's proposal was criticized as unnecessary and ineffective. Electronic Frontier Foundation staff attorney Nate Cardozo claimed, "When companies turn a blind eye [toward sales to dodgy customers for spyware and surveillance software], there are already legal tools available to hold them accountable without increasing the export control load.... If Hacking Team for instance sold surveillance tools to Sudan, the company can already be held accountable under existing laws" (Vijayan 2015).

The crypto wars of the 1990s echo strongly in these debates. The Department of Commerce's proposal's language was seen as "too broad and far-reaching, and effectively [making] it... impossible to own a zero-day and disclose a zero-day." It was also criticized for having the opposite effect of its intent: "You are going to disarm legitimate researchers and you are going to prevent them from doing that legitimate research, but you are not going to impact the bad guys" (Lemos 2015a). The proposal was unilaterally opposed by U.S. cybersecurity firms, which formed the Coalition for Responsible Cybersecurity, a single-issue group dedicated to torpedoing the Department of Commerce's proposal. Representative Jim Langevin (D-RI), who cochaired the Congressional Cybersecurity Caucus, represented their interests in a letter that stated, "The proposed rule has a number of flaws that could detrimentally affect our national security.... This could have a chilling effect on research, slowing the disclosure of vulnerabilities and impairing our nation's cybersecurity" (Bennett 2015). Opponents focused on the licensing requirement for zero-day exploits, regardless of their purpose or final destination: "Network-testing equipment sent to England would face the same potentially onerous scrutiny as spyware sent to Syria" (Uchill 2015).

The Department of Commerce's proposal would have made it more difficult and expensive to sell a wide range of web-related equipment and software overseas. Since "the only difference between an academic proof of concept and a zero-day for sale is the existence of a price tag," the principal concern of the industry was maintaining a steady supply of hacker labor for packaging hacking tools into "turnkey" suites of software. The CEO of cybersecurity vendor Netragard, Adriel Desautels, claimed the licensing and reporting requirements of the regulation would "completely [destroy] vulnerability research" (Bennett 2015) and offered a counterproposal of industry self-regulation in the trading of zero days (Lemos 2015b).[6] The Department of Commerce claimed that "vulnerability research is not controlled nor would the technology related to choosing, finding, targeting, studying and testing a vulnerability be controlled." Perhaps lending weight to industry concerns, the department's regulator for technology controls stated that the agency wanted merely to control "the development, testing, evaluating and productizing of an exploit or intrusion software, or of course the development of zero-day exploits for sale" (Bennett 2015). In practice, however, intentionality is difficult to ascertain. It is virtually impossible to discriminate between efforts to develop and test software that probes vulnerabilities and those to develop zero-day exploits and intrusion software. The 2015 Department of Commerce's proposal, and its 2017 revision, acknowledged these difficulties and, in the end, preserved "light touch" regulation for export controls. The 2015 language defined intrusion software as "software that either surreptitiously spies on data from another computer or changes the processes of another program," but "if it were only defined as software that steals information, it would still squarely restrict all spyware, but completely avoid adversely affecting research or security software, which don't need to steal data" (Bratus, qtd. in Uchill 2015).

THE CFAA AND THE SYSTEMATIC REPRODUCTION OF ERROR

We have previously described how laws such as the Digital Millennium Copyright Act defined and "protected" trusted systems. The Computer Fraud and Abuse Act (CFAA) also protects trusted systems in conflicted ways that serve to heighten risks. The CFAA operates as law even though it fails to effectively distinguish between cybersecurity researchers and cybercriminals and even though it was written before the proliferation of trusted systems, malware, and botnets (much less common access to the internet). Legend has it that the CFAA stemmed from the 1983 film *WarGames,* in which young Matthew Broderick correctly guessed a programmer's password and infiltrated the Pentagon's computer systems, possibly triggering thermonuclear world melt (a four-minute clip was screened at a 1983 congressional hearing) (Wolff 2016a). The CFAA, introduced in April 1986 and signed into law on October 16 of that year, was modeled on wire- and mail-fraud statutes in the Racketeer Influenced and Corrupt Organizations (RICO) Act. It amended existing computer fraud law to apply to situations when "someone intentionally accesses a protected computer without authorization or exceeds authorized access" (Tuma 2011, 156). The main provisions of the CFAA may be found in the seven paragraphs of subsection 1030(a), which outlaw

- computer trespassing (e.g., hacking) in a government computer;
- computer trespassing (e.g., hacking) resulting in exposure to "certain governmental, credit, financial, or computer-housed information";
- damaging (or threat to damage) a government computer, a bank computer, or a computer used in, or affecting, interstate or foreign commerce (e.g., a worm, computer virus, Trojan horse, time bomb, a denial of service attack, and other forms of cyberattack, cybercrime, or cyber terrorism);
- committing fraud, an integral part of which involves unauthorized access to any government computer, a bank computer, or a computer used in, or affecting, interstate or foreign commerce;
- trafficking in passwords for a government computer, or when the trafficking affects interstate or foreign commerce;
- accessing a computer to commit espionage; and
- attempting or conspiring to commit any of these offenses. (Doyle 2014, 1)

In 1994 the law was amended to add civil claims to criminal claims. But the burden of proof for the CFAA "is not the same as common law fraud. Rather, to defraud under the CFAA simply means wrongdoing and does not require proof of common law fraud" (Tuma 2011, 163). Intrusions subject to criminal prosecution under the CFAA "must result in some alteration in the use of the computer, furtherance of a fraud, damage or loss, or a breach of confidentiality (defined as 'obtain[ing] information')" (Keim 2015, 32). The CFAA does not use intent to distinguish the severity of intrusions arising from "exceeds authorization" cases or to separate out criminal from civil action. Instead, all intrusions are treated as criminally liable.[7] The CFAA's scope is also very broad for trusted systems. The phrase "protected computer" first appeared in a 1996 revision of the law, expanding the CFAA's domain to include not only "federal-interest" computers (such as those used by financial institutions or the federal government) but all private computers "used in or affecting interstate or foreign commerce or communication" (33). The Patriot Act expanded the scope further still, defining "protected computer" to include "a computer located outside of the United States" that can be shown to "affect" "interstate or foreign commerce or communication in the United States" (Doyle 2014, 7). The inventiveness of actual and potential accusations enabled by the Patriot Act, especially regarding guilt by association, leaves cybercrimes prosecutions ripe for abuse (Braman 2009, 192). In the process of federalizing computer crime through the expansion of protected-computer status, the CFAA now extends to any computer connected to the internet.[8]

While the CFAA defines many terms, including "computer," "financial institution," and "person," others are not—most notably, "access" and "authorization," which are key tenets of a law that prohibits unauthorized access. The terms "malware" and "malicious technology" are never used, much less defined, in the statute (Rodriguez 2016, 671). A broad interpretation of the CFAA includes computer activity that violates any rule, whether written (such as terms-of-service contracts) or built into a system's architecture (such as email or other programs). The CFAA's legal vagaries (reviewed in chapter 2) create unpredictability and risk for security researchers, computer and smartphone users, and targets of spyware sold as cybersecurity software or legal intercept technology. These legally sanctioned vulnerabilities contribute to broader insecurity of the public internet and its interconnected, trusted systems. Some believe that a reformed CFAA could constrain individual website operators and software vendors from imposing arbitrary terms of service and use. As it stands, depending on what part of the CFAA they violate, defendants can face maximum sentences of five to ten years (or twenty years if there is a prior CFAA conviction), for crimes in which intent is questionable and real harms may be lacking altogether (Wolff 2016a).

Courts have used the CFAA to "overcriminalize" and expand criminal liability for "malfeasance that is not obviously trespass or hacking" (Keim 2015, 33). Tor Ekeland (2017) provides an example of how the CFAA broad brushes "fraudulent" hacking: "Google searches that happen to take a computer user to an area of a website that the owner failed to secure could constitute criminal behavior in the eyes of the law. Indeed, the DOJ has prosecuted defendants for accessing and obtaining information from publicly facing servers with no password protection under the theory that it was done against the server owner's wishes."[9] Between 2011 and 2014 Department of Justice (DOJ) criminal prosecutions under the CFAA increased roughly 41 percent. As Ekeland argues, "The vague and often contradictory case law grants an inordinate amount of discretion to the DOJ to engage in politically-motivated prosecutions and allows civil litigants to clog court dockets with frivolous lawsuits.... Among the questions courts have confronted is whether the definition of authorization should depend on if a contract like an employment or terms of service agreement has been breached, like lying about your age on a dating website."

The U.S. Supreme Court sidestepped a review of the CFAA in *Nosal v. United States,* failing to resolve long-standing ambiguities including "conflicting interpretations [of the CFAA] among the various federal courts of appeal" (Tuma 2011, 154). As these examples show, the law's open-endedness enables a wide range of parties to classify even innocent online activities as "hacking" by claiming possible harms. Indeed, the CFAA's vagueness has been criticized for rendering it void or illegitimate (Kerr 2010). While the CFAA is overbroad in important respects, it is silent on others. For example, it fails to address the legality of hack-backs or other active defenses described in chapter 2, at least for those promoting the aforementioned Active Cyber Defense Certainty Bill. Some forms of hacking, such as DDoS attacks, have been used for purposes of political protest and could therefore fall outside the CFAA's purview (Sarikakis and Rodriguez-Amat 2014). These omissions raise "questions about whether the CFAA provides adequate clarity to potential defendants about what conduct is prohibited" (Keim 2015, 32). In other words, the CFAA might violate "the Fifth Amendment's due process clause, which requires that a defendant be on notice that the actions they are engaging in are illegal and that a statute gives clear guidance to law enforcement to avoid arbitrary prosecutions" (Ekeland 2017).

The fate of Aaron Swartz provides a case in point. Swartz, a Harvard Ethics Fellow who cofounded Reddit and developed the Really Simple Syndication (RSS) web aggregator, downloaded millions of articles from the proprietary JSTOR academic database in 2010, using MIT's open network.[10] JSTOR put MIT "under intense pressure" to identify the perpetrator (Bombardieri 2014), and after their cooperation the Department of Justice charged Swartz in 2011 with violating the CFAA. Reflecting the trouble prosecutors encountered with their case, every reference to "access in excess of authorization" was deleted from a superseding indictment in September 2012. But authorities also upped the number of felonies Swartz was charged with, from four to thirteen. Swartz, faced with a possible thirty-five years in prison and $1 million fine, killed himself in January 2013. A subsequent piece of legislation, known as "Aaron's Law," would have amended the CFAA to exclude terms-of-service violations as "unauthorized access." It is questionable whether the change would have benefited Swartz: "Even under a relatively narrow reading of the CFAA, Swartz could be said to have circumvented technical controls when he evaded the blocks on his computer's IP and MAC addresses that had been put in place by JSTOR and MIT to restrict his continued downloading activity." The bill failed after intense lobbying from tech companies. Oracle alone spent an average of $1.5 million per quarter over three fiscal quarters lobbying against the proposed legislation (Wolff 2016a). An attempt at resurrecting the bill in 2015 similarly failed.

FROM CISPA TO CISA

The Cyber Intelligence Sharing and Protection Act (CISPA), a proposed amendment to the National Security Act of 1947, proposed draconian measures to protect network security. CISPA would have allowed firms to pool defensive resources and proactively share information (including personal identifiers and internet traffic) with one another and the federal government to obtain "threat information." It also would have mandated that procedures be established for the intelligence community to share cyber-threat intelligence with private companies and vice versa (Kominsky 2014). The bill tipped its hand by including language that would criminalize "theft or misappropriation of private or government information, *intellectual property* or personally identifiable information" (Little 2012; italics ours). Employing an IP securitization stratagem, the bill's primary sponsor, Mike Rogers (R-MI), thundered, "We can't stand by and do nothing as US companies are hemorrhaging from the cyber looting coming from nation states like China and Russia. America will be a little safer and our economy better protected from foreign cyber predators with this legislation" (Tsukayama 2012). The bill passed the U.S. House by a vote of 248 to 168 in April 2012 but was defeated in the Senate; it was opposed by the Obama administration on grounds that it violated privacy, confidentiality, and civil-liberties safeguards ("Cyber-Security Bill" 2012).

Unsurprisingly, CISPA was favored by an array of industry players and representatives, including AT&T, Facebook, IBM, Microsoft, Oracle, Symantec, Verizon, and the U.S. Chamber of Commerce (Little 2012). Facebook vice president of public policy Joel Kaplan wrote, "When one company detects an attack, sharing information about that attack promptly with other companies can help protect those other companies and their users from being victimized by the same attack. Similarly, if the government learns of an intrusion or other attack, the more it can share about that attack with private companies (and the faster it can share the information), the better the protection for users and our systems." The usual suspects (including the Electronic Frontier Foundation and American Civil Liberties Union) opposed CISPA. The bill would have allowed government and industry to monitor individuals and share information under the vaguest definition of "cyber threat." The ACLU stated, "CISPA goes too far for little reason. Cybersecurity does not have to mean abdication of Americans' online privacy. As we've seen repeatedly, once the government gets expansive national security authorities, there's no going back. We encourage the Senate to let this horrible bill fade into obscurity" (Tsukayama 2012). The purposeful entanglement of antipiracy and cybersecurity policy required intensive and intrusive electronic surveillance to work—it required another category of legal hacking. CISPA also incorporated provisions from a failed antipiracy bill, the Stop Online Piracy Act (SOPA), to potentially implement a Hollywood-sanctioned digital-rights–management scheme that could censor websites or ban them altogether. One observer noted, "It's a little piece of SOPA wrapped up in a bill that's supposedly designed to facilitate detection of and defense against cybersecurity threats. The language is so vague that an internet service provider could use it to monitor communications of subscribers for potential infringement of intellectual property. An ISP could even interpret this bill as allowing them to block accounts believed to be infringing, block access to websites like The Pirate Bay, believed to carry infringing content, or take other measures provided they claimed it was motivated by cybersecurity concerns" (Little 2012).[11]

CISPA's incomplete status reflected ambivalence among the hunters and gatherers of personal data about committing to a new antihacking confederacy. How could firms like Facebook oppose SOPA yet favor CISPA? According to the *Los Angeles Times*,

> SOPA was focused on establishing punitive measures, mainly through revoking domains found to be hosting copyrighted content, which in turn would make Google responsible for every music video or movie clip posted to YouTube without the expressed consent of copyright holders. CISPA, on the other hand, is focused on information being made readily available

> between approved entities and the government.... CISPA includes an exemption of liability granted to those firms taking part in CISPA's information exchanges—possibly freeing tech firms from the responsibility of regulating users and the danger of being taken offline for alleged copyright violations—so long as they get approval from the government, actively divulge cyber-threat intelligence concerns and are "acting in good faith." (Little 2012)

CISPA once again passed the House in February 2013 but stalled in the Senate, which was drafting a companion bill that eventually became the Cybersecurity Information Sharing Act (CISA). CISPA had yet another resurrection in January 2015 but failed. CISA enjoyed greater success. Proving that politics do indeed create strange bedfellows, the bill was introduced by Dianne Feinstein (D-CA) in 2014 but did not reach a full vote before the end of the session; the following year it was pushed aggressively by Senate Majority Leader Mitch McConnell (R-KY) and was passed in October 2015. Like a pill wrapped in cheese, CISA was slipped into an omnibus spending bill in the House and signed into law by President Obama on December 18, 2015 (Velazzo 2015). CISA stripped out CISPA's provisions regarding intellectual property and routed information through the Department of Homeland Security rather than directly to the FBI and National Security Agency, which (theoretically) would allow some civilian oversight. CISA also requires companies to remove users' identifying information, yet that provision is waived if someone is even tangentially related to a "cyber threat"—a loophole Amie Stepanovich, an attorney with civil-liberties group Access, called "large enough to drive a semi truck through" (Craig 2014).

THE SECURITIZATION OF INTELLECTUAL PROPERTY

In most instances the hardware and software underpinning online networks are maintained and eventually replaced as they age. But the legal system is failing to keep pace with the Network Society's development and unable to perform its expected role as a mediator between technical and social processes. In social systems theory, law functions as its own "trusted system" of sorts. The legal system is designed to reduce risk in the face of overwhelming complexity; for Niklas Luhmann (1995) trust enables social systems to cope with uncertainty by coordinating social action around specific assumptions about the future behavior of others (Bachmann 2001, 342). Federalist legal systems like those in the United States or the European Union provide a framework that sets out goals and objectives for controlled social change. Law sets the boundaries for social action and in the process develops a specialized language, or "code," to communicate its rules and their scope. Legal decisions are communicative events that change the structures and norms of law; they are, in turn, informed by these norms (Teubner 1988, 4). The legal system therefore helps maintain the continuity of social norms by creating a common resource for "legitimating" social action. It also becomes a preeminent "condition for all further social evolution" (Luhmann 1983, 130).

"Autopoietic" systems, such as those found in biology, maintain themselves through self-regulation. They feature boundaries, but these boundaries are permeable and allow connection to larger ecosystems. New internal boundaries form as systems become increasingly complex and begin to "differentiate." Following Maturana, Luhmann (1988) posits law as an "autopoietic" system: a unitary, self-referencing, and self-organizing system with elements or components that are reflexively self-constituted.[12] Typically, the structures and norms of law are open to evolution and change. "Autopoietic closure" can tie legal norms and legal decisions more closely to each other. This restricts the scope of possible changes in the legal system and sets "effective limits to [its] political instrumentalization" (Teubner 1988, 4). Rules may become detached from social norms; laws may lag behind rapidly changing sociotechnical systems. This problem is particularly pronounced for hacking law and policy, as evidenced in the thirty-year gap between the development of the internet and interconnected trusted systems and the passage of U.S. law governing hacking and cybersecurity. Limits to the "political instrumentalization" of antihacking laws have not yet appeared, since, in many respects, public norms and expectations are very different from the laws on the books (for example, those involving intellectual property). This situation may help explain why the law overprotects trusted systems and avoids suppressing the proliferation of invasive software that impacts privacy.

Rather than promoting the demilitarization of cyberspace, the United States opted instead to develop offensive military cyber operations and promote defensive hardening of "critical" or infrastructurally central networks (Schiller 2014a, 217). The simultaneous pursuit of offensive and defensive military measures underscores what former White House security aide Richard A. Clarke has termed the "prerogative of offensive defense" (qtd. in Schiller 2014a, 216). Since 2015, when CISA created an information "hub" and extended "liability protection and other protections to companies that share indicators through" the hub (DOJ-CCIPS 2016), data is routinely shared between the federal government, the private sector, academic institutions, and foreign counterparts. The U.S. military shares information among NATO members to maintain geopolitical boundaries; it also promotes the centralization of de jure and de facto information policy regimes.[13]

Given the conflicts in developing a transnational or global regime for regulating hacking as cybercrime, a militarized model featuring panspectric surveillance and information sharing is taking shape. This paradigm inherits ideology, forms, and functions from an earlier cybercrime—piracy. In the early 2010s the United States began systematically treating intellectual-property theft as a national-security threat. The scope of the threat is broadly conceived to include hacking, trade-secret theft, file sharing, and even foreign students enrolling in U.S. universities. In each case U.S. national security, not just its economic competitiveness, is claimed to be at risk.[14] Intellectual property is used as a rationale for national, rather than strictly economic, security; the intellectual-property "agenda" conflates national-security threats, IP theft, and hacking by implication. As Debora Halbert notes, "The discourse that advances IP as a national security issue makes two important narrative moves. First, it blurs the lines between domestic economic innovation and the production of classified information. Second, it asserts that other states (with a focus on China) are responsible for the theft of IP, and not just hackers, criminals, and commercial enterprises" (2016, 256).

As global trade in media, software, and services grows disproportionately in relation to other sectors, international legal frameworks have codified "IP theft" as property crime in law and policy, placing piracy irredeemably outside the protections of positive law. Digital "piracy" is now punished through a highly developed free-trade system grounded in plurilateralist treaties. Corporate intellectual-property owners are in ever-stronger positions to capitalize on IP ownership and prosecute transgressors; the deregulation of the cybersecurity industry and the federalization of existing criminal hacking laws have contributed to the merging of legal treatment of accused cybercriminals and terrorists in the United States. The expansion of this trend would further the abilities of IP owners to collect on hacking debts owed. It would require the creation of "global warrants" issued for those accused of hacking and wanted for prosecution in the United States, together with expanded authority for police hacking into targeted computers. The global deregulation of telecommunications and information policies, starting with multilateral and plurilateral agreements such as the World Trade Organization, World Intellectual Property Organization, and the European Union Copyright Directive, has created new impetus for its implementation.

As the Network Society develops, global "deterritorialization" is matched by the expansion of territoriality into information topographies. The international legal system's inconsistencies accentuate the uncertain legal status of any hacking campaign coordinated by a state agent or enabled by a private technology transfer. With the legal system providing ambiguous guidance to markets and civil society, powerful risks to organizational continuity, personally identifying information, and trusted computing are being continually fed into the Network Society. Today the markets for "security" require a sociotechnical system of universal surveillance, which has been partly mapped by Edward Snowden, Glenn Greenwald, Bruce Schneier, Citizen Lab of the University of Toronto, and others. Intelligence and police surveillance systems have grown to meet the needs of government expediency while pursuing advantages for themselves and their clients through exploits, espionage, and information warfare. The profiling processes that are the product of the "panoptic sort" (Gandy 1993) in the end contribute to a restructuration of social classes, based on "suspicious" but familiar characteristics such as religion, race, country of origin, politics, and employment.

In light of the massive scale of government and corporate surveillance, as well as identity theft stemming from hacked private and public databases, it is remarkable—although not inexplicable—that legal remedies still seem largely unavailable to the victims. The hundreds of millions of citizens adversely affected by data breaches do not, as yet, possess a political interest or clout comparable to that of intellectual-property owners. Instead, policy prevents U.S. "digital subjects" from filing class-action lawsuits, while the interests of intellectual-property owners have been furthered through "policy laundering" (Sarikakis and Rodriguez-Amat 2014) or conflated with national security in numerous government reports and actions following 9/11—most notably, in the language added to the CFAA by the Patriot Act. The 2008 Center for Strategic and International Studies' *Report to the 44th President of the United States on Cybersecurity* cited IP protection as a "strategic issue on par with weapons of mass destruction and global jihad." The report clearly stipulates that violence is an acceptable response to threats to U.S. cybersecurity; if diplomatic persuasion fails, "the United States will seek to deter any possible threat to its national and economic security" (Halbert 2016, 257).

To standardize risk management for cybersecurity campaigns, Cyber Security Executive Order 13636 was issued on February 20, 2013, leading to a "framework" developed by the National Institute of Standards and Technology for threat assessment and network security. The entire U.S. administrative infrastructure would now be deployed to combat IP theft, even as the definition of "intellectual property" is never clarified.[15] Tacit knowledge is of limited value compared to deploying that knowledge, and the theft of trade secrets has a relatively limited impact on competitive economic development (Rid, qtd. in Halbert 2016)—nor does theft of trade secrets prevent the firm whose secrets were stolen from pursuing innovation. As Halbert notes, "The underlying assumption in these reports is that foreign governments steal our ideas but then take these ideas and make superior products before we can. Perhaps instead of feeling threatened, it might be worthwhile to ask why American businesses are not bringing their innovations to market more quickly—this is, after all, the entire point of a free-market competitive system" (2016, 261).

Despite the likelihood that intellectual-property theft or exfiltration has minimal or moderate strategic value (Klimburg 2017, 276–80), the antiespionage rhetoric surrounding IP security has become increasingly loud and shrill.[16] The link of intellectual-property law and policy to national-security policy advances a tentative rationale for war in cyberspace, however unjust. In Alexander Klimburg's analysis, Chinese military hacking activities have generated low returns on investment (notwithstanding some high-profile cases such as plans for the F-35 fighter jet) for the high cost involved in generating useful business or military applications for stolen data (294–95). While the Pentagon has claimed that some cyberattacks could be considered acts of war, it noted that "routine theft of intellectual property" was "generally" not considered to be in that category (Michaels, qtd. in Halbert 2016, 263). The United Nations' *Tallinn Manual* also explicitly excludes IP protection as an "activity governed by the law of armed conflict" (263–64).

CONCLUSION

States impose hacking and cybersecurity law and policy regimes inconsistently, incompletely, and also arbitrarily for reasons of political expediency. Major international players such as the United States, European Union, China, Russia, India, Brazil, and Israel have clashing interests regarding the security of trusted systems (in an obvious example, Russian law does not criminalize attacks on foreign computers). International norms govern trade in some cyber products, but these are flexible at the behest of industries beholden to the vulnerabilities market. World Trade Organization and UN forums offer international venues regarding issues such as copyright law and policy, but not hacking and cybersecurity. In the absence of agreement over hacking regulation, precedents in intellectual-property law have created a path for recodifying hacking law and policy. This path dependency reflects the growing trend of corporations to act as state proxies and defend their own interests. Intellectual property is framed in terms of national security with attendant policy laundering in law masquerading as cybersecurity, and the postprivacy ethos is extended and deepened through increasingly ubiquitous surveillance.

U.S. law enables a flourishing market for dual-use goods in hacking and spyware even as federal prosecutors target Aaron Swartz and others who stumble on errors in the confusing legal code. Legal remedies for victims of hacks are weak and perhaps weakening further still, while international law and policy targeting hackers remains ad-hoc, inconsistent, and largely uncodified. No comprehensive international agreement for hacking exists outside of the "symbolic" (Marion 2014) Budapest Convention, the military umbrella of NATO, or the police umbrella of Interpol. In contrast, as global trade in media, software, and services continues to grow disproportionately in relation to other sectors, digital "piracy" is punished through a highly developed free-trade system grounded in plurilateral treaties.

Cybersecurity has apparently hitched its wagon to the global antipiracy crusade. As cybersecurity standards are molded by the Global War on

Terror, hacking is increasingly framed in the language of terrorism (Halbert 2016). While terrorists undoubtedly may press hacking into service, the codification of hacking or cybersecurity law within a totalizing national-security framework has numerous repercussions. It lengthens the lag of legal norms behind social norms and heightens attendant legitimation problems; it also generates ongoing social conflicts over the security of the public internet and trusted systems. The CFAA's transmogrification into an instrument of the Global War on Terror is likely to be increasingly perceived as unjust, as social norms become further detached from the norms governing the cybernetic social system.

In sum, national and international legal systems are not yet harmonized for consistent treatment of hacking or cybersecurity practices, partly to preserve prerogatives of national security and partly to leave global markets for hacking technologies unencumbered. Therefore, hacking, as a normal practice of large, complex, and intermingled social systems, is freer to "steer" interactions between political systems, markets, and the state than would be possible in a more tightly regulated market for cybersecurity and component exploits. The consequences of hacking for the information-based commodity are more than merely technically disruptive; they are also normative, indicating profound social transformations. As Klimburg notes, "The wide-scale unknowns in cyber operations means that we probably now have a level of strategic uncertainty never before experienced in the history of Post Westphalian state conflict" (2017, 155n121).

In the medieval world political authority was shared by institutions with different levels of authority (feudal knights, kings, guilds, city-states, and the papacy). Today we find the global order increasingly characterized by overlapping and pluralistic authority structures. In this sense the world is headed back to the future, returning to a premodern organization of overlapping authorities, with a crucial difference: these authorities now place their subjects under increasingly ubiquitous surveillance. The desire to reduce risk increases the application of surveillance; the web of surveillance opens greater possibilities for hacking, which then heightens the need for security to reduce risk. The state cannot insure against a proliferation of systemic risks—to the environment, to financial systems, to infrastructures—and so it shifts responsibility for risk management increasingly to individuals and firms (Beck 1992b). Linkages between corporate partners and state agencies are tightened, strong states follow exceptionalist or extralegal rules, and international policy arbitrage is reflected in antihacking legal harmonizations wrapped up in multilateral or plurilateral trade agreements. In the conflict between stakeholders and legal classes, policy becomes feudalized, complicating the ability to develop a coordinated legal regime concerning hacking and cybersecurity. The resulting "fog of war" stems in large part from a lack of transparency, accountability, and checks and balances. Yet measures to address these issues are highly problematic and compounded by the very nature of dual-use technologies. Risks can be mitigated but never eliminated; while these technologies are rationalized in the name of countering terrorism and criminal activity, their implementation more often than not is dedicated to surveillance of private citizens. They have become so invasive that oversight is nearly impossible and attempts at regulation likely will drive the market for such products still deeper underground.

CHAPTER FIVE

Activism beyond Hacktivism

Uncertainty characterizes the state of affairs in the Network Society, where trusted systems are shot through with innumerable technical vulnerabilities and attack vectors. Many observers consider 2013 a watershed, "the year that the Internet lost its innocence for nearly everyone" (Guarnieri and Marquis-Boire 2013). Mass data breaches of government agencies and corporations holding personally identifiable information accelerated; there was a growing awareness that an unknown international actor could launch the takeover of a phone or computer. The postprivacy era began in earnest. In both the United States and Europe, internet service provider (ISP) surveillance by corporations pursuing evidence of digital piracy or online file sharing became standard practice (Burkart and Andersson Schwarz 2014, 218).[1] Also in 2013 Edward Snowden revealed the widespread use of surveillance domestically and abroad by governments. Two years later, in 2015, the *Wall Street Journal* found that at least twenty-nine countries had formal military or intelligence units dedicated to offensive hacking efforts. To citizens of North Atlantic Treaty Organization (NATO) countries and adjacent states, their trusted systems and networks seemed to be part of a new military theater. An official at the NATO Cooperative Cyber Defence Centre of Excellence in Tallinn, Estonia, stated, "In the nuclear arms race, the acronym was MAD—mutually assured destruction—which kept everything nice and tidy. Here you have the same acronym, but it's 'mutually assured doubt,' because you can never be sure what the attack will be" (Paletta, Yadron, and Valentino-DeVries 2015, A1). The abstraction and intangibility of normalized hacking, normalized surveillance, and the "new MAD" of cyber war continue to amplify these uncertainties for everyone dependent on trusted systems.

The relentless demand for networking pulls the net ever outward. At the same time the need to maintain boundaries in the face of pervasive risk requires systems to monitor and surveil themselves at all times, which increases their density. Our growing dependence on trusted systems for information and communication carries systemic risks including catastrophic data loss and multiple, cascading aftereffects. P. W. Singer (2015) proposes three strategies to address these risks. The first involves setting norms through formal treaties or codes of behavior that would prohibit certain hacks (i.e., attacking nuclear power plants), with a tacit understanding that adversaries will continue to engage in cyber espionage and theft. Yet by these criteria the Stuxnet episode, in which malware disabled Iranian centrifuges, could be construed as an act of war. A second involves "diverse responses," including retaliation through stealing assets or sanctioning companies that benefit from stolen IP, as well as exfiltration of financial data, akin to the Panama Papers hack. Aside from the difficulty of determining what firms benefit from stolen IP, retaliation and exfiltration lead to a slippery slope. A third requires "resilience," including extending cyber insurance as well as identifying and protecting key assets. But cyber insurance carries cost penalties, and "hardening key assets" may well reduce transparency and diminish access to public goods and services.

The loss of personal and social control over the security of our information and communication environment has come to characterize cyber risk in general while also undermining trust in the institutions meant to control for this risk. Several trends involving law, politics, and the economy help explain why this is happening. As we have shown, key actors maintain shrouds of secrecy and indeterminacy over their operations and prioritize private property when addressing risk and cybersecurity. In trying to understand the development of phenomena like mass hacking, cyber risk, and cyber insurance, we have followed second-generation critical theory, informed by Jürgen Habermas's (1984, 1987) theory of communicative action. This theory posits that complex social systems develop through self-guided processes, principally those that introduce changes and distinctions in law, regulation, and politics that offer greater rights and liberties to individuals.[2] Because the market does not provide these rights and liberties–and frequently forecloses opportunities for their development—the burden falls on the political system and civil society. Collective actions by new social movements have made greater strides in this area than political parties in the past fifty years, particularly in Europe and the former Soviet states. In addition to market failure, however, the resurgence of authoritarian government in many states has effectively diminished collective action for claiming new rights, as has the practice of individuating and atomizing the public to reduce market uncertainty—commodifying their resources for communicating and sharing information in the process.[3]

We have also identified problems of legitimation in chapter 4, which occur when law is detached from its normative bases in social institutions. We have focused on cases in the United States, where unreformed cybercrime laws perpetuate uncertainty and distrust. The coincidence of post-9/11 security and Napster antipiracy reforms created a temporal break with popular expectations and new legal norms regarding privacy, a break that is now being cemented juridically with the securitization of intellectual property. This doubling down on punitive policies requires even more intensive surveillance. The journalistic reporting on National Security Agency mass surveillance, the targeting of journalists and political opposition leaders abroad, the legal attack on Aaron Swartz, and other abuses of power clearly indicate areas of much-needed reform. Collective action is still necessary for making progressive reforms to the way we use and regulate trusted systems. This is particularly true in countries like the United States, where the political impacts of domestic reforms can have global repercussions.

REPERTOIRES OF RESISTANCE

We have postulated the deep hack as something like an "ideal type," a transformative hack that affects multiple social domains in meaningful ways. In certain respects its effects could be compared to those of a social movement. We developed the deep-hack concept from critical systems theory in chapter 2, but new social movement theory has already covered some of this ground from a sociological standpoint. Some computer coding for purposes other than profit or entertainment can be understood as "activist," and some sociologists have come to include "hacktivism" (hacking activism) as part of the action repertoires of new social movements. Hacktivism in the service of alternative political projects occurs simultaneously in multiple formal and informal contexts (Jordan and Taylor 2004). As a type of symbolic politics, it is typically tailored for single-issue campaigns by otherwise unrepresented groups in civil society. While we do not offer an ethical theory of hacking or cybersecurity technology practices, our critical systems theory is not hostile to normative theory—indeed, the two are compatible and complementary. We have noted several ways (especially privacy) in which corporate responsibility and state laws and policies diverge from long-standing norms and beliefs. We also have presented normative theories that have developed from scholarship on international law and policy close to the domain of hacking and cybersecurity. These include Saskia Sassen's (2006) alternatives to law and policy based on territories, Debora Halbert's (2016) alternative norms for handling cyber conflicts, and Helen Nissenbaum's (2004b) situational ethics of personal privacy. These normative frameworks can inform hacktivist strategies for social influence in a number of domains.

Hacktivism, like culture jamming, can be seen to be a variety of direct action, or politics using weapons of the weak. But unlike more traditional modes of demonstration and political messaging, it is not to be trusted as an agenda-setting activity, since it may not be an expression of collective action or the social solidarity that collective action requires. Its radical potentials also may not align ideologically with progressive or even reformist political goals, which is, of course, also the case with new social movements. Outside of motivating or influencing empowered actors in the system, hacktivism has tenuous, if any, connections to the institutions responsible for affecting reforms in law or industry. The seclusion of hacktivists to civil society, and their reluctance to join their social roles with responsibility to the system, is one of the principal reasons they do not appear in our analysis. The disclaiming of official responsibilities to political duties has also been a characteristic of pirate politics (Burkart 2014). But, by our own model, if hacktivists could effect a deep hack that reverberated throughout politics and the economy at multiple and interconnected layers of communication, then that hack might have broad social consequences. It might resemble some of the effects of a social movement—but without the social psychological changes that accompany changing norms and social attitudes. Here a potential risk from hacktivism emerges: that it substitutes for, rather than guiding or enabling, collective learning, thereby setting up a basis for rejection and backlash.

Reforms to law and policy that might reduce the catastrophic risks of cyber insecurity are available (Mills 2017, 230–42; Mandel 2017). Regulatory reforms that added spyware (intrusion software) to the restricted export list in 2017 offer an example, even during a period of political transition. But in the United States, the political system is largely ineffective in getting in front of science and technology policy. Instead, it is focused on head butting (exemplified by recurring government shutdowns over budget brinksmanship). At the same time we recognize that legislation cannot solve all, or even most, of the problem areas of law and policy. The 2017 export reforms restricting spyware and cyber weapons may not make a real difference in the end. They may even exacerbate uncertainty and risk by driving more business to black markets.

Collective action oriented to the risk society has spawned new social movements since the 1960s, with participation from ecology, environmentalism, anti–nuclear energy, antiwar, and feminist groups. Some of these movements have achieved transnational scope and influence in the ensuing decades. While autopoietic systems theory doesn't recognize new social movements to be part of the social system, we think of these movements as straddling the system and the cultural lifeworld. This also is consistent with second-generation critical theory, which conceives of progressive social movements (especially ecology) as stimulating episodes of "collective learning" in society (Eder 1985). Seen within a law and policy framework, European civil society groups have devoted their missions to the "learning games" required to play within the EU frameworks (Bomberg 2007). The social movements championing digital rights in our era have done so in a self-restricting and incomplete way, although they began with broader political traction. For example, the Pirate Parties International used effective and appropriate communication strategies for influencing reforms to certain aspects of the European copyright system and digital privacy protections. After registering some visible electoral successes in Europe and Iceland, it still remains a largely "submerged network" (Burkart 2014, 10–23, 144–48). As of this writing, pirate politics has mostly receded from participatory forums. It continues as a shared ethos and a knot of professional discourses in the fields of media technology and information science.[4]

As with previous efforts, the contemporary push for technology reform by engineers in the United States and European Union is characterized by fits and starts and is limited in focus. In what Edwin Layton Jr. (1986) termed the "revolt of the engineers," two generations of U.S. professional engineers sought reforms through calls for greater professionalism and social responsibility among their ranks. The movement peaked prior to the Great Depression and faded with antiunion legislation and other counterreforms following World War II. In the 1980s and 1990s, Computer Professionals for Social Responsibility and its Directions and Implications in Advanced Computing Conferences emphasized moral-ethical reasoning. In 2018 the Association of Computing Machinery's "future of computing academy" issued its first proposal to "address the downsides of our innovations," to press for peer review and promotion policies based partly on social responsibility (Hecht et al. 2018). If this is a commitment to reform, it is weak beer indeed. But the message signals that opportunities for reform can be had within firms and industry, as well as from independent sites in civil society. Today groups such as Electronic Frontier Foundation and the American Civil Liberties Union continue to focus on the preservation and expansion of "cyber liberties."

OPPORTUNITIES FOR REFORMS

We have identified several areas in which the structures of social systems are in flux as the hacking and cybersecurity dialectic is normalized and escalated. These uncertainties are further impacted by political shifts, including the Trump presidency in the United States, Brexiteering in the United Kingdom, and the rise of populist and authoritarian movements globally. These uncertainties thrive in the absence of broad public participation in policy making, as well as a lack of transparency and accountability on the part of agencies participating in cybersecurity. While institutional secrecy and obscurity are endemic to the domain, we propose that a politics of hacking and cybersecurity can focus on the unveiling of risks to personal privacy and security, in a permanent and thoroughgoing campaign of research and reporting—only then can transparency force issues to the table and thematize political problems that can be addressed through law and policy reform. We consolidate a short list of representative examples and projects here.

The overarching concerns are (1) the global security assemblage and the self-selection of elites participating in this assemblage; (2) the prevalence of growth hacks in competitive markets for software, news, advertising, and consumer products using trusted systems; (3) the persistence of vulnerabilities in trusted systems; (4) the permanent expansion of intrusive surveillance by state and corporate actors using dual-use technology such as deep-packet inspection and Stingrays; and (5) the merging of antipiracy and cybersecurity technology, law, and policy, especially stemming from the cyber-threat intelligence and enterprise risk-management strategies described in chapter 3. The global security assemblage is a domain of social action claimed exclusively by the state and cyber mercenaries. Its claims should be challenged and its influences attenuated at every turn. The torrents of public money flowing into private security operations and surveillance should be accounted for and audited by elected representatives. Debates about the social value of these expenditures can then be raised. The growth hack poses special problems because of the confidentiality of business strategies in unregulated or lightly regulated industries. Growth hacks exposing customers, regulators, and the public at large to cyber insecurity are difficult to catch and curtail. To contain their potential impact, protections for proprietary "business models" should be reined in. Firms increasingly have relied on these IP protections to restrict access to their operations by courts and others since the turn of the twenty-first century.

The persistence of vulnerabilities in trusted systems is related to growth hacks in the sense that the legal protections for proprietary trusted systems allow them to evade accountability through safety auditing and testing. Standards and practices that require critical infrastructures to use free and open-source software can address the intrinsic problem of bugs by broadening social participation in providing timely fixes and patches. The warrantless surveillance practices that became normalized after 9/11 can be challenged legally, if anything like an electronic bill of rights with privacy protections against state intrusion can pass the U.S. Congress. Many challenges to warrantless surveillance have failed owing to "lack of standing" in court cases, where plaintiffs cannot offer forensic evidence that the government has violated their privacy. The trend toward a recombination of antipiracy and cybersecurity policy can be singled out for greater attention by lawmakers. "IP securitization" is designed to remove legislative agency and legal oversight from the domains of cybersecurity and intellectual-property–rights law. If this securitization is allowed to expand in the federal criminal code, rooting it out will become increasingly difficult over time.

With these dynamics in mind, we present some ongoing initiatives that have already informed activism affecting internet governance. These initiatives are presented as elements of "political opportunity structures" (Kitschelt 1986, 57) in the making, perhaps awaiting a historical conjuncture with social events. The Free Software Foundation's mission is to wean the world off proprietary software code, which is an especially important objective for computer-security research and development. Entrusting giant corporations with the security of our trusted systems has failed repeatedly.[5] Alternate business models are required to develop and disseminate operating systems and applications, which have auditable security. The Free Software Foundation has a running list of "high priority" campaigns, which have attracted more interest from computer professionals than from communication researchers.[6] Its Defective by Design campaign organizes action alerts and boycotts of popular trusted systems using digital-rights–management hardware and software.

The International Consortium of Investigative Journalists (ICIJ) uses cooperating investigators to review the documents released in some of the giant data breaches described here (including the Panama Papers). These documents have been archived online in bulk formats; the ICIJ parses and organizes these "big data" datasets into accessible investigations, which have yielded important insights about global finance, political corruption, and criminal enterprises. Unlike WikiLeaks, which also provides summaries of the data dumps it publishes, the ICIJ is an independent collective of professional investigative journalists.

The University of Toronto's Citizen Lab operates a virus and malware research laboratory that examines samples of spyware and other forms of invasive software found "in the wild" and submitted by other researchers or individuals who suspect that they have been targeted. The Citizen Lab also publishes research on technology, law, and policy developments in encryption, ISP privacy, and internet filtering. The Citizen Lab provides a model for opening up, rather than enclosing and privatizing, actionable knowledge about real-time threats to the public network and their indicators. These disclosures can undermine the secrecy that preserves the advantages of spyware vendors who hoard vulnerabilities. An analogy can be made to the open-source cryptography community, which puts an "open and unowned network, rather than a corporation, at the center" of responsibilities for developing new products. "Users join these networks and open source software aligns their incentives toward cooperation and, ultimately, agreement over every scrap of data needed" to make a trusted system (Van Valkenburgh 2017).

The Pirate Parties of Europe, which began as single-issue national political parties focused on online privacy and surveillance, may still be well prepared to shape debates over cybersecurity as they did authoritarian antipiracy laws. Specifically, they can help research and translate for regulators and politicians some of the policy dilemmas that have bedeviled us here: reforms to export regulations for cyber weapons; licensing of Vx-ers (virus creators) and cybersecurity researchers; and updated practices related to the "freedom to tinker" (Samuelson 2016) and fix one's own broken trusted systems. The Pirates have a track record of mobilizing youth participation around digital rights, especially privacy rights, through single-issue campaigns and effective political communication.

Documents that would codify or recodify laws and norms related to hacking, cybersecurity, and cyber defense are in a continual state of negotiation. We summarize the most important of these here. "Aaron's Law" reforms to the Computer Fraud and Abuse Act (CFAA) were introduced in the U.S. Congress in 2013 by Representative Zoe Lofgren

(D-CA) and Senator Ron Wyden (D-OR). After the bill failed, it was reintroduced with support from Senator Rand Paul (R-KY) in 2015. It failed to get a vote in the House Judiciary Committee and has not been reintroduced at the time of this writing. Analysts note that "Aaron's Law would have ensured that breaching of terms of service, employment agreements or contracts would not be automatically deemed as violations of the CFAA. It would also look to remove the potential for duplicate charges for the same offence and bring 'greater proportionality' to sentences" (Brewster 2014). A revised and updated Aaron's Law could provide an important patch to a broken law that resembles malware in its many potentials for disruption.

Tallinn Manual 2.0 offers an example of juridical thinking based on extending Westphalian concepts to an "unbounded landscape in which anything and everything is likely to become fair game, from blowing up nuclear plants to posting medical records online" (Leetaru 2017). The dystopian visions presented as hypothetical threats are evaluated, in part, on the basis of existing privacy norms, the wartime prohibitions from the United Nations' Geneva conventions, NATO's reciprocal defense posture, and information sharing as a model for cyber defense. As an educational text, *Tallinn Manual 2.0* should become required reading for digital literacy, media and communication, and political science classes in higher education. Hacktivists also may envision a *Tallinn Manual 3.0*.

The European Union's General Data Protection Regulation (GDPR) is likely to have spillover effects into the rest of the Western world, if it does not first balkanize Chinese and U.S. digital communications. The juridical creation of the data subject brings upsides and challenges too: new digital privacy rights also heighten risks of running afoul of a complex system for regulating data in motion and at rest. Electronic privacy advocates should lobby the U.S. Congress about the advantages of U.S. harmonization to GDPR privacy standards. The GDPR requires privacy by design and privacy by default in information technologies deployed in the European Union to protect the rights of data subjects.

CONCLUSION

Tracking so many moving targets mandates a politically coordinated campaign across political and institutional boundaries and time frames. Successful campaigns promoting digital privacy and state and corporate accountability will involve searching for new political opportunities, support and resources, and attack vectors. They will require thinking like a hacker.

NOTES

PREFACE

1. We conceive the Network Society in terms of what Braman (2009) refers to as the "informational state," in which welfare states are transformed into an interconnected, information-based form of governance, and laws and other official codes manage risk through technocratic systems. We also draw on Schement and Curtis's (1995) definition of the "Information Society" as all the "tendencies and tensions of the information age" as expressed in social and political institutions that are organized technologically. Similarly, Kellner (1999) refers to "Technocapitalism" as a stage of capitalism, characterized by the overproduction of cybernetic commodities or information- or knowledge-based goods and services.

2. Although servers and networks can be hacked without using malware or botnets, we limit our empirical cases largely to those methods to illustrate how communication systems are affected by the technical application of force. While their social implications are obvious, we also leave aside cases of propaganda, "making" and "makers," and cultural varieties of "social hacking." Instead, we focus on the distinctions between legal and illegal (or "black hat") hacking, some of which may in fact be legal or of uncertain legal character.

3. The system is defined as intellectual property (especially software patents and copyrights), a set of technical specifications for end-to-end uses, and a collection of interfaces to other systems. Trusted systems include the iPhone, the iTunes Store, the Google Play store, the Spotify and Netflix platforms, the

PayPal and Visa payment platforms, and voice mail. Microsoft's Digital Rights Management suite, its "explorer.exe" process, and its acceptance of digital certificates for signature authority offer another example of a trusted system for media. Apple and Android provide competing trusted systems. For further discussions of trusted systems, see Gillespie (2004).

4. Many states organized on public welfare principles, including Canada and countries in Europe and Latin America, have shed responsibilities in favor of group insurance and increasingly market-oriented mechanisms for managing collective risk. The United States also increasingly has replaced public obligations for managing risk with discretionary policies for media and communication, personal and public health, and the environment (among other areas).

5. Wiretapping, in its most basic sense, is hacking a utility for private conversation, whether by telephone or internet application. Wiretapping by police and government agents is a long-standing legal prerogative, supported with built-in technical features and facilities. But states with strong privacy norms restrict wiretapping when consent is lacking and where theft of government or business secrets is concerned. Although hacks can have a wiretap component (for example, to access networked surveillance cameras or to capture audio and video streams from exploited cell phones), it is also quite common for hacks to have objectives other than surveillance (for example, to permanently disable a device).

1. ON THE STRUCTURES AND FUNCTIONS OF HACKING

1. These changes are also called "core" hacking crimes, as they violate "CIA" (confidentiality, integrity, and access) of data. This definition is necessarily vague as a technical denominator for our study. But, as a working definition, it is useful enough to characterize hacking as a form of communicative action as recognized in political, legal, economic, and military systems.

2. As described in the preface, trusted systems, or "walled gardens," are end-to-end proprietary networks. These closed or restricted systems require authentication of users to access goods and services. Although hacking may include other methods to approve or deny attacking servers and networks, we restrict our selection of empirical cases largely to malware and botnets for purposes of brevity and clarity.

3. In DDoS attacks a flood of superfluous information disrupts systems. A botnet is created by hacking a system of interconnected devices, allowing

them to be controlled by a third party. The largest DDoS attack to date occurred in October 2016, when the Mirai botnet attacked Dyn, a company that manages a significant part of the internet's infrastructure. The attack temporarily disabled much of the internet in the United States (Shaw 2018).

4. A famous doxxing incident from 2015 targeted thirty-seven million members of the Ashley Madison virtual community, in which individuals in problematic relationships were matched for new affairs without their partner's knowledge.

5. Besides malware, common types of attacks include Structured Query Language (SQL) injection attacks, brute-force account password–cracking attacks, distributed denial-of-service (DDoS), cross-site scripting, session hijacking, and social engineering of credentials. Many of these may be combined to achieve a successful exploit, and the field is advancing rapidly.

6. In September 2018 Facebook acknowledged that a breach had exposed personal information on nearly 50 million of its 2.2 billion users: "Once in, the attackers could have gained access to apps like Spotify, Instagram and hundreds of others that give users a way to log into their systems through Facebook. The software bugs were particularly awkward for a company that takes pride in its engineering: The first two were introduced by an online tool meant to improve the privacy of users. The third was introduced in July 2017 by a tool meant to easily upload birthday videos" (Isaac and Frankel 2018, A1).

7. The hack flickered the lantern's light to pulse disparaging messages in Morse code, spelling out "rats" repeatedly and also a ribald limerick about the highly publicized lecture itself: "There was a young fellow of Italy, who diddled the public quite prettily" (Marks 2011; Raboy 2016, 223).

8. Other examples of scientific hooliganism in the analog domain include pirate broadcasters and low-power FM operators, who competed with and sometimes interrupted licensed broadcasters. John McDougall's (Captain Midnight's) 1986 hack of HBO spurred the development of the Automatic Transmitter Identification System, which enabled satellite operators to identify unauthorized uplink transmissions.

9. Self-identified hackers are collectively depicted in popular communication as libertarian or anarchistic, competitive, meritorious, materialistic, and antiauthoritarian. Culture industries (including journalism) valorize and vilify hackers to suit the needs of the day, but the desire for personal narratives leads to the development of hacker types. From the self-made cowboy hacker John Perry Barlow to the redeemed hacker Kevin Mitnick, to the international playboy Kim Dotcom, to the fictionalized hero hacker played by

Matthew Broderick in *WarGames,* role-playing and dramatic personae fill representational voids left by the multitude of unknown and unknowable figures who populate the agencies and markets for hacking.

10. Jann Horn, a security analyst at Google Project Zero, discovered Meltdown in June 2017 and alerted Intel, who played down the flaw after it was revealed. The company claimed, "Intel and other technology companies have been made aware of new security research describing software analysis methods that, when used for malicious purposes, have the potential to improperly gather sensitive data from computing devices that are operating as designed. Intel believes these exploits do not have the potential to corrupt, modify or delete data" (Metz and Perlroth 2018, B1).

11. This admission followed a write-down of $350 million after Yahoo! disclosed an earlier data breach affecting half a billion user accounts. In the United States many companies are not required by federal law to report data breaches that result in mass exfiltration or publication of personally identifying information. This situation creates incentives for companies to suppress information about hacks that could jeopardize their customers' privacy and security.

12. As security scholar Bruce Schneier points out, "'state-sponsored actor' is often code for 'please don't blame us for our shoddy security because it was a really sophisticated attacker and we can't be expected to defend ourselves against that'" (Schneier 2016).

13. The Data Security and Breach Notification Act of 2015 remains draft legislation from the U.S. House Committee on Energy and Commerce.

14. Warren cited the former CEO of Equifax as having previously claimed that "fraud is a huge opportunity for us—it's a massive, growing business for us." Equifax shares revenue with its customers such as LifeLock and charges its own subscription costs for credit monitoring. When news of the 2017 breach was made public, Equifax offered a free, one-year credit protection service to its victims, yet no time limit exists for the breached information that hackers can buy and sell. Warren calculated that if only one half of 1 percent of people affected by Equifax's carelessness purchased a year's subscription, Equifax stood to earn over $200 million in revenue (Leonhardt 2017). Equifax's chief financial officer, John Gamble, strapped on a golden parachute shortly after the breach was discovered. Gamble sold nearly $1.8 million in company shares—a sale that was not planned in advance (Siegel Bernard et al. 2017, A1).

15. The Health Insurance Portability and Accountability Act (HIPAA) and Family Educational Rights and Privacy Act (FERPA) are examples of federal

laws governing secure access controls, with penalties available for patients and students to remedy privacy violations from data breaches.

16. Google's Be Internet Awesome education program for elementary schools includes a Google-branded cartoon game. In addition to serving as an extended advertising vehicle, the program drew fire for emphasizing hacking dangers over privacy concerns, including tracking. As one researcher stated, "'Be Internet Awesome' generally presents Google as impartial and trustworthy, which is especially problematic given that the target audience is impressionable youth" (Singer and Maheshwari 2018, B1).

17. Once these actions were revealed, the NSA's legal authority to hack phone and internet records in warrantless dragnet operations was challenged domestically and abroad. Although this authority was formally rescinded when the U.S. budget bill was passed in late 2015, the original operations continue with a revised data-retention policy. Rather than retain mass surveillance records in-house, the NSA now stores them on the servers of telecommunications carriers. In another state-orchestrated hacking campaign, "the Central Intelligence Agency improperly accessed computers used by the Senate committee investigating the agency's use of torture following the September 11, 2001 terrorist attacks, according to the CIA Inspector General Office … [confirming] … accusations made by Senator Dianne Feinstein (D-CA), who chairs the Senate Select Committee on Intelligence, that CIA employees accessed computers used by her committee's staff as they pored over documents pertaining to the CIA's detention and interrogation program" (P. Levy 2014).

18. At the same time that AT&T was colluding with NSA, some of the firm's employees were engaged in entrepreneurial activities of their own: "Employees at AT&T call centers in Mexico, Colombia and the Philippines were found to have stolen the names and full or partial Social Security numbers of about 280,000 of the wireless carrier's customers in the United States. The workers sold that information to third parties … trafficking stolen cellphones they sought to activate" (Ruiz 2015, B3). In 2015 the Federal Communications Commission fined AT&T $25 million for failing to protect the personal information of customers—the largest penalty to date the FCC had issued for violations of privacy and data security.

19. Insider threats are prioritized in corporate intelligence. Besides hacking, corporate intelligence can also be based on "open source" intelligence (OSINT) and "big data" collection (Lyon 2014). We have presented cases where hacks were believed to have provided expedient corporate intelligence.

20. As of 2017 Uber (a privately held company) was estimated for a potential $69 billion valuation (Abbaoud 2017). News Corporation's market capitalization was $8.8 billion in 2018 (Stoller 2018).

21. In November 2017 a letter revealed that Uber had attempted to steal trade secrets from Waymo, the self-driving car unit of Google's parent company, Alphabet. The letter, from former Uber employee Richard Jacobs to Uber's deputy general counsel, Angela Padilla, described the workings of Uber's "marketplace analytics team." The team would gather intelligence about competitors from the GitHub code-sharing site as well as "evade, impede, obstruct, [and] influence several ongoing lawsuits against Uber." The team used "anonymous" servers separate from Uber's network, along with devices that encrypted or automatically deleted messages after a fixed of time. Jacobs testified that the system "was to ensure there was no paper trail that would come back to haunt the company in any criminal or civil litigation" (Metz 2017, B1).

22. Evidence presented at court included a threat made from News America Marketing's CEO to a Floorgraphics executive: "If you ever get into any of our businesses, I will destroy you. . . . I work for a man [Rupert Murdoch] who wants it all and doesn't understand anybody telling him he can't have it all" ("News Corp Shareholders" 2011).

23. News Corp shuttered *News of the World,* taking a $122 million write-down in 2012 for settlements and business costs of the voice-mail–hacking scandal. It also used the opportunity to restructure its business into a more shareholder-friendly division between media and entertainment companies.

24. In this regard, the case reprised many of the themes from the Felten–Secure Digital Music Initiative saga from a decade earlier (see Burkart and McCourt 2006).

25. Phishing fraudsters can and do face prosecutions by the FBI in the United States and the National Crime Agency in the United Kingdom, for example, but they are rarely prosecuted because their cases require international coordination and often large expenditures of scarce resources.

26. The "two-judge majority seems to have no intention of making it illegal to share any passwords, ever; they explicitly dismiss such concerns as 'hypotheticals about the dire consequences of criminalizing password sharing.' But the dissenting judge is clearly concerned the majority's ruling will 'make the millions of people who engage in this ubiquitous, useful, and generally harmless conduct into unwitting federal criminals.' In other words, the Ninth Circuit decision really seems to offer very little clarity about whether it's legal for you to use your roommate's Netflix password" (Wolff 2016b).

27. The United States increasingly has "harmonized up" its legal standards to a more comprehensive and specific set of European standards that criminalized illegal access and interception, data and system interference, misuse of devices, computer-related forgery and fraud, offences related to child pornography, and infringement of copyright and related rights, as well as attempts at aiding and abetting these offenses. The updated list of ratifications, reservations, declarations, and authorities is available at Council of Europe (2001). The United States has not been held accountable for additional provisions of the protocol—accusations of xenophobia and racism—though it had agreed to abide by them (Rutkowski 2018).

28. It may not be a coincidence that malware forums cluster in a similar overlap of geopolitical regions or that Chinese-, Russian-, and Portuguese-language markets partly underpin regional political economies of software and media.

2. HACKING AND RISK TO SYSTEMS

1. Critical theorists working in the Frankfurt School tradition have used Habermas's (1984, 1987) theory of communicative action to study law and policy, economics, politics, and culture. They include Nancy Fraser, Jean Cohen, Andrew Arato, Axel Honneth, Claus Offe, Klaus Eder, Albrecht Wellmer, and Agnes Heller. Their work, which goes back to the mid-1980s, contributed to continental Marxism concerned with new social movement theory. Additionally, Teubner (1988) and others have developed a critical legal sociology focusing on autopoietic communication systems.

2. Adobe Flash has provided numerous attack vectors over the years, and Microsoft will not provide regular updates and security patches to older versions of software such as Windows XP, first released in 2001, unless customers pay for additional "custom support" (Wingfield 2017, A9). In addition to the planned obsolescence of software, which requires consistent upgrading or repurchase, the bug problem is complicated by the widespread use of bootlegged software: "A study last year by BSA, a trade association of software vendors, found that 70 percent of software installed on computers in China was not properly licensed in 2015. Russia, at 64 percent, and India, 58 percent, were close behind" (Mozuer 2017, A8)

3. Spear phishing is a targeted form of "phishing" expedition or deceptive email sent to trick or lure recipients into sending log-in credentials or other personal account information. "Phishing" is probably a play on the spelling of "phreaking" applied to "fishing."

4. In a 2018 lawsuit the U.S. Democratic National Committee argued that the aforementioned spear-phishing attacks that led to data breaches and email exfiltrations to WikiLeaks in 2016 "destabilize[ed] the US political environment" (Democratic National Committee 2018). A hack may have contributed to a system-level political crisis. Of course, attributing causes and effects to specific hacking incidents is highly problematic, as the court trial for this case would have shown, had it transpired.

5. Shaw (2018) defines "information warfare" as "the exploitation of information technology for the purposes of propaganda, disinformation, and psychological operations." The disclosures that Cambridge Analytica and others used Facebook for information warfare attracted the attention of U.S. legislators in 2018, raising questions about for whom Facebook is a trusted system.

6. Hackers can participate in politics as symbolic action or operate outside of political or economic norms entirely, finding artistic or emotional satisfaction in doing their work "for the lulz." To improve access to new digital media formats, for example, competing teams of software "crackers" began removing commercial video-game copy protections beginning in the 1980s (Reunanen 2015), and an anonymous hacker published "unfuck.exe" to unlock all ripped and otherwise tradeable music files with the Windows .wma encoding, the day after Microsoft's release of the standard for its new Digital Rights Management (Hu 2002). These efforts may have antisystemic or even altruistic intentions, in the shopworn sense of "information wants to be free," but they have also provided grist for the mill for royalties industries and others seeking to bring antihacking law ever closer to the legal code base for antipiracy.

7. For example, the independent "patriotic hacker" has emerged as an imputed actor working on behalf of countries whose state hacking agencies require plausible deniability (McKirdy 2017).

8. Many commercial technologies are rooted in military research and development, including computers and the internet itself. As with so many markets for new technology, policies (where they exist) default to routines that "socialize the risk and privatize the profits." Today, however, the extent of public and private partnerships is unprecedented. For example, the Small Business Innovation Research program serves as "the largest source of seed and early-stage funding for high-technology firms in the United States" (Weiss 2014, 59). National-security agencies supply 97 percent of the funding for SBIR; the government and public receive no equity ownership in return. Numerous government agencies (including the CIA, Department of Defense,

army, navy, National Geospatial-Intelligence Agency, NASA, and Department of Homeland Security) all have their own venture-capital funds to pour into private companies. These wrappers allow the government to develop new technologies for surveillance and cyber war while keeping risk at arm's length. At the same time they promote commercial spinoffs, such as driverless cars based in technologies developed for missile guidance systems and pilotless drones. But privatization on this model places "an extraordinary array of potential cyber-weapons in the hands of unaccountable private companies" (Shaw 2018). As the Department of Defense's annual report in 2002 explains, "The ultimate goal is to achieve technically superior, affordable Defense Systems technology while ensuring that technology developed for national security purposes is integrated into the private sector to enhance the national technology and industrial base" (cited in Weiss 2014, 65)

9. European Union–based companies have produced at least eighteen deep-packet inspection products and four products using Trojan horses (Fuchs 2012).

10. Deep-packet inspection is a "technology that gives network managers and governments the ability to monitor everything you do on the Internet, including reading and recording your e-mail and other digital communications, and tracking your every move on the Web" (O'Reilly 2012).

11. Since 2008 NSA implanted software "in nearly 100,000 computers around the world that allows the United States to conduct surveillance on those machines and can create a digital highway for launching cyberattacks" (Sanger and Shanker 2014, A1). The technology relies on a covert radio channel, with signals transmitted via circuit boards and USB cards planted in computers; briefcase-sized NSA relay stations can be set up as far as eight miles away from targets.

12. Cyber Command was created by Obama's first secretary of defense, Robert Gates, who also led the Department of Defense under George W. Bush and built up thousands of "cyber attack teams" (Kaplan 2016, 4). The Trump administration has embraced deterrence through preemptive cyberattacks rather than strengthening defenses and minimizing impacts from breaches, as reflected in their avowed intent to scrap the Obama administration's Presidential Policy Directive 20. PPD-20 required the use of cyber weapons to be coordinated among the Department of Commerce, Department of State, and intelligence agencies; now U.S. Cyber Command will be able to operate with far less oversight. Jason Healey, an expert in cybersecurity, stated, "The military is asking politicians to give them authority and then get out of the way

forever." Healey viewed the former "friction" between agencies as a positive: "Friction is how you avoid bombing Afghan weddings. This interagency process is in place to ensure civilian control over the military, limit potential escalation, and ensure other agencies that might be affected by cyberoperations have a say in the decision" (DeGeurin 2018). In mid-2018 U.S. Cyber Command policy adopted a more aggressive stance, including "nearly daily raids on foreign networks" (Sanger 2018a).

13. Immigration politics and the militarization of borders have subsequently increased demand. Amazon has entered the government market for real-time facial recognition in the service of militarized borders, offering its surveillance system to the U.S. Immigrations and Customs Enforcement agency. In an independent test of its system using photos of U.S. congressional members, Amazon "misidentified 28 US lawmakers as people who had been arrested for a crime, a shortcoming that disproportionately affected [lawmakers] . . . of color" (Locklear 2018).

14. Panoptic surveillance is also referred to as "panspectric" (Palmås 2011) and "omnichannel" (Turow 2017, 108) surveillance.

15. NSA and Cyber Command have conflicting strategies over whether implants should serve an active or passive role. While the NSA penetrates foreign networks with implants for eavesdropping, Cyber Command wants to use them to strike adversaries. But "N.S.A. officials complained that once the implants were used to attack, the Islamic State militants would stop the use of a communications channel and perhaps start one that was harder to find, penetrate or de-encrypt" (Sanger 2016, A1).

16. In response to a breach of its Gmail servers, Google is reported to have hacked back in a "secret counter-offensive" against those believed to be responsible (Sanger and Markoff 2010). But Google has subsequently publicly disclaimed proposed legislation authorizing certain "hack-backs" (Shoorbaji 2018).

17. Schmidle (2018) notes another potential application of "legalized hacking." In 2004 Eran Reshef, a former Israeli intelligence officer, cofounded a company called Blue Security, which he marketed as the ultimate antispamming service. Subscribers to Blue Security became part of a mutually protective community; whenever a member received a piece of spam, it was automatically forwarded to all the others, which simultaneously returned the message to its sender, overwhelming the spammer's server. It was essentially a distributed denial-of-service attack in reverse.

18. "Dual use" refers to technologies with both military and civilian applications. For example, nuclear fission is deployed in both weapons and reactors.

19. Rootkits surreptitiously provide administrator, or "root," access to systems they infect, providing full access and permissions for changing and controlling the information and software on the system. Once rootkits are installed, trusted systems become vulnerable to malware and botnet infections.

20. Attribution for the hacks varied from the Lizard Squad, LulzSec, and Anonymous hacker collectives; to disgruntled ex-employees; to the North Korean military. Then FBI director James Comey suggested that the initial attack vector was a successful spear-phishing exploit (Elkind 2015).

21. Sony was champing at the bit to hack back against an attributed source of the hacks, but the strategy could have brought it into direct conflict with North Korea and multiple unknown hacker groups. The North Korean internet outage that followed the hack of the century was disclaimed by the United States but was intended to send a signal to the perpetrators: expect hack-backs.

22. Samuelson (2016) reflects on these liberties broadly as a "freedom to tinker."

23. Indeed, where overreaching IP law has been exposed to political pressures, such as in the case of the Stop Online Piracy Act in the United States, the French Haute Autorité pour la Diffusion des Œuvres et la Protection des droits d'auteur sur Internet (HADOPI) escapade, and Spanish experiments with copyright maximalism, maximalist policies do not always survive the political process. Although laws protecting personal privacy vary widely by region, the United States historically has exerted an outsized influence in shaping trade agreements governing markets for information and privacy, such as the Anti-Counterfeiting Trade Agreement. The United States favors strong intellectual-property rights; indeed, the expansion of markets and technical and legal protection for owners of information commodities has been a key part of U.S. policy since the nineteenth century. Handicapping potential counterclaims to consumer privacy is central to this strategy, and EU privacy laws have been cited as a nontariff barrier to information trade with information-intensive U.S. companies, such as airlines and social media sites.

24. Auernheimer, a hacker who operates under the alias "weev" and subsequently embraced the neo-Nazi movement, exploited a flaw in AT&T servers and revealed the email addresses of 114,000 iPad users in 2010. Auernheimer and an accomplice were arrested in January 2011 and charged with violating the CFAA (Foresman 2011). Although Auernheimer was sentenced to forty-one months in prison, his conviction was overturned by the Third U.S. Circuit

Court of Appeals in April 2014 on grounds that he was charged in the wrong federal court (the court sidestepped his conviction under CFAA). Auernheimer's accomplice, Daniel Spitler, received three years' probation (Kravets 2014). In April 2016 Keys was sentenced to two years in prison for providing the hacker group Anonymous with a user name and password that allowed them to infiltrate the *Los Angeles Times'* parent company, the Tribune Company, and alter headlines on the *Times* website in 2010. According to the *New York Times,* "The charges had shocked the social media circles where he was considered a wunderkind of new media. He was named one of *Time*'s 140 best Twitter feeds" (Mele 2016, B8).

25. Regan, Monahan, and Craven (2013) have critiqued the operation of seventy-seven DHS fusion centers, which share surveillance records and generate "suspicious activity reports" for law-enforcement and counterterrorism organizations.

26. The modern nation-state, created by the Treaty of Westphal in 1648, has been the defining unit of global political organization for the past 370 years.

27. The impetus for public diplomacy and international-relations literature seems to come from the gradual codification of norms related to the public development and internationalization of cyber defenses. Examples of these include a prototreaty by the Committee of Experts on Crime in Cyberspace from 1997 to 2000 and formalized by the Council of Europe in 2001 (in the so-called Budapest Convention). The European Union's Directives on Cybersecurity and Network and Information Systems have harmonized some basic concepts as well as their problematics (Haase 2015).

3. THE POLITICAL ECONOMY OF THE HACK

1. This chapter is based in part on Burkart and McCourt (2017).

2. The "crypto wars" refer to the struggle between U.S. vendors of strongly encrypted software and federal government efforts to control the exports of hardware and software using strong encryption. The deregulation occurred around 1994.

3. According to a complaint filed with Israeli police, NSO "offered Saudi Arabia a system that hacks cellphones, a few months before Crown Prince Mohammed bin Salman began his purge of regime opponents" (Levinson 2018).

4. Among those promoting Hacking Team was Innogest, an Italian venture-capital firm headed by Ronald Spogli, a former U.S. ambassador to Italy (Currier and Marquis-Boire 2014).

5. To "pwn" is hacker slang for "own" or take over a trusted system.

6. Fisher used a zero-day exploit to access HT's network. He then hacked his way to the code base to access the company's premier product, RCS. Since the HT hack, Fisher has leaked FinFisher spyware documents and publicized antivirus software that could detect Gamma International's malware. A self-professed "black hat" hacker, in 2017 Fisher published a detailed "DIY guide" on how to attack cyber-mercenary systems and included tips on how to avoid capture through encryption and using "virtual" machines to connect indirectly to the Tor network. Fisher dedicated his guide "to the victims of the raid on Armando Diaz school and to all those who have had their blood spilled by Italian fascists." He concluded, "That's all it takes to take down a company and stop their human rights abuses. That's the beauty and asymmetry of hacking: with 100 hours of work, one person can undo years of work by a multi-million-dollar company. Hacking gives the underdog a chance to fight and win" (Smith 2017). In early 2017 Spanish police claimed to have captured Fisher, but the wily hacker responded, "I think [they] just arrested some people that retweeted the link to their personal info, or maybe just arrested some activisty/anarchisty people to pretend they are doing something" (Uchill 2017b).

7. Political activists promoting soda tax in Mexico became one of the Hacking Team's "odd targets" (Perlroth 2017, A1).

8. In addition to a basic service fee of nearly $1 million, NSO charges $150,000 for ten targets, $250,000 for twenty, $500,000 for fifty, and $800,000 for a hundred additional targets. Like HT, NSO claims to have an internal ethics committee of "employees and external counsel" (Perlroth 2016b, A1) to vet prospective clients.

9. NSO's founders insisted that the firm remain an independent subsidiary, which Verint opposed: "Hulio and Lavie … argued that the deal, which included a $600 million payment in Verint shares that could not be sold during the first year, was not worthwhile because it depended on the future success of the merged company" ("Israeli Cyber Startup" 2018).

10. According to the *New York Times,* "The unit, whose name has now been changed to Computer Network Operations, is the N.S.A.'s fastest-growing component. Its hackers break into foreign computer networks to gather intelligence, often leaving behind software implants that continue to collect

documents and other data and forward it to the agency for months or years" (Shane and Goldman 2017, A16).

11. Metasploit is a commercially available tool used in all corners of the cybersecurity world, and Kali Linux provides an open-source version of the same.

12. Targets of offensive CTI include underground economies, Internet Relay Chat channels, and, especially, hacker forums, which are known to disseminate "freely accessible, malicious tools such as Zeus, Ransomware, SQL injections, and DDoS, among others" (Samtani et al. 2017, 1025).

13. CrowdStrike was founded in 2011 by two former executives of McAfee. The company, with more than 650 employees, claimed subscriptions grew 476 percent in 2016. Interestingly, while cloud systems would seem to draw hackers pursuing "one-stop shopping," CrowdStrike espoused cloud systems over individual storage on grounds of "smarter defenses and faster responses" (de la Merced 2017).

14. Verizon publishes an annual *Data Breach Investigations Report,* which is widely regarded as the best and most respected industry report on breach detections and time to discovery.

15. For example, in April 2017 American International Group joined other insurers by offering "Family CyberEdge," which includes "public relations and legal services, as well as at-home assessments of family electronic devices" for "wealthy, high-profile individuals" (Barlyn 2017). The emergence of ransomware attacks, which hold proprietary data hostage for payment, has swelled markets for cyber insurance, although a ransomware claim made by Mondelez was denied by its cyber insurer, Zurich, as being an "act of war" and not insurable ("Mondelez/Cyber Hackers" 2019, 10).

16. Prices continue to fall. By mid-2018 personally identifying information commanded the following rates on the Tor, I2p, and Freenet anonymous networks: social security numbers, one dollar; credit card and CVV numbers and debit cards with bank information, five dollars; driver's licenses and identifiers for payment services such as PayPal, twenty dollars (Cornfield 2018).

4. ANTIHACKING LAW AND POLICY

1. The "right to be forgotten" is an EU juridical experiment intended to provide legal remedies for people who claim to have erroneous, malicious, or otherwise objectionable information published about them online. But its efficacy is questionable, since the internet's repository of content transcends the

EU political domain. Furthermore, the early experience with GPRS has already sharpened U.S.-EU trade disputes.

2. While creators may be held criminally liable for publishing or distributing their malware-based products, the United States does not treat the creation of malware as a criminal offense. Rodriguez (2016) notes that malware may be treated as intellectual property, offering an inducement for its creation. Some nominally criminal "Vx-ers" are also noted cybersecurity researchers, including Marcus Hutchins, the so-called WannaCry Hero who discovered a solution to stopping the spread of the WannaCry ransomware in the UK-NHS health system. Marcy Wheeler has analyzed the legal case supporting the arrest of Hutchins in an FBI sting operation targeting hackers: "Hutchins' defense had raised a slew of legal challenges that, together, showed the government stretching to use wiretapping and CFAA statutes to encompass writing code so as to include Hutchins in the charges" (qtd. in Burton 2018).

3. Wassenaar also commits signatories to extradition and mutual assistance in pursuing cases, including intercepting and sharing traffic and content data from service providers in real time.

4. This problem is endemic in the field. In another case in point, the European Directive 2013/40/EU lacks definitions for key terms such as "security measure" and "attack against [an] information system" altogether; offers vague definitions for terms such as "minor case"; and contains no mention of identity theft or spamming (Březinová 2017, 24).

5. As a rule, EU laws require firms to first report breaches to "Competent Authorities" rather than affected individuals (unlike common U.S. practice) (Laube and Böhme 2016, 30–31).

6. This response probably owes in part to the company's history. Netragard, founded in 1999, had sold zero-day exploits to the Hacking Team. The firm first contacted Netragard in July 2011 but did not establish a working relationship until October 2013 (WikiLeaks 2015c). Netragard's Exploit Acquisition Program claimed to serve only U.S.-based buyers; however, in March 2015 CEO Adriel Desautels wrote to Hacking Team, "We've been quietly changing our internal customer policies and have been working more with international buyers.... We do understand who your customers are both afar and in the US and are comfortable working with you directly" (WikiLeaks 2015b). After the Hacking Team hack, Netragard shut down its Exploit Acquisition Program, and Desautels claimed to be shocked, absolutely shocked, to learn the full extent of the company's dealings: "After the hack, when we saw Hacking Team's customer list was exposed and I saw who they were working with, at

first I was angry, and then I realized that, despite our efforts, we could not control their ethics. There is no framework in place to control that, and we could not rely on the contracts that we had" (Lemos 2015a).

7. A reformed law could use willful violations to elevate proof requirements to punish "the willful violation of an owner's right to exclude others from property, not the mere misuse of information" (Keim 2015, 34).

8. Hacking also became embedded in cyber warfare through the Authorization for Use of Military Force, introduced by then senator Thomas Daschle and signed by then president George W. Bush in September 2001. This authorization, which expanded the use of military force from kinetic to cybernetic warfare, facilitated the turning of NSA surveillance on U.S. citizens.

9. As Bratus and colleagues note, "Even accessing your own data on a Web portal in a manner unforeseen by the portal operator ... may similarly be a crime under CFAA" (2014, 6).

10. In 2008 Swartz published a "Guerrilla Open Access Manifesto," in which he "avowed a 'moral imperative' to share scholarship locked behind exorbitant subscription walls. 'It's time to come into the light and, in the grand tradition of civil disobedience, declare our opposition to this private theft of public culture' he wrote" (Bombardieri 2014).

11. The Stop Online Piracy Act was intended to expand U.S. legal capabilities against online copyright infringement (including streaming of copyrighted material) and trafficking in counterfeit goods. Among other things, SOPA would require internet service providers to block access to infringing websites, as well as bar advertisers and search engines from linking to them. Introduced in the U.S. House in 2011, the bill was defeated the following year after massive resistance from a broad coalition of organizations, activists, and legislators.

12. Using autopoiesis as a conceptual model for telecommunications regulations, Cherry views the "patching" function of federalized law in the United States (with processes operating at state and national levels) and the coevolution of "coupled" law and markets as features of autopoietic law. These processes can then provide sustainable legal norms with some freedom left for "innovation and resilience" (2007, 382). Since the CFAA's most problematic features remain unreformed, it is not yet possible to develop a history of the legal system's self-healing or patching functions with respect to resolving its internal contradictions.

13. These members include the Five Eyes partners in mass surveillance programs such as PRISM and its predecessor, Echelon.

14. In 2017 Dennis Blair, the former director of National Intelligence, and Keith Alexander, the former National Security Agency director, claimed that "all together, intellectual-property theft costs America up to $600 billion a year, the greatest transfer of wealth in history.... Driving down intellectual-property theft by China and other countries is vital for America's economic well-being and national security.... A broad, sustained campaign bringing together the government, the private sector and our allies is the only way to halt this hemorrhaging of America's economic life blood" (Blair and Alexander 2017, A23).

15. The Center for a New American Security, a Washington, DC–based think tank of the "best and brightest" in the Department of State, NSA, and Department of Defense, was founded in 2007 and placed many of its members into key positions in the Obama administration (Lozada 2009). In 2013 the center issued a report on cybersecurity that further underscored the growing link between cybersecurity, national security, and intellectual-property theft. The report's author, Irving Lachow, avers that an active cyber defense is necessary because the threat now comes from state-sponsored spies and sophisticated criminals who create what he calls an "advanced persistent threat" regarding "stealing intellectual property and defrauding individuals and businesses" (2013, 2).

16. Ex post facto hack public-relations campaigns by cybersecurity consultancies such as Mandiant have fanned the flames. In 2013 the company released a report in which it claimed to have evidence linking Unit 61398 of the People's Liberation Army in Shanghai to a global cyber-espionage campaign against nearly 150 companies from twenty economic sectors "designed to steal large volumes of valuable intellectual property." Mandiant's report garnered widespread press coverage in the West, prompted angry responses from China, and catalyzed the Obama administration's release of a new strategy to combat theft of U.S. trade secrets (Fidler 2013, 2). Obama met with Chinese president Xi Jinping in a 2015 summit to reach an honor agreement involving U.S. accusations of Chinese mass hacking and theft of IP (Wiseman and Dilanian 2015).

5. ACTIVISM BEYOND HACKTIVISM

1. ISP surveillance has been implemented under the French Haute Autorité pour la Diffusion des Œuvres et la Protection des droits d'auteur sur Internet (HADOPI) experiences, the Spanish Ley Sinde, and the Swedish Försvarets Radioanstalt (FRA) law. But these have since been challenged and altered.

Website blocking (which monitors and intercepts user requests) has been legally enforced by ISPs in the United Kingdom, Netherlands, Belgium, Italy, Finland, Spain, and Denmark, and the European Court of Justice has expressed official approval (Mezei 2018, 4). The UK Investigative Powers Act of 2016 required ISPs to keep user logs, and many ISPs are now blocking the use of VPNs. Copyright maximalism in the United States–Mexico-Canada Agreement (the "new NAFTA") seem likely to provide opportunities for future surveillance justified as intellectual-property securitization in North American treaty law.

2. Habermasian critical theory recognizes "communicative rationality" to be an experience of the "lifeworld," in which language and communication enable meaning making and consensus building. Complex communication systems evolve to handle the riskiest and most uncertain processes (for example, legitimating political and legal systems).

3. Facebook's "scraping" and sale of user data is but one example. Others are more deeply embedded, with a more overt political mission. For example, "The Koch brothers' data firm, i360, whose funding rivals that of both parties, has spent years developing detailed portraits of 250 million Americans and refining its capacities for influence operations through 'message testing' to determine what kinds of advertisements will have traction with a given audience. It employs 'mobile ID matching,' which can link users to all of their devices—unlike cookies, which are restricted to one device—and it has conducted extensive demographic research over social media. Google's DoubleClick and Facebook are listed as i360's featured partners for digital marketing" (Shaw 2018).

4. Pirate politics has made trace appearances in the United States and Canada and has a precursor movement in Mexico (Burkart and Corona 2016).

5. In April 2018 thirty-one tech companies signed an agreement in which they refused to help any government mount cyberattacks against "innocent civilians and enterprises from anywhere." They also pledged to assist any nation so attacked, whether the attack was "criminal or geopolitical." Signatories included Microsoft, Facebook, Cisco, Dell, Oracle, Hewlett Packard, Juniper Networks, Symantec, and FireEye. Two foreign firms, Spain's Telefónica and Finland's Nokia, also signed. Notably, Google, Apple, and Amazon refused to sign, as did any Chinese or Russian companies (Sanger 2018b). Microsoft, whose software was compromised by the WannaCry ransomware used in countless cyber-ransom attacks, has advocated the creation of a digital Geneva Convention to protect against cyberattacks by nations and states—

while placing the very tech companies whose security was compromised in charge of enforcing security. As Evgeny Morozov notes, "Thus, in addition to regularly extracting rent from the users of its software, Microsoft can now also extract additional rent from those very users for protecting the very software that they are renting in the first place" (2017b).

6. The campaigns include Free JavaScript, Secure Boot versus Restricted Boot, Upgrade from Windows, Surveillance, Working Together for Free Software, GNU, Defective by Design (anti-DRM), PlayOgg, End Software Patents, Campaign for OpenDocument, Campaign for Hardware That Supports Free Software, and the Free BIOS Campaign.

REFERENCES

Abbaoud, Leila. 2017. "Uber's $69 Billion Dilemma." Bloomberg.com. March 16, 2017. www.bloomberg.com/gadfly/articles/2017-03-16/uber-needs-to-get-real-about-that-69-billion-price-tag.

Abrahamsen, Rita, and Michael C. Williams. 2009. "Security beyond the State: Global Security Assemblages in International Politics." *International Political Sociology* 3:1–17. https://pdfs.semanticscholar.org/24d5/138fb85cc264e28403fd9711fbc06a6b7a95.pdf.

Acohido, Byron. 2016. "Despite Changing Landscape, VC Investment in Cybersecurity Still Strong." Third Certainty. October 1, 2016. http://thirdcertainty.com/featured-story/despite-changing-landscape-vc-investment-in-cybersecurity-still-strong/#.

Ahmed, Azam. 2017. "Spyware Trailed Investigators in Mexico." *New York Times,* July 10, 2017, A1.

Ahmed, Azam, and Nicole Perlroth. 2017. "Using Texts as Lures, Government Spyware Targets Mexican Journalists and Their Families." *New York Times,* June 19, 2017. www.nytimes.com/2017/06/19/world/americas/mexico-spyware-anticrime.html.

Akdeniz, Yaman. 2008. "The Council of Europe's Cyber-Crime Convention 2001 and the Additional Protocol on the Criminalization of Acts of a Racist or Xenophobic Nature Committed through Computer Systems." Cyber-Rights and Cyber-Liberties. May 2008. www.cyber-rights.org/cybercrime/coe_handbook_crcl.pdf.

Angwin, Julia, Charlie Savage, Jeff Larson, Henrik Molton, Laura Poitras, and James Risen. 2015. "AT&T Helped US Spy on Internet on a Vast Scale." *New York Times,* August 16, 2015, A1.

"Appleby Reaction to Media Coverage." 2017. Appleby. May 11, 2017. www.applebyglobal.com/media-statements/appleby-reaction-to-media-coverage.aspx.

Arrington, Michael. 2006. "AOL Proudly Releases Massive Amounts of Private Data." Techcrunch. August 16, 2006. https://techcrunch.com/2006/08/06/aol-proudly-releases-massive-amounts-of-user-search-data/.

Auchard, Eric, and Joseph Menn. 2015. "Surveillance Software Maker Hacking Team Gets Taste of Its Own Medicine." Reuters. July 6, 2015. www.reuters.com/article/us-cybersecurity-hacking-team/surveillance-software-maker-hacking-team-gets-taste-of-its-own-medicine-idUSKCN0PG16720150706?virtualBrandChannel = 11563.

Bachmann, Reinhard. 2001. "Trust, Power, and Control in Trans-organizational Relations." *Organizational Studies* 22 (2): 337–65.

Bailey, Dawn. 2016. "Baldrige for Detection and Prevention of Corporate Espionage." National Institute of Standards and Technology. July 21, 2016. www.nist.gov/blogs/blogrige/baldrige-detection-and-prevention-corporate-espionage.

Balko, Radley. 2016. "Surprise! NSA Data Will Soon Routinely Be Used for Domestic Policing That Has Nothing to Do with Terrorism." *Washington Post,* March 10, 2016. www.washingtonpost.com/news/the-watch/wp/2016/03/10/surprise-nsa-data-will-soon-routinely-be-used-for-domestic-policing-that-has-nothing-to-do-with-terrorism/.

Barlyn, Suzanne. 2017. "AIG Taps into Consumer Fears with New Cybersecurity Product." Reuters. April 3. http://mobile.reuters.com/article/technologyNews/idUSKBN1751E0.

Batey, Angus. 2011. "The Spies behind Your Screen." *Sunday Telegraph,* November 24, 2011. www.telegraph.co.uk/technology/8899353/The-spies-behind-your-screen.html.

———. 2015. "Stolen Emails Provide Cyberwarfare Lessons." *Aviation Week and Space Technology,* September 8, 2015. https://aviationweek.com/defense/stolen-emails-provide-cyberwarfare-lessons-0.

Beck, Ulrich. 1992a. "From Industrial Society to the Risk Society: Questions of Survival, Social Structure and Ecological Enlightenment." *Theory, Culture and Society* 9 (1): 97–123.

———. 1992b. *Risk Society: Towards a New Modernity.* Thousand Oaks, CA: Sage.

———. 1996. “The Cosmopolitan Manifesto.” *New Statesman* 127, no. 4377 (March): 28–30.

———. 2004. “Cosmopolitan Reason: On the Distinction between Cosmopolitanism in Philosophy and the Social Sciences.” *Global Networks* 4 (2): 132.

———. 2006. “Living in the World Risk Society.” *Economy and Society* 35 (3): 329–45.

———. 2009. *World at Risk*. Cambridge: Polity.

Beck, Ulrich, Anders Blok, David Tyfield, and Joy Yueyue Zhang. 2013. “Cosmopolitan Communities of Climate Risk: Conceptual and Empirical Suggestions for a New Research Agenda.” *Global Networks* 13, no. 1 (January): 1–21.

Bellovin, Steven M., Matt Blaze, Sandy Clark, and Susan Landau. 2014. “Lawful Hacking: Using Existing Vulnerabilities for Wiretapping the Internet.” *Northwestern Journal of Technology and Intellectual Property* 12, no. 1 (April): 1–64.

Bennett, Cory. 2015. “Cyber Industry Assails Anti-hacking Regulations.” *Hill,* July 21, 2015. https://thehill.com/regulation/cybersecurity/248579-cyber-industry-assails-anti-hacking-regulations.

Bennhold, Katrin, and Mark Scott. 2017. “How to Catch Hackers? Old-Fashioned Sleuthing, with a Digital Twist.” *New York Times,* May 15, 2017, A6.

Berke, Jeremy. 2015. “The Freakiest TV Hack of the 1980s: Max Headroom.” Atlas Obscura. July 27, 2015. www.atlasobscura.com/articles/the-freakiest-tv-hack-of-the-1980s-max-headroom.

Biddle, Sam. 2017. “Leaked NSA Malware Threatens Malware Windows Users around the World.” *Intercept,* April 14, 2017. https://theintercept.com/2017/04/14/leaked-nsa-malware-threatens-windows-users-around-the-world/.

Blair, Dennis C., and Keith Alexander. 2017. “Cracking Down on I.P. Theft.” *New York Times,* August 15, 2017, A23.

Bombardieri, Marcella. 2014. “The Inside Story of MIT and Aaron Swartz.” *Boston Globe,* March 30, 2014. www.bostonglobe.com/metro/2014/03/29/the-inside-story-mit-and-aaron-swartz/YvJZ5P6VHaPJusReuaN7SI/story.html.

Bomberg, Elizabeth. 2007. “Policy Learning in an Enlarged European Union: Environmental NGOs and New Policy Instruments.” *Journal of European Public Policy* 14 (2): 248–68.

Braman, Sandra. 2009. *Change of State: Information, Policy, and Power.* Cambridge, MA: MIT Press.

Branford, Robert. 2017. “Information Warfare: Is Russia Really Interfering in European States?” BBC News. March 31, 2017. www.bbc.com/news/world-europe-39401637.

Bratus, Sergey, Ivan Arce, Michael E. Locasto, and Stefano Zanero. 2014. "Why Offensive Security Needs Engineering Textbooks or How to Avoid a Replay of 'Crypto Wars.'" *Login* 39, no. 4 (August): 6–11. www.usenix.org/system/files/login/articles/02_bratus.pdf.

Brewster, Thomas. 2013. "RSA 2013: Hacking Team Defends Its Surveillance Software." *Techweek,* February 28, 2013. www.silicon.co.uk/workspace/rsa-2013-hacking-team-surveillance-uae-morocco-tor-project-109101.

———. 2014. "Aaron's Law Is Doomed Leaving US Hacking Law 'Broken.'" *Forbes,* August 6, 2014. www.forbes.com/sites/thomasbrewster/2014/08/06/aarons-law-is-doomed-leaving-us-hacking-law-broken/.

———. 2015a. "Meet the Hacking Team Alumni Fighting Their Old Overlord and Its Spyware." *Forbes,* July 15, 2015. www.forbes.com/sites/thomasbrewster/2015/07/15/hacking-team-ex-employers-legal-fight/#56d3d8f17551.

———. 2015b. "Wikileaks Release: Hacking Team Says It Sold Spyware to FSB, Russia's Secret Police." *Forbes,* July 9, 2015. www.forbes.com/sites/thomasbrewster/2015/07/09/wikileaks-hacking-team-fsb-sales/#77297136 55c7.

———. 2016. "Hacking Team in Trouble Again—Loses License to Sell Malware Outside Europe." *Forbes,* April 6, 2016. www.forbes.com/sites/thomasbrewster/2016/04/06/hacking-team-loses-sales-license/.

———. 2018a. "'Disturbing' Smartphone Hacks Hit Saudi Activists via WhatsApp." *Forbes,* August 1, 2018. www.forbes.com/sites/thomasbrewster/2018/08/01/amnesty-activist-targeted-in-whatsapp-based-hack/#66b5b9906353.

———. 2018b. "King iPhone Hacker NSO Group Robbed by Employee—Spyware on Dark Web Sale for $50 Million, Israel Claims." *Forbes,* July 5, 2018.www.forbes.com/sites/thomasbrewster/2018/07/05/apple-iphone-hackers-nso-group-hacked/#68cocdf174b1.

Březinová, Kristýna. 2017. "Company Criminal Liability for Unlawful Attacks against Information Systems within the Scope of EU Law." Prague Law Working Papers 2017/II/3. *SSRN.* June 20, 2017. https://ssrn.com/abstract=2989005.

Burkart, Patrick. 2010. *Music and Cyberliberties.* Middletown, CT: Wesleyan University Press.

———. 2011. "Hacking, Jamming, Boycotting, and Out-Foxing the Markets for New Media." In *Online Territories: Mediated Practice and Social Space,* edited by Miyase Christensen, André Jansson, and Christian Christensen, 185–204. New York: Lang.

———. 2014. *Pirate Politics: The New Information Policy Contests.* Cambridge, MA: MIT Press.

Burkart, Patrick, and Jonas Andersson Schwarz. 2014. "Post-Privacy and Ideology." In *Media, Surveillance and Identity: Social Perspectives*, ed. André Jansson and Miyase Christensen, 218–37. New York: Lang.

Burkart, Patrick, and Antonio Corona. 2016. "Developments in Mexican Digital Rights Activism." Presentation, Global Studies Association, Austin, Texas, 2016.

Burkart, Patrick, and Tom McCourt. 2006. *Digital Music Wars: Ownership and Control of the Celestial Jukebox*. New York: Rowman and Littlefield.

———. 2017. "The International Political Economy of the Hack: A Closer Look at Markets for Cybersecurity Software." *Popular Communication* 15 (1): 37–54.

Burns, Christine. 1998. "Locking Down NT Networks; Third-Party Developers Have Rushed in to Plug NT Security Holes." *Network World*, October 19, 1998, 30.

Burton, Graeme. 2018. "WannaCry Hero Marcus Hutchins Hit with More Federal Malware Charges." *Inquirer*, June 7, 2018. www.theinquirer.net/inquirer/news/3033753/wannacry-hero-marcus-hutchins-hit-with-more-federal-malware-charges.

Camp, L. Jean. 2001. *Trust and Risk in Internet Commerce*. Cambridge, MA: MIT Press.

Chait, Jonathan. 2017. "The Consumer Financial Protection Bureau Was Designed to Stop Donald Trump." *Intelligencer*, November 27, 2017. http://nymag.com/daily/intelligencer/2017/11/the-cfpb-was-designed-to-stop-donald-trump.html.

Chandrasekaran, Rajit. 1998. "The Guardians of Computer Security." *Washington Post*, March 17, 1998, 12–14.

Cherry, Barbara A. 2007. "The Telecommunications Economy and Regulation as Coevolving Complex Adaptive Systems: Implications for Federalism." *Federal Communications Law Journal* 59:369–402.

Coleman, E. Gabriella. 2011. "Hacker Politics and Publics." *Public Culture* 23 (3): 511–16.

———. 2013. *Coding Freedom: The Ethics and Aesthetics of Hacking*. Princeton, NJ: Princeton University Press.

Commonwealth of Australia. 2016. *Cyber Security: US Clusters*. White paper. Sydney: Australian Trade and Investment Commission, Government of Australia.

Constantin, Lucian. 2017. "How Much Are Vendor Security Assurances Worth after the CIA Leaks?" *Computerworld.com*, March 13, 2017. www.computerworld

.com/article/3180029/security/how-much-are-vendor-security-assurances-worth-after-the-cia-leaks.html.

Cook, James, and Rob Price. 2017. "Uber Reportedly Used a Secret Program Called 'Hell' to Track Rival Lyft Drivers." *Business Insider,* April 13, 2017. www.businessinsider.com/uber-used-program-called-hell-to-track-lyft-drivers-2017-4?op = 1&r = UK&IR = T.

Corkery, Michael. 2016. "Once Again, Thieves Enter Financial Network and Steal." *New York Times,* May 12, 2016. www.nytimes.com/2016/05/13/business/dealbook/swift-global-bank-network-attack.html.

Cornfield, Jill. 2018. "Your Private Data Goes for as Little as a $1 on the Dark Web." MSN. July 7, 2018. www.msn.com/en-us/money/personalfinance/your-private-data-goes-for-as-little-as-a-dollar1-on-the-dark-web/ar-AAzuFQE.

Council of Europe. 2001. "Convention on Cybercrime." European Treaty 185. November 23, 2001. www.coe.int/en/web/conventions/full-list/-/conventions/rms/0900001680081561.

———. 2018. "Chart of Signatures and Ratifications of Treaty 185." Accessed May 5, 2019. www.coe.int/en/web/conventions/full-list/-/conventions/treaty/185/signatures?p_auth = zlv1ClzA.

Cox, Joseph. 2016. "Dropbox Forces Password Resets after User Credentials Exposed." *Vice,* August 26, 2016. https://motherboard.vice.com/en_us/article/78kevq/dropbox-forces-password-resets-after-user-credentials-exposed.

Craig, Caroline. 2014. "CISPA Returns as CISA—and It's Just as Terrible for Privacy." *Infoworld,* June 20, 2014. www.infoworld.com/article/2607981/federal-regulations/cispa-returns-as-cisa-and-it-s-just-as-terrible-for-privacy.html.

Currier, Cora, and Morgan Marquis-Boire. 2014. "Secret Manuals Show the Spyware Sold to Despots and Cops Worldwide." *Intercept,* October 30, 2014. https://theintercept.com/2014/10/30/hacking-team/.

"Cyber-Security Bill CISPA Passes US House." 2012. BBC News. April 27, 2012. www.bbc.co.uk/news/world-us-canada-17864539.

"Cyber Security Investment Grows, Resilient to Market Turmoil." 2015. *Fortune,* September 23, 2015. http://fortune.com/2015/09/23/cyber-security-investing/.

"Cyber Security Markets." 2017. MarketsandMarkets. Accessed January 21, 2019. www.marketsandmarkets.com/PressReleases/cyber-security.asp.

"A Darknet Site Currently Offers 42,497 U.S. Credit Cards." 2016. CuriousGnu. September 6, 2016. www.curiousgnu.com/darknet-credit-cards.

DeGeurin, Mack. 2018. "U.S. Silently Enters New Age of Cyberwarfare." *Intelligencer,* September 11, 2018. http://nymag.com/intelligencer/2018/09/us-rescinds-ppd-20-cyber-command-enters-new-age-of-cyberwar.html.

Deibert, Ronald J. 2002. "Circuits of Power: Security in the Internet Environment." In *Information Technologies and Global Politics: The Changing Scope of Power and Governance,* edited by James N. Rosenau, and Jaswinder P. Singh, 115–42. Albany: State University of New York Press, 2002.

De la Merced, Michael J. 2017. "Digital Security Provider Raises $100 Million to Tackle Booming Market." *New York Times,* May 17, 2017. www.nytimes.com/2017/05/17/business/dealbook/crowdstrike-hacking-investment.html.

Democratic National Committee v. Russian Federation et al. 2018. 1:18-cv-03501. District Court, S.D. New York. Accessed May 5, 2019. https://drive.google.com/file/d/142q1Yg5CodDYps8DgJe1FkIhcE9LEflW/view.

Dewar, Robert S. 2017. *Active Cyber Defense.* White paper. Center for Security Studies, ETH Zurich. Accessed May 15, 2019. www.researchgate.net/publication/321057804_Active_Cyber_Defense.

DiDio, Laura. 1998. "Major Hacks Raise Hackles, Spur Defenders." *Computerworld* 3, no. 17 (March 30): 25.

"Documents Reveal Top NSA Hacking Unit." 2013. *Spiegel Online,* December 29, 2013. www.spiegel.de/international/world/the-nsa-uses-powerful-toolbox-in-effort-to-spy-on-global-networks-a-940969.html.

DOJ-CCIPS (Department of Justice–Computer Crime and Intellectual Property Section). 2015. "About CCIPS." U.S. Department of Justice. Accessed May 15, 2019. www.justice.gov/criminal-ccips/about-ccips.

Douglas, Susan. 1987. *Inventing American Broadcasting, 1899–1922.* Baltimore: Johns Hopkins University Press.

Doyle, Charles. 2014. *Cybercrime: An Overview of the Federal Computer Fraud and Abuse Statute and Related Federal Criminal Laws.* Congressional Research Service. October 15, 2014. https://fas.org/sgp/crs/misc/97-1025.pdf.

Ducklin, Paul. 2013. "Anatomy of a Password Disaster: Adobe's Giant-Sized Cryptographic Blunder." Naked Security. November 4, 2013. https://nakedsecurity.sophos.com/2013/11/04/anatomy-of-a-password-disaster-adobes-giant-sized-cryptographic-blunder/.

Dursht, Kenneth A. 1997. "From Containment to Cooperation: Collective Action and the Wassenaar Arrangement." *Cardozo Law Review* 19:1079–123.

Eakin, Hugh. 2017. "The Swedish Kings of Cyberwar." *New York Review of Books,* January 19, 2017, 56.

Eder, Klaus. 1985. "'The New Social Movements': Moral Crusades, Political Pressure Groups, or Social Movements?" *Social Research* 52, no. 4 (Winter): 869–90.

Edwards, Jim. 2009. "News America Marketing Group Buys Floorgraphics Just Hours after Settling Spying Lawsuit." *MoneyWatch,* March 12, 2009. www.cbsnews.com/news/news-america-marketing-group-buys-floorgraphics-just-hours-after-settling-spying-lawsuit/.

EFF (Electronic Frontier Foundation). 2015. "NSA Spying." Accessed May 15, 2019. www.eff.org/nsa-spying.

———. n.d. "Felten, et al., v. RIAA, et al." Accessed May 15, 2019. www.eff.org/cases/felten-et-al-v-riaa-et-al.

Eichensehr, Kristen E. 2017. "Public-Private Cybersecurity," *Texas Law Review* 95 (3): 467–538.

Ekeland, Tor. 2017. "How to Reform the Outdated Federal Anti-hacking Law." *Christian Science Monitor,* March 24, 2017. www.csmonitor.com/World/Passcode/Passcode-Voices/2017/0324/How-to-reform-the-outdated-federal-anti-hacking-law.

Elgin, Ben, and Vernon Silver. 2011. "Syria Crackdown Gets Italy Firm's Aid with U.S.-Europe Spy Gear." Bloomberg. November 5, 2011. www.bloomberg.com/news/articles/2011-11-03/syria-crackdown-gets-italy-firm-s-aid-with-u-s-europe-spy-gear.

Elkind, Peter. 2015. "Inside the Hack of the Century." *Fortune,* July 1, 2015. http://fortune.com/sony-hack-part-1/.

Elliott, Anthony. 2002. "Beck's Sociology of Risk: A Critical Assessment." *Sociology* 36 (2): 293–315.

Espiner, Tom. 2007. "Wi-Fi Hack Caused TK Maxx Security Breach." ZDNet. May 8, 2007. www.zdnet.com/article/wi-fi-hack-caused-tk-maxx-security-breach/.

Estes, Adam Clark. 2017. "Uber's Secret App for Tracking Cops Sounds Creepy as Hell." *Gizmodo,* March 3, 2017. https://gizmodo.com/ubers-secret-app-for-tracking-cops-sounds-creepy-as-hel-1792949962.

European Commission. 2013. *Cybersecurity Strategy of the European Union: An Open, Safe, and Secure Cyberspace.* February 7, 2013. https://ec.europa.eu/home-affairs/sites/homeaffairs/files/e-library/documents/policies/organized-crime-and-human-trafficking/cybercrime/docs/join_2013_1_en.pdf.

Evers, Joris. 2005. "Credit Card Breach Exposes 40 Million Accounts." CNET. July 18, 2005. www.cnet.com/news/credit-card-breach-exposes-40-million-accounts/.

Farivar, Cyrus. 2015. "Hacking Team Goes to War against Former Employees, Suspects Some Helped Hackers." Ars Technica. July 20, 2015. http://arstechnica.com/security/2015/07/italian-prosecutors-investigate-former-hacking-team-employees-for-role-in-hack/.

Faulconbridge, Guy, and Michael Holden. 2018. "Cyber Worm Attack Propels Health Funding to Center of British Election Campaign." Reuters. May 15, 2018. www.reuters.com/article/us-cyber-attack-britain/britain-worked-through-night-to-counter-cyber-attack-on-health-service-minister-idUSKCN18B0QZ.

Fidler, David P. 2013. "Economic Cyber Espionage and International Law: Controversies Involving Government Acquisition of Trade Secrets through Cyber Technologies." *Insights* 17, no. 10 (March): 1–6. www.asil.org/sites/default/files/insight130320.pdf.

"Film Group Backs Antipiracy Curriculum for Schools." 2013. Associated Press. November 11, 2013. www.yahoo.com/entertainment/news/film-group-backs-antipiracy-curriculum-schools-194201911.html.

Finkle, Jim. 2015. "Cyber Insurance Premiums Rocket after High-Profile Attacks." Reuters. October 12, 2015. www.reuters.com/article/us-cybersecurity-insurance-insight/cyber-insurance-premiums-rocket-after-high-profile-attacks-idUSKCN0S609M20151012.

———. 2017. "Blackstone Ends Talks for NSO Group Stake That Prompted Protest: Sources." Reuters. August 1, 2017. www.reuters.com/article/us-nso-group-blackstone-group-protests-idUSKCN1AV234.

Fischer-Lescano, Andreas. 2012. "Critical Systems Theory." *Philosophy and Social Criticism* 38 (1): 3–23. https://doi.org/10.1177/0191453711421600.

Foresman, Chris. 2011. "Goatse Security Trolls Were after 'Max Lols' in AT&T iPad Hack." Ars Technica. January 11, 2011. https://arstechnica.com/gadgets/2011/01/goatse-security-trolls-were-after-max-lols-in-att-ipad-hack/.

Franceschi-Bicchierai, Lorenzo. 2016a. "Hacker Tries to Sell 427 Million Stolen MySpace Passwords for $2,800." *Vice,* May 27, 2016. https://motherboard.vice.com/en_us/article/pgkk8v/427-million-myspace-passwords-emails-data-breach.

———. 2016b. "How Hackers Broke into John Podesta and Colin Powell's Gmail Accounts." *Motherboard,* October 20, 2016. https://motherboard.vice.com/en_us/article/mg7xjb/how-hackers-broke-into-john-podesta-and-colin-powells-gmail-accounts.

"Fraud and Related Activity in Connection with Computers." n.d. 18 U.S. Code § 1030. Legal Information Institute. Cornell Law School. www.law.cornell.edu/uscode/text/18/1030#e_6.

Frizell, Sam. 2014. "Here's How Sony Is Hacking Back to Defend Itself." *Time*, December 11, 2014. http://time.com/3629768/sony-hack-hackers/.

Fuchs, Christian. 2012. *Implications of Deep Packet Inspection (DPI) Internet Surveillance for Society.* Privacy and Security Research Paper Series. http://fuchs.uti.at/wp-content/uploads/DPI.pdf.

Gallagher, Ryan. 2011. "Governments Turn to Hacking Techniques for Surveillance of Citizens." *Guardian,* November 1, 2011. www.theguardian.com/technology/2011/nov/01/governments-hacking-techniques-surveillance.

Galperin, Eva, and Nate Cardozo. 2015. "What Is the U.S. Doing about Wassenaar, and Why Do We Need to Fight It?" Electronic Frontier Foundation. May 28, 2015. www.eff.org/deeplinks/2015/05/we-must-fight-proposed-us-wassenaar-implementation.

Gandy, Oscar H., Jr. 1993. *The Panoptic Sort: A Political Economy of Personal Information—Critical Studies in Communication and in the Cultural Industries.* Boulder, CO: Westview.

Garcia, Flavio D., David Oswald, Timo Kasper, and Pierre Pavlidès. 2016. "Lock It and Still Lose It: On the (In)Security of Automotive Remote Keyless Entry Systems." Paper presented at the Twenty-Fifth USENIX Security Symposium, Austin, TX, August 10–12, 2016. www.usenix.org/system/files/conference/usenixsecurity16/sec16_paper_garcia.pdf.

Garcia, Flavio D., Roel Verdult, and Baris Ege. 2013. "Dismantling Megamos Crypto: Wirelessly Lockpicking a Vehicle Immobilizer." Paper presented at the Twenty-Second USENIX Security Symposium, Washington, DC, August 14–16, 2013. www.usenix.org/sites/default/files/sec15_supplement.pdf.

Gartner Research. 2017. *Magic Quadrant for Security Information and Event Management.* White paper. December 4, 2017. www.softshell.ag/wp-content/uploads/2017/12/magic_quadrant_for_security__315428.pdf.

Geller, Eric. 2018. "China, EU Seize Control of the World's Cyber Agenda." *Politico,* July 22, 2018. www.politico.com/story/2018/07/22/china-europeglobal-cyber-agenda-us-internet-735083.

General Data Protection Regulation. 2016. "Article 82: Right to Compensation and Liberty." Intersoft Consulting. Accessed May 22, 2019. https://gdpr-info.eu/art-82-gdpr/.

Gibbs, Samuel. 2014. "Sony Uses Hacker Techniques to Fight Back over Stolen Data." *Guardian,* December 11, 2014. www.theguardian.com/technology/2014/dec/11/sony-uses-hacker-techniques-to-fight-back-over-stolen-data.

———. 2015a. "Hacking Team: Police Investigate Employees over Inside Job Claims." *Guardian,* July 21, 2015. www.theguardian.com/technology/2015/jul/20/hacking-team-police-investigate-employees-inside-job-claims.

———. 2015b. "Uber Denies Security Breach Despite Reports of Logins for Sale Online." *Guardian,* March 30, 2015. www.theguardian.com/technology/2015/mar/30/uber-denies-security-breach-logins-for-sale-dark-web.

Gilbert, David. 2013. "Hacking Team and the Murky World of State-Sponsored Spying." *International Business Times,* March 13, 2013. www.ibtimes.co.uk/hacking-team-murky-world-state-sponsored-spying-445507.

Gillespie, Tarleton. 2004. "Copyright and Commerce: The DMCA, Trusted Systems, and the Stabilization of Distribution." *Information Society* 20 (4): 239–54.

Glinton, Sonari. 2015. "How a Little Lab in West Virginia Caught Volkswagen's Big Cheat." *Morning Edition.* National Public Radio. September 24, 2015. www.npr.org/2015/09/24/443053672/how-a-little-lab-in-west-virginia-caught-volkswagens-big-cheat.

Goodin, Dan. 2015. "Massive Leak Reveals Hacking Team's Most Private Moments in Messy Detail." Ars Technica. July 6, 2015. http://arstechnica.com/security/2015/07/massive-leak-reveals-hacking-teams-most-private-moments-in-messy-detail/.

———. 2017. "An NSA-Derived Ransomware Worm Is Shutting Down Computers Worldwide." Ars Technica. May 12, 2017. https://arstechnica.com/information-technology/2017/05/an-nsa-derived-ransomware-worm-is-shutting-down-computers-worldwide/.

Goyett, Jared. 2015. "For This Group of Ethiopian Journalists, the Hacking Team Revelations Are Personal." Public Radio International. July 8, 2015. www.pri.org/stories/2015-07-08/these-ethiopian-journalists-exile-hacking-team-revelations-are-personal.

Graham, Thomas Wallace. 1986. *Public Attitudes towards Active Defense: ABM and Star Wars, 1945–1985.* Cambridge, MA: Center for International Studies, Massachusetts Institute of Technology, 1986.

Greenberg, Andy. 2016. "A New Wireless Hack Can Unlock 100 Million Volkswagens." *Wired,* August 10, 2016. www.wired.com/2016/08/oh-good-new-hack-can-unlock-100-million-volkswagens/.

Greene, Tim. 2015. "Biggest Data Breaches of 2015." *Network World,* December 2, 2015.www.networkworld.com/article/3011103/security/biggest-data-breaches-of-2015.html.

Greenwald, Glenn. 2014. *No Place to Hide: Edward Snowden, the NSA, and the U.S. Surveillance State.* New York: Macmillan.

———. 2016. "Three New Scandals Show How Pervasive and Dangerous Mass Surveillance Is in the West, Vindicating Snowden." *Intercept,* November 4, 2016. https://theintercept.com/2016/11/04/three-new-scandals-show-how-pervasive-and-dangerous-mass-surveillance-is-in-the-west-vindicating-snowden/.

Guarnieri, Claudio, and Morgan Marquis-Boire. 2013. "To Protect and Infect: The Militarization of the Internet." Chaos Computer Club. Video, 45:52. December 29, 2013. https://media.ccc.de/v/30C3_-_5439_-_en_-_saal_1_-_201312292105_-_to_protect_and_infect_-_claudio_guarnieri_-_morgan_marquis-boire.

Haase, Adrian. 2015. "Harmonizing Substantive Cybercrime Law through European Union Directive 2013/40/EU: From European Legislation to International Model Law?" In *2015 First International Conference on Anti-Cybercrime,* 1–6. Institute of Electrical and Electronics Engineers. November 10–12, 2015. https://ieeexplore.ieee.org/document/7351931/.

Habermas, Jürgen. 1975. *Legitimation Crisis.* Boston: Beacon.

———. 1984. *The Theory of Communicative Action.* Vol. 1, *Reason and the Rationalization of Society.* Boston: Beacon.

———. 1987. *The Theory of Communicative Action.* Vol. 2, *Lifeworld and System: A Critique of Functionalist Reason.* Boston: Beacon.

Halbert, Debora. 2016. "Intellectual Property Theft and National Security: Agendas and Assumptions." *Information Society* 32 (4): 256–68. https://doi.org/10.1080/01972243.2016.1177762.

Halpern, Sue. 2014. "Partial Disclosure." *New York Review of Books,* July 10, 2014. www.nybooks.com/articles/2014/07/10/glenn-greenwald-partial-disclosure/.

Harcourt, Bernard E. 2018. *The Counterrevolution: How Our Government Went to War against Its Own Citizens.* New York: Basic Books.

Harding, Luke. 2016. "What Are the Panama Papers? A Guide to History's Greatest Data Leak." *Guardian,* April 5, 2016. www.theguardian.com/news/2016/apr/03/what-you-need-to-know-about-the-panama-papers.

Harley, Brian. 2010. "A Global Convention on Cybercrime?" *Columbia Science and Technology Law Review,* March 23, 2010. http://stlr.org/2010/03/23/a-global-convention-on-cybercrime.

Hecht, Brent, Lauren Wilcox, Jeffrey P. Bigham, Johannes Schöning, Ehsan Hoque, Jason Ernst, Yonathan Bisk, et al. 2018. "It's Time to Do Something: Mitigating the Negative Impacts of Computing through a Change to the Peer Review Process." *ACM-Future Computing Academy,* March 29, 2018. https://acm-fca.org/2018/03/29/negativeimpacts/.

Hern, Alex. 2015a. "Hacking Team Hack Casts Spotlight on Murky World of State Surveillance." *Guardian,* July 11, 2015. www.theguardian.com/technology/2015/jul/11/hacking-team-hack-state-surveillance-human-rights.

———. 2015b. "Hacking Team Hacked: Firm Sold Spying Tools to Repressive Regimes, Documents Claim." *Guardian,* July 7, 2015. www.theguardian.com/technology/2015/jul/06/hacking-team-hacked-firm-sold-spying-tools-to-repressive-regimes-documents-claim.

High, Peter. 2017. "A Board Member's Top Five Recommendations for Cybersecurity and Risk Management." *Forbes,* October 30, 2017. www.forbes.com/sites/peterhigh/2017/10/30/a-board-members-top-five-recommendations-for-cybersecurity-and-risk-management/#369fc4df70e5.

Hinck, Garrett. 2018. "Wassenaar Export Controls on Surveillance Tools: New Exemptions for Vulnerabilities Research." *Lawfare,* January 5, 2018. www.lawfareblog.com/wassenaar-export-controls-surveillance-tools-new-exemptions-vulnerability-research.

Hoelscher, Christoph, and Hans-Michael Wolffgang. 1998. "The Wassenaar-Arrangement between International Trade, Non-proliferation, and Export Controls." *Journal of World Trade* 32 (45): 45–63.

"How the U.S. Cyber Insurance Market Is Performing: Aon Report." 2018. *Insurance Journal,* July 10, 2018. www.insurancejournal.com/news/national/2018/07/10/494552.htm.

Hu, Jim. 2002. "Windows Media Hits Sour Note." CNET. January 2, 2002. www.cnet.com/news/windows-media-hits-sour-note/.

Hunt, Troy. 2016. "Observations and Thoughts on the LinkedIn Data Breach." May 24, 2016. www.troyhunt.com/observations-and-thoughts-on-the-linkedin-data-breach/.

ICIJ (International Consortium of Investigative Journalists). 2017. "The 'Paradise Papers' and the Long Twilight Struggle against Offshore Secrecy." December 27, 2017. www.icij.org/investigations/paradise-papers/paradise-papers-long-twilight-struggle-offshore-secrecy/.

Infosec Institute. 2016. *Panama Papers: How Hackers Breached the Mossack Fonseca Firm.* White paper. April 20, 2016. http://resources.infosecinstitute.com/panama-papers-how-hackers-breached-the-mossack-fonseca-firm/.

Irby, Latoya. 2019. "What Everyone Should Do after the Equifax Data Breach." *Balance.* February 4, 2019. www.thebalance.com/equifax-data-breach-what-to-do-4150508.

Isaac, Mike. 2017. "How Uber Deceives the Authorities Worldwide." *New York Times,* March 4, 2017, A1.

Isaac, Mike, Katie Benner, and Sheera Frenkel. 2017. "Uber Breach, Kept Secret for a Year, Hit 57 Million Accounts." *New York Times,* November 22, 2017, B1.

Isaac, Mike, and Sheera Frankel. 2018. "Facebook's Woes Rise as Hackers Expose Data of 50 Million Users." *New York Times,* September 29, 2018, A1.

Isidore, Chris. 2016. "Top Volkswagen Executives Accused of Fraud in Emissions Scandal." CNN. July 19, 2016. http://money.cnn.com/2016/07/19/news/companies/volkswagen-top-executives-emissions-fraud/?iid = EL.

"Israeli Cyber Startup NSO 'Kills Merger Talks' with Software Company Verint." 2018. Reuters. July 23, 2018. www.haaretz.com/israel-news/business/verint-merger-talks-with-israeli-cyber-firm-nso-reportedly-terminated-1.6310700.

"The John Podesta Emails Released by WikiLeaks." 2016. CBS News. October 13, 2016. www.cbsnews.com/news/the-john-podesta-emails-released-by-wikileaks/.

Jordan, Tim, and Paul Taylor. 2004. *Hacktivism and Cyberwars: Rebels with a Cause?* New York: Routledge.

Kaplan, Fred. 2016. *Dark Territory: The Secret History of Cyber War.* New York: Simon and Schuster.

Kaspersky Lab. 2018. "What Is a Botnet?" Accessed May 15, 2019. https://usa.kaspersky.com/resource-center/threats/botnet-attacks.

Keim, Jim. 2015. "Updating the Computer Fraud and Abuse Act." *Engage* 16, no. 3 (October): 31–37.

Kellner, Douglas. 1999. "New Technologies: Technocities and the Prospects for Democratization." In *Technocities: The Culture and Political Economy of the Digital Revolution,* edited by John Downey and James McGuigan, 186–204. Thousand Oaks, CA: Sage.

Kelty, Christopher M. 2008. *Two Bits: The Cultural Significance of Free Software.* Durham, NC: Duke University Press.

Kerr, Orin S. 2010. "Vagueness Challenges to the Computer Fraud and Abuse Act." *Minnesota Law Review* 94:1561–87. www.minnesotalawreview.org/wp-content/uploads/2012/03/Kerr_MLR.pdf.

Khandelwal, Swati. 2014. "Uber's Android App Is Literally Malware?" *Hacker News,* November 28, 2014. https://thehackernews.com/2014/11/ubers-android-app-is-literally-malware_28.html.

Kirkpatrick, David D. 2018. "Kashoggi Ally Sues Saudis for Hacking His Cellphone." *New York Times,* December 3, 2018, A9.

Kirkpatrick, David D., and Azam Ahmed. 2018. "How United Arab Emirates Used Israeli Technology to Spy on Rivals." *New York Times,* August 31, 2018, A7.

Kitschelt, Herbert P. 1986. "Political Opportunity Structures and Political Protest: Anti-nuclear Movements in Four Democracies." *British Journal of Political Science* 16 (1): 57–85.

Klimburg, Alexander. 2017. *The Darkening Web: The War for Cyberspace.* New York: Penguin.

Kominsky, Mitchell. 2014. "The Current Landscape of Cybersecurity Policy: Legislative Issues in the 113th Congress." *Harvard Law School National Security Journal,* February 6, 2014. http://harvardnsj.org/2014/02/the-current-landscape-of-cybersecurity-policy-legislative-issues-in-the-113th-congress/.

Korolov, Maria. 2016. "Black Market Medical Record Prices Drop to under $10, Criminals Switch to Ransomware." CSO. December 22, 2016. www.csoonline.com/article/3152787/data-breach/black-market-medical-record-prices-drop-to-under-10-criminals-switch-to-ransomware.html.

Kravets, David. 2014. "Appeals Court Reverses Hacker/Troll 'Weev' Conviction and Sentence." Ars Technica. April 11, 2014. https://arstechnica.com/tech-policy/2014/04/appeals-court-reverses-hackertroll-weev-conviction-and-sentence/.

Kuchler, Hannah. 2015. "Cyber Insecurity: Hacking Back." *Financial Times,* July 27, 2015. www.ft.com/content/c75a0196-2ed6-11e5-8873-775ba7c2ea3d.

Kumar, Mohit. 2017. "Proposed Bill Would Legally Allow Cyber Crime Victims to Hack Back." *Hacker News,* March 8, 2017. https://thehackernews.com/2017/03/hacking-back-hackers.html.

Kuranda, Sarah. 2017. "The New Old Guard: Symantec and McAfee Fight to Regain Dominance in the New World of Security." CRN. June 12, 2017. www.crn.com/news/security/300086891/the-new-old-guard-symantec-and-mcafee-fight-to-regain-dominance-in-the-new-world-of-security.htm.

Kushner, David. 2016. "Fear This Man: David Vincenzetti Built a Spyware Empire; Is the Italian Mogul a Code Breaker or an Arms Dealer?" *Foreign Policy.* April 26, 2016. https://foreignpolicy.com/2016/04/26/fear-this-man-cyber-warfare-hacking-team-david-vincenzetti/.

Lachow, Irving. 2013. "Active Cyber Defense: A Framework for Policymakers." Center for a New American Security. February 22, 2013. www.cnas.org/publications/reports/active-cyber-defense-a-framework-for-policymakers.

Landau, Susan. 2013. *Surveillance or Security: The Risks Posed by New Wiretapping Technologies.* Cambridge, MA: MIT Press.

Lapsley, Phil. 2013. *Exploding the Phone: The Untold Story of the Teenagers and Outlaws Who Hacked Ma Bell.* New York: Grove.

Larson, Serena. 2017a. "Every Single Yahoo Account Was Hacked: 3 Billion in All." CNN. October 4, 2017. https://money.cnn.com/2017/10/03/technology/business/yahoo-breach-3-billion-accounts/index.html.

———. 2017b. "Uber's Massive Hack: What We Know." CNN. November 23, 2017. http://money.cnn.com/2017/11/22/technology/uber-hack-consequences-cover-up/index.html.

Laube, Stefan, and Rainer Böhme. 2016. "The Economics of Mandatory Security Breach Reporting to Authorities." *Journal of Cybersecurity* 2 (1): 29–41.

Layton, Edwin T., Jr. 1986. *The Revolt of the Engineers. Social Responsibility and the American Engineering Profession.* Baltimore: Johns Hopkins University Press.

Lee, Kyung-bok, and Jong-in Lim. 2016. "The Reality and Response of Cyber Threats to Critical Infrastructure: A Case Study of the Cyber-Terror Attack on the Korea Hydro and Nuclear Power Co., Ltd." *KSII Transactions on Internet and Information Systems* 10 (2): 857–80.

Lee, Timothy B. 2013. "How the FBI's Wiretapping Plan Could Get Your Computer Hacked." *Washington Post,* May 17, 2013. www.washingtonpost.com/news/wonk/wp/2013/05/17/how-the-fbis-online-wiretapping-plan-could-get-your-computer-hacked/?utm_term=.18630b22e914.

Leetaru, Kalev. 2017. "What Tallinn Manual 2.0 Teaches Us about the New Cyber Order." *Forbes,* February 9, 2017. www.forbes.com/sites/kalevleetaru/2017/02/09/what-tallinn-manual-2-0-teaches-us-about-the-new-cyber-order/#4e4753b9928b.

Leigh, David, Harold Frayman, and James Ball. 2012. "Nominee Directors Linked to Intelligence, Military." International Consortium of Investigative Journalists, Center for Public Integrity. November 28, 2012. www.icij.org/offshore/nominee-directors-linked-intelligence-military.

Lemos, Robert. 2015a. “Hacking Team Leak Could Lead to Policies Curtailing Security Research.” *Eweek*, August 1, 2015. www.eweek.com/security/hacking-team-leak-could-lead-to-policies-curtailing-security-research.html.

———. 2015b. “Leak Shows That Hacking Team Targeted Cryptocurrency.” *Eweek*, July 20, 2015. www.eweek.com/security/leak-shows-that-hacking-team-targeted-cryptocurrency.html.

Leonhardt, Megan. 2017. “Equifax Is Going to Make Millions Off Its Own Data Breach.” *Time*. October 4, 2017. http://time.com/money/4969163/equifax-hearing-elizabeth-warren-richard-smith/.

LeRiche, Matthew. 2017. “Mercenaries Gone Legit: Private Security Professionals and Private Military Security Companies as Transnational Actors.” In *Transactional Actors in War and Peace: Militants, Activists, and Corporations in World Politics*, edited by David Malet and Miriam J. Anderson, 146–67. Washington, DC: Georgetown University Press.

Lewis, Dave. 2015. “Heartland Payment Systems Suffers Data Breach.” *Forbes*, May 31, 2015. www.forbes.com/sites/davelewis/2015/05/31/heartland-payment-systems-suffers-data-breach/#230f6c72744a.

Levinson, Chaim. 2018. “Report: Israel Authorized NSO’s Sale of Spyware to Saudi Arabia.” Haaretz. December 9, 2018. www.haaretz.com/israel-news/report-israel-authorized-nso-s-sale-of-spyware-to-saudi-arabia-1.6725044.

Levy, Pema. 2014. “CIA Hacked Senate Computers.” *Newsweek*, July 31, 2014. www.newsweek.com/cia-hacked-senate-computers-262387.

Levy, Steven. 1984. *Hackers: Heroes of the Computer Revolution*. New York: Doubleday.

Limer, Eric. 2016. “How Hackers Wrecked the Internet Using DVRs and Webcams.” *Popular Mechanics*, October 21, 2016. www.popularmechanics.com/technology/infrastructure/a23504/mirai-botnet-internet-of-things-ddos-attack/.

Little, Morgan. 2012. “CISPA Legislation Seen by Many as SOPA 2.0.” *Los Angeles Times*, April 9, 2012. http://articles.latimes.com/2012/apr/09/news/la-pn-cispa-legislation-seen-by-many-as-sopa-20-20120409.

Locklear, Mallory. 2018. “Amazon Pitched ICE on Its Facial Recognition Technology.” Engadget. October 23, 2018. www.engadget.com/2018/10/23/amazon-pitched-ice-rekognition-facial-recognition-technology/.

Lohr, Steve. 2016. “Stepping Up Security for an Internet-of-Things World.” *New York Times*, October 17, 2016, B3.

Longstreth, Andrew, and Tom Hals. 2011. “News Corp Shareholders File New Allegations.” Reuters. September 13, 2011. www.reuters.com/article/us-newscorp-lawsuit/news-corp-shareholders-file-new-allegations-idUSTRE78C3XY20110913.

Lou, Ethan. 2015. "Canadian Lab a Nightmare for Italian Spyware Firm: Leaked Files." *Hamilton Spectator,* July 26, 2015. www.thespec.com/news-story/5752033-canadian-lab-a-nightmare-for-italian-spyware-firm-leaked-files/.

Lowe, Josh. 2017. "Who Is Spying on the U.S.? German Intelligence Had American Surveillance Targets, Says Report." *Newsweek,* June 22, 2017. www.newsweek.com/germany-spying-white-house-628254.

Lozada, Carlos. 2009. "Setting Priorities for the Afghan War." *Washington Post,* June 7, 2009. www.washingtonpost.com/wp-dyn/content/article/2009/06/05/AR2009060501967.html.

Lucas, George R. 2017. *Ethics and Cyber Warfare: The Quest for Responsible Security in the Age of Digital Warfare.* New York: Oxford University Press.

Luhmann, Niklas. 1983. *The Differentiation of Society.* New York: Columbia University Press.

———. 1988. "The Unity of the Legal System." In *Autopoietic Law: A New Approach to Law and Society,* edited by Gunther Teubner, 12–35. Berlin: De Gruyter.

———. 1995. *Social Systems.* Translated by John Bednarz. With Dirk Baecker. Stanford, CA: Stanford University Press.

———. 2000. "Familiarity, Confidence, Trust: Problems and Alternatives." In *Trust: Making and Breaking Cooperative Relations,* edited by Diego Gambetta, 94–107. Electronic ed. Department of Sociology, University of Oxford. Accessed January 25, 2019. https://web.archive.org/web/20060918113704/http://www.sociology.ox.ac.uk/papers/luhmann94-107.pdf.

Lyall, Sarah. 2011. "British Inquiry Is Told Hacking Is Worthy Tool." *New York Times,* November 29, 2011. www.nytimes.com/2011/11/30/world/europe/british-hacking-scandal-widens-to-government-secrets.html.

Lyon, David. 2014. "Surveillance, Snowden, and Big Data: Capacities, Consequences, Critique." *Big Data and Society* 1 (2): 1–13. https://doi.org/10.1177/2053951714541861.

Macdonald, Mitch, and Richard Frank. 2017. "The Network Structure of Malware Development, Deployment and Distribution." *Global Crime* 18 (1): 49–69. https://doi.org/10.1080/17440572.2016.1227707.

Mandel, Robert. 2017. *Optimizing Cyberdeterrence: A Comprehensive Strategy for Preventing Foreign Cyberattacks.* Washington, DC: Georgetown University Press.

Manjoo, Farhad. 2017. "Scrambling to Dig Out of the Equifax Mess." *New York Times,* September 9, 2017, B1.

Marczak, Bill, and Sarah McKune. 2015. "What We Know about the South Korea NIS's Use of Hacking Team's RCS." Citizen Lab. August 9, 2015. https://citizenlab.ca/2015/08/what-we-know-about-the-south-korea-niss-use-of-hacking-teams-rcs/.

Marczak, Bill, and John Scott-Railton. 2016. "The Million Dollar Dissident: NSO Group's iPhone Zero-Days Used against a UAE Human Rights Defender." Citizen Lab. August 24, 2016. https://citizenlab.ca/2016/08/million-dollar-dissident-iphone-zero-day-nso-group-uae/.

Marion, Nancy E. 2014. "The Council of Europe's Cyber Crime Treaty: An Exercise in Symbolic Legislation." *International Journal of Cyber Criminology* 4 (1–2): 699–712.

Market Research Media. 2018. *Deep Packet Inspection: US Government Market Forecast, 2019–2024.* White paper. February 15, 2018. www.marketresearchmedia.com/?p = 450.

Markoff, John. 2005. *What the Dormouse Said: How the 60s Counterculture Shaped the Personal Computer.* New York: Viking.

Marks, Paul. 2011. "Dot-Dash-Diss: The Gentleman Hacker's 1903 Lulz." *New Scientist,* December 20, 2011. www.newscientist.com/article/mg21228440-700-dot-dash-diss-the-gentleman-hackers-1903-lulz/.

McCarthy, Kieren. 2017. "Volkswagen Pleads Guilty to Three Dieselgate Criminal Charges." *Register,* March 10, 2017. www.theregister.co.uk/2017/03/10/volkswagen_pleads_guilty_three_diseselgate_felonies/.

McIntosh, Neil. 2000. "Could You Pass the Tiger Test? Their Mission Is All Too Possible: To Rip Your Security System to Shreds." *Guardian,* March 9, 2000. www.theguardian.com/technology/2000/mar/09/onlinesupplement9.

McKirdy, Euan. 2017. "Putin: 'Patriotic' Russian Hackers May Have Targeted US Election." CNN. June 2, 2017. www.cnn.com/2017/06/01/politics/russia-putin-hackers-election/index.html.

McMillan, Robert. 2016. "Firm Manipulated iPhone Software to Allow Spying, Report Says." *Wall Street Journal,* August 25, 2016, B1.

McMullan, Thomas. 2015. "The World's First Hack: The Telegraph and the Invention of Privacy." *Guardian,* July 15, 2015. www.theguardian.com/technology/2015/jul/15/first-hack-telegraph-invention-privacy-gchq-nsa.

Mele, Christopher. 2016. "Journalist Gets Two Years for Assistance to Hackers." *New York Times,* April 14, 2016, B8.

Metz, Cade. 2017. "Uber Trial Is Delayed as Letter Roils Case." *New York Times,* November 24, 2017, B1.

Metz, Cade, and Nicole Perlroth. 2018. "Two Big Flaws Discovered in Nearly All Computers." *New York Times,* January 4, 2018, B1.

Mezei, Péter. 2018. "Platform Economy vs. Piracy: The (Un)Expected Consequences of Online Media Consumption." PhD diss., Faculty of Law and Political Sciences, University of Szeged. September 28, 2018. https://ssrn.com/abstract=3208038.

Miller, Charlie. 2007. *The Legitimate Vulnerability Market: Inside the Secretive World of 0-Day Exploit Sales.* White paper. Independent Security Evaluators. May 6, 2007. www.econinfosec.org/archive/weis2007/papers/29.pdf.

Mills, Jon L. 2017. "The Future of Privacy in the Surveillance Age." In *After Snowden: Privacy, Secrecy, and Security in the Information Age,* edited by Ronald Goldfarb, 193–251. New York: Dunne Books.

Mishkin, Jeremy D. 2016. "Prosecutorial Discretion under the CFAA Gets More Discretionary: US v. Nosal." *White Collar Alert* (blog). July 18, 2016. https://whitecollarblog.mmwr.com/2016/07/18/prosecutorial-discretion-cfaa-gets-discretionary-us-v-nosal/.

"Mondelez/Cyber Hackers: More Duck Than Cover." 2019. *Financial Times,* January 9, 2019, 10.

Morbin, Tony. 2015. "Defending against the Known Unknowns." *SC Magazine: For IT Security Professionals,* UK ed. March–April, 2015, 16-19.

Moroney, Mic. 2014. "Computer Security Industry Adds State Agencies to Global Malware Blacklist." *Irish Times,* December 18, 2014. www.irishtimes.com/business/technology/computer-security-industry-adds-state-agencies-to-global-malware-blacklist-1.2041234.

Morozov, Evgeny. 2017a. "Cyber-Insecurity Is a Gift for Hackers, but It's Our Own Governments That Create It." *Guardian,* May 6, 2017. www.theguardian.com/technology/2017/may/06/cyber-insecurity-hackers-data-theft-protection.

———. 2017b. "Why Do We Need 'Accidental Heroes' to Deal with Global Cyber-Attacks?" *Guardian,* May 20, 2017. www.theguardian.com/commentisfree/2017/may/20/cyber-attack-ransomware-microsoft-tech-giants-are-only-winners?CMP = share_btn_link.

Morris, David Z. 2016. "Sharing Passwords Can Now Be a Federal Crime, Appeals Court Rules." *Fortune,* July 10, 2016. http://fortune.com/2016/07/10/sharing-netflix-password-crime.

Mosco, Vincent. 1996. *The Political Economy of Communication: Rethinking and Renewal.* Thousand Oaks, CA: Sage.

———. 2015. *To the Cloud: Big Data in a Turbulent World.* New York: Routledge.

Mozuer, Paul. 2017. "Addiction to Pirated Software Leaves China Vulnerable to Malware Assaults." *New York Times,* May 16, 2017, A8.

"MPAA Links Online Piracy to Obama's Cybersecurity Plan." 2015. TorrentFreak. January 14, 2015. https://torrentfreak.com/mpaa-links-online-piracy-to-obamas-cybersecurity-plan-150114/

Mueller, Milton. 2017. "Is Cybersecurity Eating Internet Governance? Causes and Consequences of Alternative Framings." *Digital Policy, Regulation and Governance* 19 (6): 415–28. https://doi.org/10.1108/DPRG-05-2017-0025.

Mueller, Milton, and Andreas Kuehn. 2013. "Einstein on the Breach: Surveillance Technology, Cybersecurity, and Organizational Change." Paper presented at the Twelfth Workshop on the Economics of Information Security, Washington, DC, June 11–12, 2013.

Muller, Lilly Pijnenburg. 2016. "How to Govern Cyber Security? The Limits of the Multi-stakeholder Approach and the Need to Rethink Public-Private Cooperation." In *Conflict in Cyber Space,* edited by Karsten Frijs and Jens Ringsmose, 132–45. New York: Routledge.

"Murdoch Begins Series of Apologies in Phone-Hacking Scandal." 2011. CNN. July 16, 2011. www.cnn.com/2011/WORLD/europe/07/15/uk.phonehacking.scandal/index.html.

Murnane, Kevin. 2016. "How John Podesta's Emails Were Hacked and How to Prevent it from Happening to You." *Forbes,* October 21, 2016. www.forbes.com/sites/kevinmurnane/2016/10/21/how-john-podestas-emails-were-hacked-and-how-to-prevent-it-from-happening-to-you/#5f87d9d92476.

Nakashima, Ellen, and Ashkan Soltani. 2014. "The Ethics of Hacking 101." *Washington Post,* October 8, 2014. www.washingtonpost.com/postlive/the-ethics-of-hacking-101/2014/10/07/39529518-4014-11e4-b0ea-8141703bbf6f_story.html?utm_term = .02999dc3924e.

National Audit Office. 2017. "Investigation: WannaCry Cyber Attack and the NHS." April 25, 2017. www.nao.org.uk/report/investigation-wannacry-cyber-attack-and-the-nhs/.

NCSL (National Conference of State Legislatures). 2017. "Security Breach Notification Laws." April 12, 2017. www.ncsl.org/research/telecommunications-and-information-technology/security-breach-notification-laws.aspx.

"News Corp Shareholders Bring Fresh Charges against Company's Senior Management and Board of Directors." 2011. *Cision,* September 13, 2011. www.prnewswire.com/news-releases/news-corp-shareholders-bring-fresh-charges-against-companys-senior-management-and-board-of-directors-129719673.html.

Nieland, Andrew E. 2007. "National Security Letters and the Amended Patriot Act." *Cornell Law Review* 92, no. 6 (September): 1201–38.

Nissenbaum, Helen. 2004a. "Hackers and the Contested Ontology of Cyberspace." *New Media and Society* 6 (2): 195–217.

———. 2004b. "Privacy as Contextual Integrity." *Washington Law Review* 79 (2004): 101–39.

O'Reilly, Dennis. 2012. "How to Use VPN to Defeat Deep Packet Inspection." CNET. February 21, 2012. www.cnet.com/how-to/how-to-use-vpn-to-defeat-deep-packet-inspection/.

Paletta, Damian, Danny Yadron, and Jennifer Valentino-DeVries. 2015. "Cyberwar Ignites New Arms Race: Countries Amass Digital Weapons, Reconfigure Militaries to Meet Threat." *Wall Street Journal,* October 11, 2015, A1. www.wsj.com/articles/cyberwar-ignites-a-new-arms-race-1444611128.

Palmås, Karl. 2011. "Predicting What You'll Do Tomorrow: Panspectric Surveillance and the Contemporary Corporation." *Surveillance and Society* 8 (3): 338–54.

Panton, Bradley C., John M. Colombi, Michael R. Grimaila, and Robert F. Mills. 2014. "Strengthening DoD Cyber Security with the Vulnerability Market." *Defense ARJ* 21, no. 1 (January): 466–84. https://apps.dtic.mil/docs/citations/ADA582734.

Perlroth, Nicole. 2016a. "Intimidating Dissidents with Spyware." *New York Times,* May 30, 2016, B5.

———. 2016b. "Phone Spying Is Made Easy: Choose a Plan." *New York Times,* September 3, 2016, A1.

———. 2016c. "Shopping for Bugs That Sting." *New York Times,* June 9, 2016, F5.

———. 2017. "Spyware's Odd Targets: Backers of Mexico's Soda Tax." *New York Times,* February 11, 2017, A1.

Perlroth, Nicole, and Vindu Goel. 2016. "Defending against Hackers Took a Back Seat at Yahoo, Insiders Say." *New York Times,* September 29, 2016, B1.

Perlroth, Nicole, and Mike Isaac 2018. "Inside Uber's $100,000 Payment to a Hacker, and the Fallout." *New York Times,* January 13, 2018, A1.

Perlroth, Nicole, and David Sanger. 2017a. "Hackers Use Tool Taken from N.S.A. in Global Attack." *New York Times,* May 3, 2017, A1.

———. 2017b. "Hacks Raise Fear of N.S.A. Arsenal." *New York Times,* June 29, 2017, A1.

Peterson, Andrea. 2014. "eBay Asks 145 Million Users to Change Passwords after Data Breach." *Washington Post,* May 21, 2014. www.washingtonpost.com/news/the-switch/wp/2014/05/21/ebay-asks-145-million-users-to-change-passwords-after-data-breach/?utm_term=.143f991e4b56&utm_term%20=%20.3716b31f9643.

Pilkington, Ed. 2011. "Newscorp Shareholders Lodge Complaint against Rupert Murdoch." *Guardian,* September 13, 2011. www.theguardian.com/media/2011/sep/13/news-corporation-shareholders-complaint.

"Pirate Sites Are Rife with Malware and Scams, Report Claims." 2014. TorrentFreak. April 30, 2014. https://torrentfreak.com/pirate-sites-rife-malware-credit-card-fraud-report-claims-140430/.

Popper, Nathaniel. 2015. "A Hacking Epidemic That Hits Few Consumers in the Wallet." *New York Times,* August 2, 2015, BU-6.

Preimesberger, Chris. 2016. "Encryption Finally Gaining Widespread Enterprise Adoption." *Eweek,* July 11, 2016. www.eweek.com/security/encryption-finally-gaining-widespread-enterprise-adoption.

Quintin, Cooper. 2018. "Our Cellphones Aren't Safe." *New York Times,* December 27, 2018, A19.

Raboy, Marc. 2016. *Marconi: The Man Who Networked the World.* New York: Oxford University Press.

Radianti, Jaziar, Eliot Rich, and Jose J. Gonzalez. 2007. "Using a Mixed Data Collection Strategy to Uncover Vulnerability Black Markets." Paper presented at the Workshop on Information Security and Privacy, Montreal, Canada, December 9, 2007. www.albany.edu/~er945/publications/Radianti-MixedDataCollectionStrategiesforVBM-WISP2007-Submitted.pdf.

Regan, Priscilla M., Torin Monahan, and Krista Craven. 2013. "Constructing the Suspicious: Data Production, Circulation, and Interpretation by DHS Fusion Centers." *Administration and Society* 47 (6): 740–62. https://doi.org/10.1177/0095399713513141.

Reunanen, Markku. 2015. "Crack Intros: Piracy, Creativity, and Communication." *International Journal of Communication* 9:798–817. http://ijoc.org/index.php/ijoc/article/view/3731/1345.

Richtel, Matt. 2015. "A Police Gadget Tracks Phones? Shhh! It's Secret." *New York Times,* March 16, 2015, B4.

Risen, James. 2000. "Ex-Soviet Spy Takes on Internet Mission in U.S., Using Old Skills." *New York Times,* June 8, 2000, A14.

———. 2015. "A Syrian Case Reflects a Battle on Tech Exports." *New York Times,* November 1, 2015, A1.

Risen, James, and Laura Poitras. 2014. "N.S.A. Collecting Millions of Faces from Web Images." *New York Times,* June 1, 2014, A1.

Risse, Thomas, ed. 2013. *Governance without a State? Policies and Politics in Areas of Limited Statehood.* New York: Columbia University Press.

Roberts, Jeff John. 2017. "Uber Growth Hacks the Government." *Fortune,* March 4, 2017. http://fortune.com/2017/03/04/uber-greyball-hacking/.

Rodriguez, Miranda. 2016. "All Your IP Are Belong to Us: An Analysis of Intellectual Property Rights as Applied to Malware." *Texas A&M Law Review* 3:663–89.

Rosenbaum, Ron. 1971. "Secrets of the Little Blue Box." *Esquire* 76 (October 1971): 117–25.

Ruddick, Graham. 2017. "Murdoch Papers Hid Evidence of Illegality, Say Phone-Hacking Victims." *Guardian,* October 11, 2017. www.theguardian.com/media/2017/oct/11/murdoch-papers-hid-evidence-of-illegality-say-phone-hacking-victims.

Ruiz, Rebecca R. 2015. "AT&T Fined $25 Million for Failing to Shield Data." *New York Times,* April 9, 2015, B3.

"Russia Warned U.S. about Boston Marathon Bomb Suspect Tsarnaev: Report." 2014. Reuters. March 25, 2014. www.reuters.com/article/us-usa-explosions-boston-congress/russia-warned-u-s-about-boston-marathon-bomb-suspect-tsarnaev-report-idUSBREA2P02Q20140326.

Rutkowski, Anthony. 2018. "Trump's Tweets Flouting the Cybercrime Treaty Curbs on Racist and Xenophobic Incitement." *CircleID,* July 2, 2018. www.circleid.com/posts/20180702_trumps_tweets_flouting_the_cybercrime_treaty_curbs_on_racist/.

Sale, Kirkpatrick. 1996. *Rebels against the Future: The Luddites and Their War on the Industrial Revolution: Lessons for the Computer Age.* New York: Basic Books.

Salton, Daniel M. 2013. "Starving the Dark Markets: International Injunctions as a Means to Curb Small Arms and Light Weapons Trafficking." *Connecticut Law Review* 46, no. 1 (November): 369–414.

Samtani, Sagar, Ryan Chinn, Hsinchun Chen, and Jay F. Nunamaker. 2017. "Exploring Emerging Hacker Assets and Key Hackers for Proactive Cyber Threat Intelligence." *Journal of Management Information Systems* 34 (4): 1023–53. https://doi.org/10.1080/07421222.2017.1394049.

Samuelson, Pamela. 2016. "Freedom to Tinker." *Theoretical Inquiries in Law* 17 (2): 562–600.

Sandvik, Kristin Bergtora. 2016. "Law in the Militarization of Cyber Space: Framing a Critical Research Agenda." In *Conflict in Cyber Space: Theoretical,*

Strategic and Legal Perspectives, edited by Karsten Friis and Jens Ringsmose, 175–97. New York: Routledge.

Sanger, David E. 2016. "Questions Loom over a Response to Cyberattacks." *New York Times*, July 31, 2016, A1.

———. 2018a. "Pentagon Puts Cyberwarriers on the Offensive, Increasing the Risk of Conflict." *New York Times*, June 17, 2018. www.nytimes.com/2018/06/17/us/politics/cyber-command-trump.html.

———. 2018b. "Tech Firms Sign 'Digital Geneva Accord' Not to Aid Governments in Cyberwar." *New York Times*, April 17, 2018. www.nytimes.com/2018/04/17/us/politics/tech-companies-cybersecurity-accord.html.

Sanger, David E., Sewell Chan, and Mark Scott. 2017. "Aftershock Feared as U.S. Warns of Malware Attack's Complexity." *New York Times*, May 5, 2017, A1.

Sanger, David E., and David Markoff. 2010. "After Google's Stand on China, U.S. Treads Lightly." *New York Times*, January 14, 2010. www.nytimes.com/2010/01/15/world/asia/15diplo.html?ref = technology.

Sanger, David E., and Thom Shanker. 2014. "N.S.A Devises Radio Pathway into Computers." *New York Times*, January 25, 2014, A1.

Sankin, Aaron. 2015. "Forget Hacking Team—Many Other Companies Sell Surveillance Tech to Repressive Regimes." *Daily Dot*, July 9, 2015. www.dailydot.com/layer8/hacking-team-competitors/.

Sarikakis, Katharine, and Joan Rodriguez-Amat. 2014. "Intellectual Property Law Change and Process: The Case of Spanish Ley Sinde as Policy Laundering." *First Monday* 19 (3). Accessed May 15, 2019. http://journals.uic.edu/ojs/index.php/fm/article/view/4854/3847.

Sassen, Saskia. 2006. *Territory, Authority, Rights: From Medieval to Global Assemblages*. Princeton, NJ: Princeton University Press.

Sauer, Maddy, and Len Tepper. 2008. "Murdoch: Media Mogul or Corporate Pirate?" ABC News. May 13, 2008. http://abcnews.go.com/print?id=4841347.

Savage, Charlie. 2010. "U.S. Is Working to Ease Wiretaps on the Internet." *New York Times*, September 27, 2010, A1.

———. 2018. "Big Jump in Phone and Text Records Collected by the N.S.A." *New York Times*, May 5, 2018, A11.

Savage, Charlie, Julia Angwin, Jef Larson, and Henrik Moltke. 2015. "In a Secret Step, N.S.A. Expanded Internet Spying." *New York Times*, June 5, 2015, A1.

Savides, Matthew. 2015. "The Diaries of a Digital Mercenary." *Press-Reader*, July 12, 2015. www.pressreader.com/south-africa/sunday-times/20150712/281552289534197.

Schement, Jorge, and Terry Curtis. 1995. *Tendencies and Tensions of the Information Age.* New Brunswick, NJ: Transaction.

Schiller, Dan. 2000. *Digital Capitalism: Networking the Global Market System.* Cambridge, MA: MIT Press.

———. 2014a. *Digital Depression: Information Technology and Economic Crisis.* Chicago: University of Illinois Press.

———. 2014b. "The Militarization of US Communications." In *The Handbook of Political Economy of Communications,* edited by Janet Wasko, Graham Murdock, and Helena Sousa, 264–82. West Sussex, UK: Blackwell.

Schmidle, Nicholas. 2018. "The Digital Vigilantes Who Hack Back." *New Yorker,* May 7, 2018. www.newyorker.com/magazine/2018/05/07/the-digital-vigilantes-who-hack-back.

Schmitt, Michael N., ed. 2013. *Tallinn Manual on the International Law Applicable to Cyber Warfare.* Cambridge: Cambridge University Press.

Schneier, Bruce. 2015. "What's Next in Government Surveillance: A Future Awaits Where Countries Share Intelligence One Minute, and Hack and Cyberattack Each Other the Next." *Atlantic,* March 2, 2015. www.theatlantic.com/international/archive/2015/03/whats-next-in-government-surveillance/385667/.

———. 2016. "The Hacking of Yahoo." *Schneirer on Security* (blog). September 30, 2016. www.schneier.com/blog/archives/2016/09/the_hacking_of_.html.

Sciutto, Jim, and Zachary Cohen. 2017. "US Official: Erik Prince Proposed Private Spy Network to Trump Administration." CNN. December 5, 2017. www.cnn.com/2017/12/05/politics/erik-prince-private-spy-network-trump-administration/index.html.

Segal, Adam, and Matthew C. Waxman. 2011. "Why a Cybersecurity Treaty Is a Pipe Dream." Council on Foreign Relations. October 27, 2011. www.cfr.org/cybersecurity/why-cybersecurity-treaty-pipe-dream/p26325.

Shackelford, Scott J., and Scott Russell. 2015. "Risky Business: Lessons for Mitigating Cyber Attacks from the International Insurance Law on Policy." *Minnesota Journal of International Law* 24:1–15.

Shane, Scott. 2018. "Ex-N.S.A. Worker Accused of Stealing Trove of Secrets Offers to Plead Guilty." *New York Times,* January 3, 2018. www.nytimes.com/2018/01/03/us/politics/harold-martin-nsa-guilty-plea-offer.html.

Shane, Scott, Matt Apuzzo, and Jo Becker. 2016. "Hacking Tools among Data Stolen from U.S." *New York Times,* October 20, 2016, A1.

Shane, Scott, and Adam Goldman. 2017. "Former NSA Employee Pleads Guilty." *New York Times,* December 2, 2017, A16.

Shane, Scott, Nicole Perlroth, and David Sanger. 2017. "Deep Security Breech Cripples NSA." *New York Times,* November 13, 2017, A1.

Shaw, Tamsin. 2018. "Beware the Big Five." Review of *The Darkening Web: The War for Cyberspace,* by Alexander Klimburg. *New York Review of Books,* April 5, 2018. www.nybooks.com/articles/2018/04/05/silicon-valley-beware-big-five/.

Shenk, David. 1997. *Data Smog: Surviving the Information Glut.* New York: HarperCollins.

Shoorbaji, Zaid. 2018. "Google and Microsoft Ask Georgia Governor to Veto 'Hack Back' Bill." Cyberscoop. April 27, 2018. www.cyberscoop.com/georgia-sb-315-hack-back-google-microsoft/.

Siegel Bernard, Tara, Tiffany Hsu, Nicole Perlroth, and Ron Lieber. 2017. "Equifax Attack Exposes Data of 143 Million." *New York Times,* August 8, 2017, A1.

Silver, Vernon. 2012. "When Cyber Tools Become Weapons." *Citizen* (Ottawa), October 18, 2012. www.pressreader.com/canada/ottawa-citizen/20121018/281981784828455.

Singel, Ryan. 2010. "Netflix Cancels Recommendation Contest after Privacy Lawsuit." *Wired,* March 12, 2010. www.wired.com/2010/03/netflix-cancels-contest/.

Singer, Natasha, and Sapna Maheshwari. 2018. "Internet Safety, Taught by an Internet Giant." *New York Times,* October 24, 2018, B1.

Singer, P. W. 2015. "How the United States Can Win the Cyberwar of the Future." *Foreign Policy,* December 18, 2015. https://foreignpolicy.com/2015/12/18/how-the-united-states-can-win-the-cyberwar-of-the-future-deterrence-theory-security/.

Singh, Amitpal. 2015. "FinFisher Lawsuit to Be Heard in Pakistan's Lahore High Court." Citizen Lab. March 30, 2015. https://citizenlab.ca/2015/03/finfisher-lawsuit-to-be-heard-in-pakistans-lahore-high-court/.

Siudak, Robert, ed. 2017. *European Cybersecurity Market: Research, Innovation, Investment.* White paper. Kosciuszko Institute. Accessed May 15, 2019. http://cybersechub.eu/files/ECM_regional_small.pdf.

Slater, Jeff. 2016. "Volkswagen's Promise." *Marketing Sage* (blog). February 19, 2016. www.themarketingsage.com/volkswagens-promise/.

Smith, Ms. 2015. "Leaked Emails Show Florida Police Interested in Buying Hacking Team Surveillance Tech." CSO. July 12, 2015. www.csoonline.com/article/2947392/microsoft-subnet/leaked-emails-show-florida-police-interested-in-buying-hacking-team-surveillance-tech.html.

———. 2017. "Hacker Who Hacked Hacking Team Published DIY How-to Guide." CSO. April 17, 2017. www.csoonline.com/article/3057200/security/hacker-who-hacked-hacking-team-published-diy-how-to-guide.html.

Solove, Daniel J. 2008. *Understanding Privacy.* Cambridge, MA: Harvard University Press.

Stallman, Richard. 2002. *Free Software, Free Society: Selected Essays of Richard M. Stallman.* Edited by Joshua Gay. Boston: GNU. www.gnu.org/philosophy/fsfs/rms-essays.pdf.

Statista. 2018. "Annual Number of Breaches and Exposed Records in the United States from 2005 to 2017 (in Millions)." Accessed May 15, 2019. www.statista.com/statistics/273550/data-breaches-recorded-in-the-united-states-by-number-of-breaches-and-records-exposed/.

Staufenberg, Jess. 2016. "9/11 Report: Secret 28 Pages Reveal 'Indirect Link' to Saudi Prince." *Independent,* August 6, 2016. www.independent.co.uk/news/world/americas/911-report-secret-28-pages-al-qaeda-suspect-saudi-royal-family-prince-bandar-abu-zubaydah-a7176011.html.

Sterling, Bruce. 1992. *The Hacker Crackdown: Law and Disorder on the Electronic Frontier.* Cambridge, MA: MIT. www.mit.edu/hacker/hacker.html.

Stoller, Kristin. 2018. "Global 2000: The World's Largest Public Companies 2018." *Forbes.* June 6, 2018. www.forbes.com/sites/kristinstoller/2018/06/06/the-worlds-largest-public-companies-2018/#3ea11222769f.

"Street Level Surveillance: Cell-Site Simulators/IMSI Catchers." n.d. Electronic Frontier Foundation. Accessed May 15, 2019. www.eff.org/pages/cell-site-simulatorsimsi-catchers.

Sweney, Mark. 2017. "Rupert Murdoch's Sky Bid to Be Investigated by UK Regulator." *Guardian,* March 16, 2017. www.theguardian.com/business/2017/mar/16/rupert-murdoch-sky-bid-uk-ofcom.

"SWIFT Banking System Was Hacked at Least Three Times This Summer." 2016. *Fortune,* September 26, 2016. http://fortune.com/2016/09/26/swift-hack/.

Tarrow, Sidney. 1999. "Paradigm Warriors: Regress and Progress in the Study of Contentious Politics." *Sociological Forum* 14 (1): 71–77.

Teubner, Gunther. 1988. "Introduction to Autopoietic Law." In *Autopoietic Law: A New Approach to Law and Society,* edited by Gunther Teubner, 1–11. Berlin: De Gruyter.

Timberg, Craig. 2014. "Spyware Lets Regimes Target U.S.-Based Journalists." *Washington Post,* February 13, 2014. www.washingtonpost.com/wp-srv/tablet/20140213/A01_SU_EZ_DAILY_20140213.pdf.

Traynor, Ian, Philip Oltermann, and Paul Lewis. 2013. "Angela Merkel's Call to Obama: Are You Bugging My Mobile Phone?" *Guardian,* October 24, 2013. www.theguardian.com/world/2013/oct/23/us-monitored-angela-merkel-german.

Trotman, Andrew. 2013. "Volkswagen Sues UK University after It Hacked Sports Cars." *Telegraph* (United Kingdom), July 30, 2013. www.telegraph.co.uk/finance/newsbysector/industry/10211760/Volkswagen-sues-UK-university-after-it-hacked-sports-cars.html.

Tsukayama, Hayley. 2012. "CISPA: Who's for It, Who's against It and How It Could Affect You." *Washington Post,* April 27, 2012. www.washingtonpost.com/business/technology/cispa-whos-for-it-whos-against-it-and-how-it-could-affect-you/2012/04/27/gIQA5urolT_story.html?utm_term = .4e8a3a88793e.

Tsyrklevich, Vlad. 2015. *Hacking Team: A Zero-Day Market Case Study.* White paper. July 22, 2015. https://tsyrklevich.net/2015/07/22/hacking-team-0day-market/.

Tuma, Shawn E. 2011. "What Does CFAA Mean and Why Should I Care? A Primer on the Computer Fraud and Abuse Act for Civil Litigators." *South Carolina Law Review* 63, no. 1 (September): 141–89.

Turner, Fred. 2006. *From Counterculture to Cyberculture: Stewart Brand, the Whole Earth Network, and the Rise of Digital Utopianism.* Chicago: University of Chicago Press.

Turow, Joseph. 2017. *The Aisles Have Eyes.* New Haven: Yale University Press.

Tynan, Dan. 2016. "The State of Cyber Security: We're All Screwed." *Guardian,* August 8, 2016. www.theguardian.com/technology/2016/aug/08/cyber-security-black-hat-defcon-hacking.

"Uber Faces Criminal Investigation after Evading the Law with 'Greyball' Tool." 2017. *Guardian,* May 4, 2017. www.theguardian.com/technology/2017/may/04/uber-criminal-investigation-greyball.

Uchill, Joe. 2015. "European Parliament Member Presses to Change Spyware Export Rules." *Christian Science Monitor,* September 29, 2015. www.csmonitor.com/World/Passcode/2015/0929/European-Parliament-member-presses-to-change-spyware-export-rules.

———. 2017a. "New Bill Would Allow Hacking Victims to 'Hack Back.'" *Hill,* October 13, 2017. http://thehill.com/policy/cybersecurity/355305-hack-back-bill-hits-house.

———. 2017b. "Report That Spanish Police Arrest Hacktivist Phineas Fisher Disputed." *Hill,* January 31, 2017. http://thehill.com/policy/cybersecurity/317092-spanish-police-capture-hacktivist-phineas-fisher.

UK-DIT (United Kingdom–Department for International Trade). 2018. "Cyber Security Export Strategy." March 26, 2018. www.gov.uk/government/publications/cyber-security-export-strategy.

United Nations. 1945. "Charter of the United Nations." Accessed May 15, 2019. www.un.org/en/charter-united-nations/index.html.

USA Today. 2014. "Eyes on You: Experts Reveal Police Hacking Methods." June 25, 2014. www.usatoday.com/story/tech/2014/06/25/police-hacking-methods/11348497/.

"Valve's Online Game Service Steam Hit by Hackers." 2011. BBC News. November 11, 2011. www.bbc.com/news/technology-15690187.

Van Valkenburgh, Peter. 2017. "What Is 'Open Source' and Why Is It Important for Cryptocurrency and Open Blockchain Projects?" Coin Center. October 17, 2017. https://coincenter.org/entry/what-is-open-source-and-why-is-it-important-for-cryptocurrency-and-open-blockchain-projects.

Velazzo, Chris. 2015. "Budget Bill Heads to President Obama's Desk with CISA Intact." Endgadget. December 18, 2015. www.engadget.com/2015/12/18/house-senate-pass-budget-with-cisa.

Vijayan, Jaikumar. 2015. "Hacking Team Breach Focuses Attention on Merchants of Spyware." *Christian Science Monitor*, July 8, 2015. www.csmonitor.com/World/Passcode/2015/0708/Hacking-Team-breach-focuses-attention-on-merchants-of-spyware.

Walzer, Michael. 2008. *Spheres of Justice: A Defense of Pluralism and Equality*. New York: Basic Books.

Wassenaar Arrangement. 2017. *Wassenaar Arrangement on Export Controls for Conventional Arms and Dual-use Goods and Technologies*. Vol 2, *List of Dual-Use Goods and Technologies and Munitions List*. December 7, 2017. www.wassenaar.org/app/uploads/2018/01/WA-DOC-17-PUB-006-Public-Docs-Vol.II-2017-List-of-DU-Goods-and-Technologies-and-Munitions-List.pdf.

Wassenaar Arrangement Secretariat. 2016. "Wassenaar Arrangement on Export Controls for Conventional Arms and Dual-Use Goods and Technologies." Accessed May 15, 2019. www.wassenaar.org/app/uploads/2017/12/WA_Public_Docs_Vol_IV_Background_Docs_and_Plenary-related_and_other_Statements.pdf, 1–79.

Weiss, Linda. 2014. *America, Inc.? Innovation and Enterprise in the National Security State*. Ithaca, NY: Cornell University Press.

Whitaker, Zack. 2016. "AdultFriendFinder Network Hack Exposes 412 Million Accounts." ZDNet. November 13, 2016. www.zdnet.com/article/adultfriendfinder-network-hack-exposes-secrets-of-412-million-users/.

WikiLeaks. 2015a. "0-Days." Accessed May 15, 2019. WikiLeaks.org/hackingteam/emails/emailid/335050.

———. 2015b. "Re: ***UNCHECKED*** Re: Fwd: New EAF Submission: RED-SHIFT." July 8, 2015. https://wikileaks.org/hackingteam/emails/emailid/15116.

———. 2015c. "Re: Follow Up on Phone Conversation." July 8, 2015. https://WikiLeaks.org/hackingteam/emails/emailid/15114.

———. 2017. "Vault 7: CIA Hacking Tools Revealed." March 7, 2017. https://wikileaks.org/ciav7p1/.

Wilkinson, Tracy. 2005. "Wiretaps Unfold Italian Tycoons' Dirty Laundry." *Los Angeles Times*, August 24, 2004. http://articles.latimes.com/2005/aug/24/world/fg-wiretaps24.

Willan, Phillip. 2015. "Saudi Arabia Came Close to Buying Hacking Team." CSO. September 25, 2015. www.csoonline.com/article/2986776/data-breach/saudi-arabia-came-close-to-buying-hacking-team.html.

Williams, Christopher. 2011. "Apple iTunes Flaw Allowed Government Spying for 3 Years." *Daily Telegraph*, November 24, 2011. www.telegraph.co.uk/technology/apple/8912714/Apple-iTunes-flaw-allowed-government-spying-for-3-years.html.

Williams, David. 2016. "Cyber Defence Collaboration to Be the Space Race of Our Generation." *Itwire*, September 30, 2016. www.itwire.com/enterprise-solutions/75026-cyber-defence-collaboration-to-be-the-space-race-of-our-generation.html.

Wingfield, Nick. 2002. "It Takes a Hacker." *Wall Street Journal*, March 11, 2002. www.wsj.com/articles/SB1015790823535042600.

———. 2017. "Ransomware Attack Refocuses a Light on an Old Problem for Microsoft: Security." *New York Times*, May 16, 2017, A9.

Wiseman, Paul, and Ken Dilanian. 2015. "US-China Agreement on Hackers Marks Progress on Cybertheft Issue." PBS News Hour. September 26, 2015. www.pbs.org/newshour/rundown/us-china-agreement-hackers-marks-progress-cybertheft-issue/.

Wolff, Josephine. 2016a. "The Hacking Law That Can't Hack It: The Five Cases That Show How the Frustrating and Confusing 30-Year-Old Computer Fraud and Abuse Act Is." *Slate*, September 27, 2016. www.slate.com/articles/technology/future_tense/2016/09/the_computer_fraud_and_abuse_act_turns_30_years_old.html.

———. 2016b. "Is It Really Illegal to Share Your Netflix Password?" *Slate*, July 12, 2016. www.slate.com/articles/technology/future_tense/2016/07/is_it_really_illegal_to_share_your_netflix_password.html.

Worrall, J.J. 2013. "Surveillance Software Puts European Companies in Eye of Spyware Storm." *Irish Times,* May 9, 2013, 6.
Zetter, Kim. 2008. "Hacker in Murdoch Trial Acknowledges Receiving Money from Murdoch Firm." *Wired,* April 25, 2008. www.wired.com/2008/04/hacker-in-murdo/.

INDEX

Founded in 1893,
UNIVERSITY OF CALIFORNIA PRESS
publishes bold, progressive books and journals on topics in the arts, humanities, social sciences, and natural sciences—with a focus on social justice issues—that inspire thought and action among readers worldwide.

The UC PRESS FOUNDATION
raises funds to uphold the press's vital role as an independent, nonprofit publisher, and receives philanthropic support from a wide range of individuals and institutions—and from committed readers like you. To learn more, visit ucpress.edu/supportus.